Zychlin Memorial Book
(Żychlin, Poland)

Translation of

Sefer Zychlin

Original Book Edited by: Ami Shamir

Published by the Organization of Zychliners in Israel and America

Tel Aviv, 1974

A Publication of JewishGen, INC
Edmond J. Safra Plaza, 36 Battery Place, New York, NY 10280
646.494.5972 | info@JewishGen.org | www.jewishgen.org

Zychlin Memorial Book
Translation of *Sefer Zychlin*

Editor of Original Yizkor Book: Ami Shamir
Project Coordinators: Leon Zamosc, David Goren and Lori Sandoval
Cover Design: Jan R. Fine
Name Indexing: Jonathan Wind

Printed in the United States of America by Lightning Source, Inc.

Library of Congress Control Number (LCCN): 2022941661

ISBN: 978-1-954176-51-5 (hard cover: 334 pages, alk. paper)

Credits and Captions for Book Covers:

Front cover photograph:
The center of Jewish religious life in Zychlin as depicted in a drawing by W. Reszelbach.
Source: Page 73 of this book.

Back cover photograph:
Zychlin survivors at a memorial meeting after liberation.
Source: Page 208 of this book.

About JewishGen.org

JewishGen, an affiliate of the Museum of Jewish Heritage - A Living Memorial to the Holocaust, serves as the global home for Jewish genealogy.

Featuring unparalleled access to 30+ million records, it offers unique search tools, along with opportunities for researchers to connect with others who share similar interests. Award winning resources such as the Family Finder, Discussion Groups, and ViewMate, are relied upon by thousands each day.

In addition, JewishGen's extensive informational, educational and historical offerings, such as the Jewish Communities Database, Yizkor Book translations, InfoFiles, Family Tree of the Jewish People, and KehilaLinks, provide critical insights, first-hand accounts, and context about Jewish communal and familial life throughout the world.

Offered as a free resource, JewishGen.org has facilitated thousands of family connections and success stories, and is currently engaged in an intensive expansion effort that will bring many more records, tools, and resources to its collections.

Please visit https://www.jewishgen.org/ to learn more.

Executive Director: Avraham Groll

About the JewishGen Yizkor Book Project

Yizkor Books (Memorial Books) were traditionally written to memorialize the names of departed family and martyrs during holiday services in the synagogue (a practice that still exists in many synagogues today).

Over the centuries, as a result of countless persecutions and horrific atrocities committed against the Jews, Yizkor Books (Sefer Zikaron in Hebrew) were expanded to include more historical information, such as biographical sketches of famous personalities and descriptions of daily town life.

Following the Holocaust, the idea of remembrance and learning took on an urgent and crucial importance. Survivors of the Holocaust sought out other surviving residents of their former towns to memorialize and document the names and way of life of those who were ruthlessly murdered by the Nazis. These remembrances were documented in Yizkor Books, hundreds of which were published in the first decades after the Holocaust.

Most of these books were published privately, or through landsmanshaftn (social organizations comprised of members originating from the same European town or region) that still existed, and were often distributed free of charge. Sadly, the languages used to document these crucial histories and links to our past, Yiddish and Hebrew, are no longer commonly understood by a significant percentage of Jews today. As a result, JewishGen has undertaken the sacred responsibility of translating these books into English so that the culture and way of life of these communities will be preserved and transmitted to future generations.

In 1986, a group of farsighted JewishGenners started a project to pool their efforts together in groups based upon their ancestors from each town and donate money to get the Yizkor books of their ancestral towns translated into English. As the translated material became available, it was made freely accessible at www.JewishGen.org/Yizkor.

Hardcover copies can be purchased by visiting the JewishGen Press:
https://www.jewishgen.org/Yizkor/ybip.html

It is our hope that the translation of these books into English (and other languages) will assist the countless Jewish family researchers who are so desperately seeking to forge a connection with their heritage.

Director of JewishGen Yizkor Book Project: Lance Ackerfeld

About the JewishGen Press

JewishGen Press (formerly the Yizkor Books-in-Print Project) is the publishing division of JewishGen.org, and provides a venue for the publication of non-fiction books pertaining to Jewish genealogy, history, culture, and heritage.

In addition to the Yizkor Book category, publications in the Other Non-Fiction category include Shoah memoirs and research, genealogical research, collections of genealogical and historical materials, biographies, diaries and letters, studies of Jewish experience and cultural life in the past, academic theses, and other books of interest to the Jewish community.

A list of all books available from JewishGen Press along with prices is available at:
https://www.jewishgen.org/Yizkor/ybip.html

Please visit https://www.jewishgen.org/Yizkor/ybip.html to learn more.

Director of JewishGen Press: Joel Alpert
Managing Editor: Jessica Feinstein
Publications Manager: Susan Rosin

Notes to the Reader

The images in the original book were reproduced from photographs from the time of the first edition. These reproductions were already of poor quality, being pre-war and at least 30 or more years old. As a result the images in the book are not very good and the best achievable.

Readers can view the original book online at the Yiddish Book Center website:
https://www.yiddishbookcenter.org/collections/yizkor-books/yzk-nybc314136/shamir-ami-sztokfisz-david-sefer-z-ihlin
or at the New York Public Library Digital Collections website:
https://digitalcollections.nypl.org/items/c1d5aed0-2328-0133-6337-58d385a7b928

To obtain a list of Shoah victims from Zychlin (Żychlin, Poland), the reader should access the Yad Vashem web site listed below; one can also search for specific family names using family name option. These lists are continually updated by Yad Vashem, so it is worthwhile to periodically search these lists.

There is more valuable information (including the Pages of Testimony, etc.) available on this website: https://yvng.yadvashem.org/

Geopolitical Information

Żychlin, Poland is located at 52°15' N 19°37' E and 59 miles W of Warszawa.

Period	Town	District	Province	Country
Before WWI (c. 1900):	Żychlin	Kutno	Warszawa	Russian Empire
Between the wars (c. 1930):	Żychlin	Kutno	Warszawa	Poland
After WWII (c. 1950):	Żychlin			Poland
Today (c. 2000):	Żychlin			Poland

Alternate Names for the Town:

Żychlin [Pol], Zhichlin [Yid], Zhikhlin [Rus], Zakhlin, Zekhlin, Zykhlin, Zshikhlin.

Jewish Population: 2,268 (in 1897), 2,701 (in 1921).

Nearby Jewish Communities:

Sobota 10 miles SSE
Kiernozia 11 miles E
Kutno 11 miles W
Gąbin 11 miles NNE
Sanniki 12 miles ENE
Bielawy 13 miles S
Gostynin 14 miles NNW
Piątek 14 miles SSW
Łowicz 16 miles SE
Krośniewice 18 miles W
Głowno 20 miles SSE
Płock 21 miles N
Lubień Kujawski 21 miles WNW
Łęczyca 21 miles SW
Dąbrowice 22 miles W
Dobrzyń nad Wisłą 30 miles NNW

Łyszkowice 22 miles SE
Bodzanów 24 miles NE
Ozorków 24 miles SW
Stryków 24 miles S
Bolimów 26 miles ESE
Wyszogród 26 miles ENE
Grabów 27 miles WSW
Chodecz 27 miles WNW
Parzęczew 27 miles SW
Sochaczew 27 miles E
Kowal 27 miles NW
Zgierz 29 miles SSW
Kłodawa 30 miles W
Bielsk 30 miles NNE
Skierniewice 30 miles SE

Map of Poland showing the location of **Żychlin**

TABLE OF CONTENTS

Preface to the English translation

by Leon Zamosc, David Goren and Lori Sandoval

[Not included in the original book]

In 2021, the Zychlin group of the Association of Descendants of Jewish Central Poland undertook the translation of the Zychlin Memorial Book into English as part of several initiatives to memorialize the Jewish community of Zychlin and preserve its cultural heritage. As coordinators of the translation project, we are pleased that we have been able to complete it in a relatively short time. For us, the opportunity to connect more deeply to our ancestors and help preserve their legacy for others has been a true privilege.

The original book was edited by Ami Shamir, supported by an editorial board that included Yaakov Ben-Binah, Rivka Kanarek and Moshe Zyger. It was published in Hebrew and Yiddish in 1974 by the Zychliner Organization in Israel and America, "on the 32nd anniversary that bitter day when the town's ghetto inmates were deported to the extermination camp at Chelmno and the Jewish community of Zychlin was no more." It was dedicated to the memory of "the martyrs of Zychlin, our brothers and sisters who were so tragically taken away from us. We can only hope that their sacred memory will remain an inspiration to posterity."

Zychlin, a small town in the District of Kutno in central Poland, was home to a Jewish community for more than 400 years, until the last remaining Jews were deported and murdered at the Chelmno extermination camp by the German Nazis. Of the almost 3,000 Jews who lived in Zychlin on the eve of the Second World War, only 68 survived the Holocaust. Some of them had managed to escape across the Soviet border after the German invasion, and a few others spent the war in hiding. The majority of the Zychliner survivors, however, had to endure years of torture and terror in the Nazi camps.

The Zychlin Memorial Book contains much insight about the local community and its involvement in the processes and events that shaped the fate of the Polish Jews in different historical periods and especially during the 20th century. Through personal accounts, narratives, documents and photographs, the book tells the stories of the Zychliners' difficulties and successes in their individual and collective efforts to live their lives as Jews. It also gives us a somber sense of their helplessness and despair as the community faced persecution and destruction following the occupation of Poland by Nazi Germany.

While this English edition preserves the original content of the book in its entirety, we considered that it was pertinent and justified to include some photographs and a few written materials and lists of Holocaust victims that only became available after the Hebrew and Yiddish original book was published in 1974. The new photographs have been inserted at appropriate points throughout the book, and the new written materials and lists have been placed together in a final section entitled "Additional Materials." In both cases, we took special care to specify the source of the items and indicate that they had not been published as part of the original book.

We would like to express our appreciation to those who contributed to the success of this initiative: Janie Respitz (Yiddish translator), Lance Ackerfeld (Director, JewishGen Yizkor Book Project), Joel Alpert (Director, JewishGen Press), and Susan Rosin (Publications Manager, JewishGen Press).

Finally, the speedy translation of the Zychlin Memorial Book would not have been possible without the support of a grant from Lawrence Zlatkin, honoring the memory of his father, Holocaust survivor Rafael (Ralph) Zlatkin, and the donations of Arlene Beare, Fay Bussgang, David Goren, Tobias Kaye, Thomas Laichas, Ron Merkel, Rhea Siers, Judith Simon, Roslyn Tatarka, and Samuel Tatarka. We thank you all for your JewishGen-erosity.

We dedicate this English translation of the Zychlin Memorial Book to the more than 400 years of vibrant Jewish community and life of our ancestors in Zychlin.

Introduction

Translated by Leon Zamosc

[Original book: pages VII-VIII Hebrew section, 149-150 Yiddish section]

.

The Zychlin Memorial Book is published on the 32nd anniversary of that bitter day when town's ghetto inmates were deported to the extermination camp at Chelmno and the Jewish community of Zychlin was no more.

Our beloved hometown was only a small provincial township in the middle of the vast central plain of Poland, surrounded by drowsy villages and situated several miles from the nearest railway station. Nevertheless, it was full of life. The Jews of Zychlin never numbered more than 3,000 people. But that small community, although poor and facing hardships most of the time, led a remarkably rich and active community life. There was hardly a trend in Jewish life, whether religious, Zionist or otherwise, that was not represented in the public ideological struggles that took place in Zychlin. Our townspeople took an active part in every development involving European Jewry, thus enriching their own lives and the collective life of their community.

Between the two World Wars, the Jewish community of Zychlin flourished as never before in its two-hundred year history. It was then that Zionism began taking an ever stronger hold among the people. Many Zychliners joined the Third Aliyah movement and contributed their share to the rebuilding of Israel. Others emigrated to the United States —where a Zychliner organization was soon established—and still others went to Canada and Australia, but deep in their hearts they all continued to cherish the hometown of their youth.

Those staying in Zychlin could never foresee the horrible end that was to befall them. But the unthinkable nightmare became a cruel reality. In September 1939, the henchmen of Hitler conquered Poland and in less than six years nearly all of the three million Jews of Poland were exterminated. Among the many thriving Jewish communities liquidated by the Nazis and their accomplices during the Shoah was the community of Zychlin. Nothing of it remained. Even the Jewish cemetery, where our loved ones were buried, was completely destroyed.

The following pages tell the story of the Jews of Zychlin, their history, their affairs, their joys and their sorrows. The book was written and edited—in Hebrew and Yiddish—by Zychliners who remember with deep affection their beloved hometown that is no more.

The publication of the book, undertaken by the Zychliner organization in Israel, was made possible through the generous help of landsmen in the United States, Canada and other countries.

The Memonial Book is dedicated to the martyrs of Zychlin, our brothers and sisters who were so tragically taken away from us. We can only hope that their sacred memory will remain an inspiration to posterity.

Alas, my people, you burned quietly and in silence,
And my prayer houses, all burned to the ground,
Synagogues and Jews burned together,
And my cities, my holy cities, the Jewish cities.

Yitzhak Katzenelson

לזכר עולם לקדושי קהילת
זי'כלין הי"ד
(ע"י קוטנו פלך ורשה)
שנספו בשנות השואה
ונחנקו בתאי הגזים בחלמנו תש"ב
יום הזכרון י"ד אדר
ת נ צ ב ה
מנציחים ארגון יוצאי זי'כלין
בישראל ובתפוצות

Remembrance plaque for the Zychlin martyrs in Martef HaShoah, Jerusalem.

History of Zychlin

Zychlin – Six hundred years of history

Translated by Leon Zamosc

[Original book: pages 17-20 Hebrew section, 153-157 Yiddish section]

This chapter is based on various historical sources, including the book *Miasta polskie w tysiącleciu [Polish cities of the millennium]*, by Mateusz Siuchniński, published by the National Ossolinski Institute, Wroclaw, 1965, 2 volumes.

Zychlin (which in some old documents is spelled "Szichlin" or "Sychlin") is part of Kutno county in Central Poland. The settlement lies on a plain along the banks of the Sludwia river which, after merging with the Przysowa, flows into the Bzura river near Lowicz. Paved roads link the town with Pniewo's train station on the Warsaw-Bydgoszcz line (3 km to the south), Kutno (21 km to the west), and Lowicz (24 km to the southeast).

Archaeological excavations in the area corroborate the long existence of the settlement. By 1331 there was already a village with a church belonging to Chwala, a knight from Leczyca. That same year, Zychlin was occupied by the Crusaders and, for a long time to come, it would continue to be a prize in the private property disputes of the nobility. It can be assumed that the town was granted municipal rights before 1397, since it was a Catholic parish seat, it had a castle, and was strategically located on the crossroads between Greater Poland and Mazovia. The castle, a tiny structure in the center of town, was first mentioned in the official document *Fula de Zychlino Judex* of 1332.

In 1394, at a general convention in Leczyca, an agreement was signed between Pietrasz from Widawa and the standard-bearer of Leczyca, Klemens, by which the castle of Zychlin with its dependencies (*Szichlin castrum cum aliis attinencis*) became the permanent property of Klemens, who commited to pay Pietrasz 50 gold coins by Christmas of that year as a down payment towards the total sum of 150 coins. On June 20 1397, the same Klemens transferred on his behalf and on behalf of his heirs all the villages belonging to Zychlin (*appido Sychlin*) to Wojciech of Slonsk and to his brother. As mentioned above, this would seem to indicate that Zychlin had already received municipal rights well before

1450, which some sources consider the year of its founding by Albertus of Zychlin, Chancellor of the King. On the basis of documents from 1466 and 1469, Niesiecki writes that Albertus "founded and established the town of Zychlin" and that King Kazimierz Jagiellonczyk apparently granted the town new rights as a reward for Albertus' good services to the crown. In 1418, Albertus built a community church in whose basement he was laid to rest in 1471.

Very little is known about Zychlin in the following two centuries. Wojciech, vice-chancellor of King Kazimierz Jagiellonczyk, seems to have come from the town. According to a document of 1552, Zychlin included the following land divisions: Sziul, Pasieka, Rakowo, Daszki, Dobrzelin, Buszkow Zilona, Buszkow Major, Kamieniec, Rakowiec, Skaszewo Mala, Gomina (known as Raszkewizna), Gomina Sedky, Gomin, Gomin Rafalizna, Marszewo, Chocholow, Bobrowo, Zabikow, Budzyn, and Pzikoti. In these villages, a tiny nobility of 131 subjects had settled on small plots.

Wardam, who visited the area in the years 1670-72, reported that "Zychlin is a small town, the like of which you will find many in Mazovia and all over Poland. These towns differ from the villages in that their inhabitants enjoy more freedom and are considered nobles, or peasants who submit to the king and not to the tyranny of the nobility. Yes, even in a place like Zychlin, there is an aristocracy. I met one of them, with a sword hanging from his belt, as he was driving a garbage cart to the field."

Later newcomers like the Grezinskis, the Rakowitskis and the Pruszkows, did not contribute to raising the level of the town. The only new landmark was the parish church of Saints Peter and Paul, a late Baroque brick building erected in 1782 on the site of the previous wooden church. For 30 years, beginning in 1838, the church was led by Glech Kondratski, and over time it was significantly expanded: a wing was added for the worshipers, and a new altar.

Severina Pruszkova-Dichinska, a writer, gave the church an image of Saint Stanislaus Kostka as a present. Two pictures remain of the ancient church, bearing inscriptions of Josef Sollohova (son of the Principality of Lithuania's Minister of Finance) and his wife Antonina, the Duchess Oginska.

A wall surrounds the church cemetery, where three iron tombstones stand out, corresponding to Felix Tikla (died 1847), Carol (died 1848), and Theodor Grabski. The small tombstone of Justina Orstata depicts a woman kneeling with her hands clasped in front of a statue of the Blessed Virgin Mary. It was the last work of the talented sculptor Paweł Maliński, who died in 1853.

Rather than developing, during the 17th century Zychlin had actually regressed. In 1715 it had 69 houses, a large inn and a beer and vodka tavern.

The owner of the place, Tomasz Fruszak, requested and obtained the privilege to renew the license from King Stanislaw August Poniatowski. But this did not help the revival of the town, which in 1790 had 68 houses and 250 inhabitants.

As early as 1764-65 there were Jews in Zychlin, but their number was small and they were not formally organized as a Jewish community. They were registered as members of the Jewish communities of Kutno and Gostynin, where they paid taxes. At that time, there were about 930 Jews in these three towns. The Jewish synagogue of Zychlin was built of wood in 1780, on the basis of a special license from Antoni Kazimierz Ostrowski, archbishop of Gniezno. In 1880 a new brick synagogue was built on the site.

Under the Prussians, following the 1793 second partition of Poland, the number of houses slightly increased to 77 and the population reached 743. There were 57 artisans, including 6 ironsmiths, 3 goldsmiths and 3 barbers. During the years of the Duchy of Warsaw, there was further improvement. By 1812, the town had 817 inhabitants.

In 1820, there were 104 houses in Zychlin (four of them brick buildings), inhabited by 1,391 people, including a large majority of 846 Jews. The residents engaged in handicrafts and trade and among them were shopkeepers and salaried workers. Weekly market days were held on Sundays and every year there were eight regional market fairs. In 1858, there were 94 houses in Zychlin with 1,611 residents, including 1,002 Jews.

During the January 1863 uprising, 500 peasants and townspeople occupied Zychlin, expelled the Czarist soldiers and temporarily gained control of the town. Following the uprising, Zychlin lost its municipal privileges in 1870.

Around 1890, however, Zychlin entered a new phase of development. On that year, the permanent residents numbered 4,997 including 21 Orthodox Christians, 236 Protestants, 2,201 Jews, and the rest Catholics. Spurred by the construction of the Sochaczew-Kutno road and the Warsaw-Kutno-Poznan railway, an agriculture-based industry began to thrive in the town and its surrounding rural areas, especially in the agricultural estates of Budzyn, Pasieka, and Sokolowek. At the time, the Zychlin district covered an area of 14,881 morga (1 morga = 0.6 hectare), of which 13,098 were owned by landowners, 1,397 by peasants, and 386 by townspeople. Among the industries that developed in the region, of particular note were the two sugar factories located in Dobrzelin and Budzyn (Valentinov). The other local industrial establishments included two flour mills powered by steam, a foundry, a tannery, and a factory that produced soap and candles.

By the turn of the 20th century, there were 7,830 residents in the Zychlin district (3,799 men, 4,031 women), including 6,396 permanent residents (4,018 Christians, 2,378 Jews) and 1,434 non-permanent residents (971 Christians, 363 Jews). There were five primary schools, including two in Zychlin, two near the sugar factories, and one in Pniewo.

In the town itself, there were 205 houses (105 of them brick buildings) with fire insurance in the amount of 256,200 Russian rubles. In addition to the two schools, Zychlin had a courthouse, a post office, two doctors, a pharmacy, 184 stores (7 owned by Christians) and 16 bakeries (4 owned by Christians). The livelihood of many of the town dwellers depended on work in the agriculture-based industries, but that industrial development also brought an expansion of the local crafts and trade. Among the craftsmen, the largest group was the shoemakers (about 50), who were unionized in an artisans' association. Zychlin had two marketplaces (old and new) and two squares where cattle and horses were traded. The town's main commercial streets were Warszawska, Podwal, Poznanska, Lowiczka, Zhabia and Tylna.

In 1924 Zychlin recovered the municipal status that it had lost in 1870. By then, there were 426 houses and, despite the impact of the First World War, the population had continued to grow. In 1939, before the outbreak of the Second World War, Zychlin had 8,276 inhabitants and was the second largest town in the district of Kutno.

The extermination of the Jews by the Nazis during the Second World War caused a drastic reduction in population numbers and in the level of economic activity.

In 1946, there were about 6,000 residents in Zychlin. In recent years, the town has been rebuilding with the help of the industrial plants, including the development of an electronics industry. By December 1961, Zychlin had 7,880 inhabitants, three elementary schools, four vocational schools and a high school. The town has water supply and sewage.

A "Mother Town" of the People of Israel

by Yaakov Ben-Binah

Translated by Janie Respitz
Edited by Leon Zamosc

[Original book: pages 21-31 Hebrew section, 158-173 Yiddish section]

With shivers and dread I will attempt to record my memories of Zychlin where I was born, took my mother's milk, received my first education in a *heder* like all the town's Jewish children, and got a more general education from the local parish priest. I experienced the development of the social, cultural and political life in town until my emigration to Eretz Israel in 1926.

In the following lines I want to convey my memories of the town, the social and cultural organizations, political parties and in general, the exuberant Jewish life. Yes, there was once a small Jewish town that no longer exists.

* * * *

It is difficult to find Zychlin in an encyclopedia or a geography textbook. The town is situated three kilometres from the train tracks which run from Warsaw to Torun, between Lowicz and Kutno on one side, and Gombin on the other. The distance between Zychlin and these other towns is 20-25 kilometres. The name of the train station was Pniewo, after a nearby small village. During the years 1919-1920, when Zychlin was transformed from a small village to a town, the train station was renamed Zychlin.

From the train station one would arrive in town by foot or horse cart. On the outskirts of town, in Budzyn, there was a sugar factory that later became a factory of electrical engines and transformers, a branch of a Swiss company. This undertaking was run by the president of Poland, Gabriel Narutowicz who was later murdered by nationalists from the right-wing, antisemitic party, the Endeks. (National Democrats).

In Budzyn there was a beautiful tree-lined path where young people would take walks and meet friends. Between Budzyn and Zychlin one had to cross a wooden bridge over a small river which flowed towards the Bzura. After crossing the bridge you were in Zychlin's main street, Budzyner, which was renamed after Narutowicz after his death.[1] There were Jewish shops on both sides of the street. Among them, two or three Christian shops, one of which was the pharmacy. That was the only street with a paved sidewalk. No wonder people would gather and walk there. At the end of the street was the market square, dominated by the church with its high tower from which the bell rang a few times a day.

View of Budzyner street, later renamed Narutowicza.
[Not in the original book. Image source: Fotopolska.eu]

To the right was Buszkower street, which was inhabited by the poor and led to the Jewish cemetery. To the left of the market aquare was Pasieka street, with its municipal offices, schools, and the large mill which belonged to Moshe Wojdeslawski. Podwal street stretched north beyond the church leading to two squares.

---

[1] Gabriel Józef Narutowicz was elected in 1922 as first president of the Second Polish Republic thanks to the votes of the parties of the center-left and the national minorities. He was bitterly opposed by the right-wing National Democrats, the ultra-Catholic unions, and other far right groups, who targeted him for alledged sympathy towards Polish Jews. He was assassinated five days after assuming office.

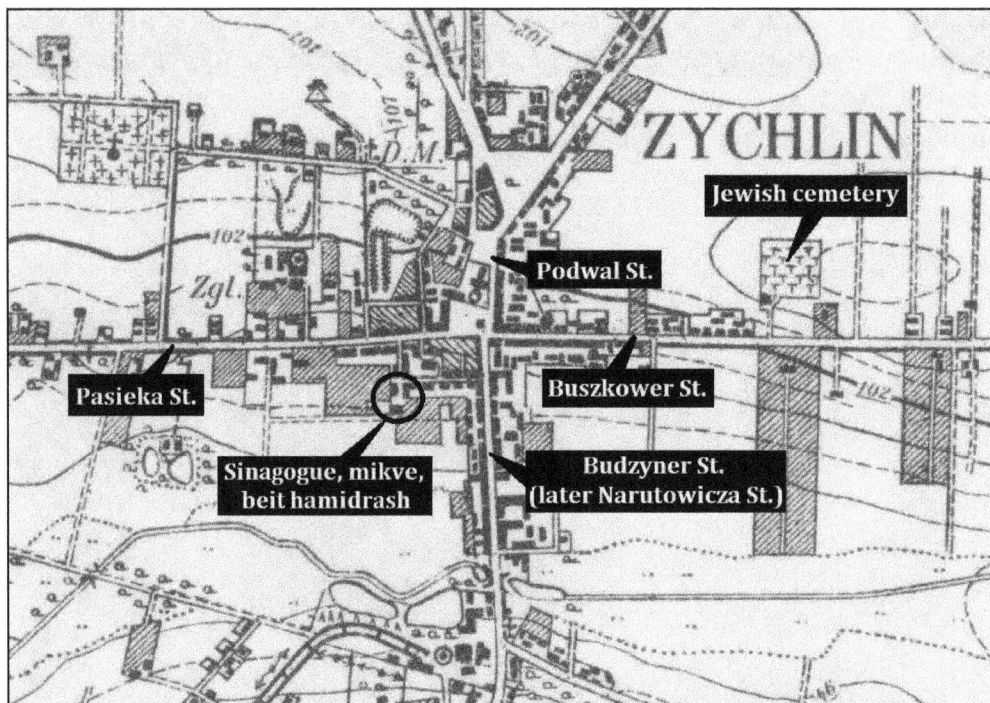

Map of Zychlin in the 1920s: main streets and Jewish places.
[Not in the original book. Image source: Leon Zamosc]

The Jewish religious centre was around Pasieka street: the large synagogue, the *beit hamidrash*, the *mikveh*, the Rabbi's house, the chicken slaughterhouse and a well from which practically the entire town drew its water.

The Rabbi prayed in the large synagogue with the most distinguished men in town, who had their own paid-for assigned seats. The women's section was on the second floor. The synagogue had an anteroom where the artisans prayed. People only prayed in the synagogue on the Sabbath and holidays, but the *beit hamidrash* was open all week for the prayers of the common folk prayed and the rabbi's assistant. Jews sat there day and night studying a page of Talmud and commentaries. Visitors would often sleep in the *beit hamidrash.*

There were also Hasidic prayer houses. The important Rebbes had their own *stiebels* and competed with each other to gain control of the Jewish street. The followers of one Rebbe would not dare enter the prayer house of another, not even to pray.

Many towns in Poland and Lithuania were known for the well known *yeshivas* or Rabbinic courts, but Zychlin did not have a *yeshiva* that would attract boys from other towns. Those who studied in the *beit hamidrash* did it on their own or with the help of older men who were learned in Talmud and commentaries. There was a rabbinic court that was not known outside of our town. The Hasidim that followed that particular Rebbe did not wear the typical fur hats or satin coats. They were simple folk types.

* * * *

In 1918-1919 a *yeshiva* was founded in Zychlin by the Agudat Israel as well as a school for religious girls, Banot Yakov.

The education of Jewish children began in early childhood. They went to the elementary *heder* and gradually began to study bible and Rashi until they could learn a page of Talmud. Not all the children had the opportunity to continue studying. Sometimes they even stopped going to *heder* because their parents could not pay even the lowest tuition. Other towns had community-subsidized, free Talmud Torah schools for poor children. But that was not the case in Zychlin. While local community leaders tried to sponsor the attendance of poor children to *heder*, few of them were able to study even bible and Rashi because at a young age they had to face the burden of earning a living in one of the typical Jewish trades, which was taught to them by their own parents or some other artisan. These young people were hired by craft masters and apprenticed for a year or two without any salaries or defined working hours.

* * * *

A small group of influential religious Jews used to run the Jewish communal affairs. Their activities were purely reduced to the maintenance of religious services. There was no elected community committee. There were only the town's Jewish notables and the plain Jews, community members who used the sanctuary, each one looking out for himself.

The religious functionaries in the community were the Rabbi, his assistant *dayan* (rabbinic judge), the cantor, the beadle of the synagogue, the beadle of the *beit hamidrash*, the caretaker of the *mikveh*, the cemetery guard, two ritual slaughterers, and the *shulklapper* who went around knocking on people's doors to call them for prayers.

The Rabbi and his *dayan* subsisted on a special tax imposed on ritual slaughtering. On Purim and other holidays it was customary to send them dishes or other gifts. The ritual slaughterers earned their living from the slaughter of cows and chickens. The cantor and the beadles would go from house to house collecting contributions every Friday and on the eve of holidays. Weddings and circumcisions were other sources of income for the religious functionaries.

Icek Majer Elechnowicz, appointed rabbi of Zychlin in 1902 after the death of Rabbi Binem Zaiderman. Rabbi Elechnowicz passed away in Zychlin in 1909.

[Not in the original book. Image source: Żychlin Historia]

There was no Jewish public school in Zychlin. Parents did not want to send their children to the municipal Polish school because they would have been required to study on Sabbath and recite a Christian prayer every morning. Therefore, Jewish children would just study in *heder* all day.

Those who ran the Jewish communal affairs did not care about general secular education. There was only a private school run by a teacher who had come from Gombin. Parents who wanted their children to learn to read and write and some arithmetic, sent them to study with that teacher. There were those who studied on their own, secretly reading books and newspapers. They were the enlightened Jews of the town. Jewish parents who wanted to give their children a broader education would send them to the town's parish priest, or to Polish students who came home to Zychlin during the vacations. At that time in Zychlin there was only one Jewish student, Avraham Toroncyk, the son of Yitzhak Toroncyk.

It was easier for the girls because they did not have to go to Heder and could study with Christian teachers, male and female, or at the Polish school.

A few newspapers reached the town. The more educated boys would get and swap books among them. In 1912 there was an attempt to open a library,

16

and it really opened, but then was closed by the Russian authorities. A few enlightened young people took the initiative and invited the author Hillel Zeitlin to Zychlin to give a lecture. In those days this was considered a daring step.

* * * *

How did the Jews make a living in Zychlin?

Most were tiny merchants, some were shopkeepers in all kinds of trades, and some roamed the neighboring villages buying produce or selling various articles to the peasants. Others waited for the market days in the town or travelled to fairs in nearby and far away places. There were also dairy men who bought milk in the villages and turned it into various products. There was no shortage of dealers who purchased poultry, eggs, cattle and grain which they sold in larger cities. A few Jews had business relations with the nobility in the region, leasing forests, buying the harvest and loaning money with interest. These Jews were wealthier and rubbed shoulders with the powerful people in the town.

Besides these there were the artisans: tailors, shoemakers, stitchers, butchers, bakers, hat makers. There were also cart owners, porters, water carriers, teachers, and barbers who in addition to giving haircuts and shaves also took care of medical problems – pulling teeth and doing other traditional therapies like cupping and leeching. They earned a good living.

The tailors' guild in Zychlin.

Most of the craftsmen worked alone, helped only by their children. There were some who hired workers. Working hours were limitless, from dawn until late at night. These craftsmen barely earned a living, except for those who worked for the nobility and the bureaucrats.

Although there were sugar factories and foundries in the region, they did not hire Jews. Only once a year, before Passover, the supervisor of kosher food would go to the sugar factory. At Wojdeslawski's flour mill only one miller and one machinist, besides the family, were Jewish. The rest of the workers were Christian.

There were also partnerships to make socks using artisanal knitting machines. This was run by sons of traditional Jews who had left the *beit hamidrash* and became independent workers. They received the raw materials and delivered the finished product. They were meticulous, intelligent workers.

* * * *

In 1905, the effects of the revolutionary wave that engulfed Russia and its Polish territories were also felt in Zychlin. The revolt in the town was led by the workers who knitted socks by machine and a few boys from the *beit hamidrash* who secretly supported the revolution. I remember that some of those who were active were the Skrobek brothers, the Chlawny brothers and others who went down the "wrong path". They sincerely believed that a new age was coming of freedom for all, for our people as well. They were called "the good guys".

The workers were not class conscious enough due to their backwardness. The more educated began to organize activities to spread socialist ideals and improve working conditions. This was all done secretly as they feared being sent to Siberia.

There were no forests near Zychlin where they would be able to meet secretly or find a hiding place. Only on the road to Gombin were there some old poplar trees. On Saturdays, the "revolutionaries" would gather there to organize and instruct. In order to disguise the political nature of the meetings they brought their children, as if they were on an excursion or having a picnic. The activists read to the group from newspapers about what was going on in Russia and the large cities of Poland and they also tried to organize underground action cells.

More than once I played the role of liaison, notifying people about the meetings and gatherings. In other places the rebellion against the Czarist oppression led to attempted assassinations on governors and police. In

Zychlin, however, there were no big rulers, just two pitiful policemen. Since we had to do something against the Czar, it was decided to try to assassinate his representative in our town, the policeman.

One Saturday night, one of the two policemen was leaving the tavern that was located in the same building where my family lived. He was shot on the spot. The policeman died, but the Czar remained in his throne and the authority decided not to tolerate this offense. A punishment battalion of armed soldiers was sent to Zychlin to repress the masses, and took revenge on the Jews. The soldiers stood on the street in the middle of the day with whips in their hands and every Jew that walked by received a lash. The Poles were delighted by this "spectacle".

There were rumours that anti-Jewish pogroms were perpetrated in other towns by the "Black Century," a right-wing extremist group that operated under the auspices and with the full assistance of the police (see Hayim Nahman Bialik's Hebrew poem "In the City of Slaughter" about the 1903 Kishinev pogrom).

In Zychlin, the revolutionaries and some other Jews organized a self-defense group to defend the community and prevent the *pogromchiks* from going wild. But in the end there were no confrontations and everything passed peacefully.

The end of this period is well-known: all those who naively believed that a new era was coming and were prepared to fight for a new, better world were bitterly disappointed. They were in a state of despair and did not want to remain in Zychlin. They scattered to all the winds of heaven: some left to the big cities and others sailed overseas, in search of a purpose in life.

The anti-Semites in Poland raised their heads and with the support of the government waged open war on Jewish merchants. They proclaimed a boycott on Jewish businesses with the slogan "Our own for our own". Polish businesses were opened throughout Poland, and this happened in Zychlin as well. The anti-Semites also organized cartels to buy milk and grain directly from the peasants, which took away the meagre livelihoods of many Jews in Zychlin. The sugar factories were organized in a separate cartel. The sugar factory in Budzyn and another factory in the area were closed. This greatly affected the economic situation in the town.

By then, the rapid development of the textile industry in Lodz, Kalisz and other cities opened new opportunities to the Jews. Many families with lots of children left Zychlin, searching for a livelihood. Zychlin was emptied out of its exuberant youth and all public activities died down – in fact, they were forbidden by law after the failed revolution. A slumber fell on the town.

* * * *

Things were stirred up by the Hasidic wars. Ger Hasidim against followers of the Rebbes of Skierniewice, Sochaczew, Aleksandrow Lodzki, etc. It was a fight for control of the Jewish street. Should the town's rabbi be elected or continue to be appointed in the old way? Who should be in charge of the affairs of the community? The Ger Hasidim had always won these battles.

In 1911-12 all the Hasidim who opposed the followers of the Ger dynasty banded together to put an end to their authority. Instead of individual prayer houses they opened a large one called Linat Tzedek, where not only Hasidim came to pray, but common folk as well. The initiators were Shmelke Biderman, Mendl Kraut, Avraham Berman and others. David Steinberger took the practical work upon himself. I believe that it was his first involvement in community work. Later, the Linat Tzedek prayer house would became the main activity center for the religious Zionists of the Mizrachi party and the activists of all the other Zionist groups.

It all started with the elections for members of the Jewish community council. For the first time the opponents of the Ger Hasidim dared to put forth a candidate of their own, Reb Yehoshua Fayvel Kelmer, against a candidate of the Ger Hasidim, Reb Moshe Chelmski.

My father was active in the anti-Ger coalition, and I was given the job of preparing some banners with slogans to encourage people to vote for Reb Yehoshua Fayvel Kelmer.

Our activists, headed by Shmeryl Berman hung the banners at night. The campaign was successful and for the first time a member of the Jewish council was chosen from among the common folk, Reb Yehoshua Fayvel Kelmer. The authority of the Ger Hasidim was broken. However Reb Yehoshua Fayvel disappointed his voters. After he was elected he joined the Ger Hasidim.

* * * *

The main cultural activities at that time were the visits of preachers who would occasionally come to town and give a speech at the *beit hamidrash* between afternoon and evening prayers. Otherwise, the town lived its usual life, except for Simchat Torah and Purim, when Jews were permitted to drink a few glasses to forget the hardships we endured all year. We celebrated and danced. On Purim, the *Purim shpilers* (actors) would perform. They were boys from the *beit hamidrash* who enacted plays on biblical themes. They performed in the homes where they knew they would be compensated. Family members and neighbours would gather to enjoy the show.

From time to time troupes would come from Lodz or Warsaw and perform in the firemen's hall. The performances would begin close to midnight because most of the audience were craftsmen and laborers who worked until late at night.

Every wedding in town brought about a sense of joy for all, not just for the families directly involved. The wedding canopy was set up in the synagogue's courtyard. The bride and groom were brought separately, led by the band followed by the guests and all the children from town.

* * * *

That was how we lived until the outbreak of the First World War in 1914. Zychlin did not suffer directly from the war. The town was far from strategic places. There was no river nearby or any other foothold for the armies to conquer. Thanks to this fact, our town was spared destruction.

As soon as the war broke out the two policemen who were supposed to keep order left Zychlin, leaving the town in lawless disarray (the older of the two policemen came back after the war and became the leader of the Polish Socialist Party's local branch). The firefighters took upon themselves the task of maintaining order and the Jews participated in the effort: dressed in firefighter uniforms they maintained order day and night. However, it was not completely smooth. One day Russian soldiers arrived in Zychlin on their way to the front and demonstrated their "heroism" by tearing apart Jewish businesses and robbing everything they could with help of the Poles. The firefighters, led by Poles, did not even try to stop the wild soldiers, despite the fact that it was their job and they were in a position to do something.

In 1915 Zychlin was occupied by the German army. The Jews welcomed the Germans with open arms, seeing them as redeemers and not as the enemy army. The Russian authorities had not shown any interest in developing the town, so that nobody was bothered by their defeat. In Zychlin, we did not have electricity. The streets were illuminated by just three kerosene lamps in the main intersections until 11 o'clock at night. After that there was darkness, pitch black. Anyone who had to walk in the streets late at night had to carry a lantern. The first accomplishment of the Germans was the installation of electric lights in the streets and in the houses, although only until midnight. This was great progress.

Installation of electric poles in Zychlin.
[Not in the original book. Image source: Żychlin Historia]

The Germans also brought order and cleanliness to our streets. The military hospital in Budzyn was open for all patients without requiring previous appointments. At the time, there was a typhus epidemic in town. The sick were taken to the firemen's hall and aid from the Red Cross was quickly organized for the hospital. A municipal garden was also planted on the side of the pond. Later, a municipal school was opened for Jewish children. Certified teachers came from Plock as well as two female teachers from Zychlin, Hella Landshnaider and Flora.

Building of the Jewish public school in Zychlin. The school, which was supported by the municipality, had 4 class levels in 1916-1918. After Polish independence, it was transformed into a 7-grade school in 1922.
[Not in the original book. Image source: Żychlin Historia]

Some of those who had left the town were now returning because of the lack of work in the big cities. They felt at home in Zychlin among their own people. Among those who returned were: the Steinberger (Shamir) family, Yehoshua Zyger, Avraham Zaiderman, Getzel, Yosef Rosengarten and others. Some people who were not originally from Zychlin came to live in the town as well, including Gombinski, Maizel and his sister, the student from Lodz Toroncyk, Kozisovitz and Bol from Warsaw, and others. Their arrival brought a new breath of life to our sleepy town. A general library was founded as well as a sports club headed by an experienced instructor from Lodz. Branches of political parties and movements were also established in the town, including Bnai Zion, Poalei Zion, the Bund, Tzeirei Zion, and a scout organization.

* * * *

Our bored youngsters were now awakened. The dams were breached and they passionately devoted themselves to self-education, with the help of the "guests" who had recently arrived. Courses were offered in Hebrew as well as private lessons in general secular education. Everyone had a strong desire to learn. It was a drastic transition, as if from darkness to light. With great thirst, the young people pounced on the books, like desert wanderers who discovered living water. Day and night, by the light of a kerosene lamp or a candle, they read everything they could get their hands on: classic literature, Jewish and general themes, science, sociology and history. This is how self-education began.

The first board of the library was not aligned with any political party. There were people from different parties. I had the privilege to be the first secretary of the library until the split, when the board was taken over by the activists of Poalei Zion. That is when the General Zionists founded their own library.

The athletics club Turen Farein was created by Gombinski. He was the lively spirit behind this organization. There were very active members who trained with a specialist from Lodz. They bought special equipment for gymnastics. The club also had more passive members who donated money. From time to time they would hold a tournament festival which brought a holiday spirit to town. Jewish sports organizations were invited from other surrounding towns. The members on the organizing committee were from different political parties.

A. Maizel and his sister organized lectures in Hebrew and Polish. They also tried to open a modern Heder, but the project foundered because most parents did not understand the concept. Among other things, they directed the Hebrew play "Yehudzn" by Schweiger which was performed by the students of the evening courses with great success.

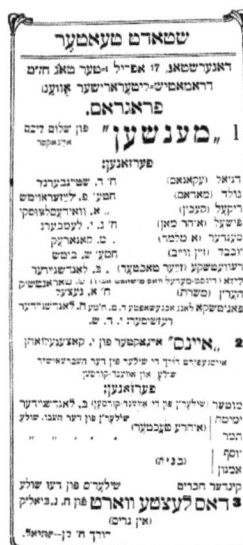

Programs for plays staged in Zychlin.

David Steinberger was very active in the town's social and cultural life and in the General Zionists' organization Bnai Zion. He organized evening courses in Hebrew and every Friday evening lectured on the history of the Jewish people to a crowded audience. He also organized performances and even directed a children's choir. The first production was Y. L. Peretz' play "Hamekubalim" with the participation of David Steinberger and Zaiderman. Then he directed Sholem Aleichem's play "Menschen". He also lectured on political and literary topics. Later on, he founded a Hebrew school with certified teachers brought from other cities.

Yehoshua Zyger, Zaiderman, Majdat and others established the local branch of the Poalei Zion party, which gained prominence in Zychlin and became a large party.

The student Toroncyk from Lodz founded branches of the Scouts Organization in Zychlin and Kutno. At the time, the organization had a strictly scouting character. In Zychlin, where I led the group, we carried out a broad range of activities organizing outings on the outskirts of town and visits to Gombin and Kutno. We were a group of idealistic young people, non-partisan, but devoted to the Zionist values which at the time seemed a distant reality. Everyday we carried out the good deed of distributing aid to the needy as well as communal tasks like serving as honour guards at various assemblies.

The main leaders of the scouts were David Steinberger, Rozenfeld, and Meir Helmer. With time, that scouts' organization turned into the Zychlin branch of Hashomer Hatzair, led by Bunim Steinberger. At that point I left the organization and, together with A. Getzel, we founded the group Tzeirei Zion, which included Avraham Wrontzberg, Yehoshua Wojdeslawski and others among its first members. Later, other activists who were not satisfied with the existing Zionist parties joined the group and Tzeirei Zion became the basis for the formation of the party Poalei Zion Right in Zychlin.

This was a rich time for activism and awakening. The atmosphere was romantic. Everything seemed hopeful. Excitement and loftiness filled the air. We all had a goal that we strove to achieve, despite the differences in philosophies.

The branches of the Jewish political parties in Zychlin were respected by the central committees in Warsaw. The most prestigious speakers from all the parties came to Zychlin, including well-known writers who lectured on literary themes.

Every Saturday there were cultural gatherings and recitals. There were choirs, a mandolin orchestra, and theatrical performances, and all of that was done with local talents.

* * * *

In 1917 we received the wonderful news about the Balfour Declaration. People were overjoyed and kissing in the streets, almost believing the Messiah had actually arrived. The General Zionists brought Rabbi Milkovsky to give a talk. His visit was an unforgettable event for those who heard him speak in the synagogue. Most Jewish shops and businesses were closed. The synagogue was filled, men and women sitting together like on Simchat Torah. The scouts served as the honour guard for our guest. He electrified the audience with his speech, which rang out like an announcement of redemption. The Zionist activists of all stripes felt celebratory and began to prepare for future events.

By the end of 1918 the First World War ended. The revolution broke out in Russia. The Czar abdicated. Kaiser Wilhelm in Germany was brought down from his throne. A new world was born with hope for a better future, without race discrimination and freedom for all nations. The Germans left and Poland became independent after a long period of enslavement. The Jewish youth believed that this new era of freedom would benefit our people as well.

The Zionist parties felt that Zionism was no longer a dream but a reality. The exception were the activists of Poalei Zion Left, which felt redemption would come from Russia. Unfortunately, the expectation that the Jewish masses in Poland would benefit from independence and receive equal rights were bitterly disappointed.

Poland celebrated its independence with pogroms, just like the Czar had done in Pinsk, Lviv and other places. The new government did not condemn the pogroms and did not try to stop the wild slaughter. To the contrary, they found excuses to justify these vile events. A dark cloud descended on Zychlin.

David Steinberger invited me to a discussion on the situation at the Poalei Zion club. They also invited Ettinger and Gombinski as non- partisan communal workers. After a long exchange of ideas it was decided to form a self-defence group with the participation of all the parties and movements. All the differences and divisions were set aside. A fund was created on the spot to purchase means of defense. We believed that we would be able to buy weapons from the Germans who were still stationed not far from Zychlin. I was chosen to lead the self-defence. That same evening I organized a group and placed them in various spots in town. There were guards all night. At dawn, through a middleman, I tried to establish contact with the Germans but when we arrived at the bridge we were met by a Polish guard.

We guarded the city for a few days and nights and there were no incidents. This experience affected everyone. Deep in our hearts we understood that freedom for other nations did not mean freedom for us. We had to be the grease for the freedom wheels of others. This feeling was one of the most important factors for the many Zychlin Jews who decided to fulfill their dream and go to the Eretz Israel. The Zionist and pioneer movements were blossoming and many youngsters from their ranks eventually emigrated to Palestine.

In Eretz Israel, the Jews from Zychlin worked in a variety of fields. Each according to his talents and inclinations. There were Zychliners in the Haganah, the Histadrut, the political parties, the *kibbutzim*, the press and even in the most important institution of the country - the Knesset. A Jew from Zychlin, Moshe Kelmer, became a member of parliament. The seeds which had been sown in Zychlin gave fruit in the Land of Israel.

* * * *

The Second World War broke out in 1939. Poland was occupied by Hitler's army. All contact with Zychlin was interrupted. In Palestine we received sporadic, unclear news about the extermination of the Jews of Europe. We could not imagine the terrible dimensions of this tragedy - that our parents, sisters and brothers and all those close to us were being murdered. In those years an association of townsfolk from Zychlin was set up in Eretz Israel to help the survivors as much as we could. But the disaster turned out to be much worse than anything we had imagined. After the Holocaust, very few remained. They went to various countries, very few came to Israel, and Zychlin was left without any Jews at all.

The Hasidic dynasty of Zychlin

by Esther Zychlinski-Zyger

Translated by Janie Respitz
Edited by Leon Zamosc

[Original book: pages 31-35 Hebrew section, 173-178 Yiddish section]

Adding my modest contribution to this book on the life and customs of the Jews of Zychlin, I will outline the history of Zychlin rabbinic dynasty, of which I am a survivor and actually the only one who remained alive. The first Zychlin Rebbe was Reb Shmuel Abba of blessed memory. As a child, his father took him to visit Reb Fishel Strikover, who had studied with Reb Dov Ber the Maggid of Mezeritch and the Rebbe Elimelech of Lizhensk.

The Rebbe Shmuel Abba Zychlinski was born in 1810. He was known as a great Talmudic scholar. He was a great patriot and during the Polish uprising of 1831 he called the Hasidim to help the Poles, because he recognized that the Czar and the Russians were great enemies of the Jews. Unfortunately, his opponents the Kotzk Hasidism and the Peshischa Hasidim denounced him to the Russians. He was arrested and imprisoned in the Leczyca jail in 1845. After intervention by the Warsaw Hasidim he was released on the same year.

Nahum Sokolow wrote in *Ishim* (chapter on Eliezer Ben-Yehuda, page 13) that the first person he ever heard speaking Hebrew was the Zychlin Rebbe:

> "Truth be told, the first spoken Hebrew word I heard in my childhood and left a lasting impression were the Hebrew words of the great Talmudic scholar Rebbe Shmuel Abba of blessed memory from Zychlin who on the Sabbath would only speak the Holy Tongue. He was a student of my grandfather of blessed memory, and he received me as a grandchild. I was seven years old when he examined me with questions on the Talmud. They were not too difficult and I was able to answer. His speaking the Holy Tongue with a Talmudic accent simply enchanted me. Since that day I never lost the enthusiasm to speak Hebrew, not only on the Sabbath, but during the week as well. I established societies to pursue this goal more than 50 years ago" (Jerusalem, 20th of Tevet, 1933).

The Rebbe Shmuel Abba passed away in 1879 and his son Reb Moshe Natanel Zychlinski became the Rebbe in Zychlin. When the Rebbe Moshe Natanel passed away in 1912, he was succeeded by my grandfather Reb Menachem Yedidah Zychlinski.

The family of the Zychlin Rebbe Menachem Yedidah.

The Rebbe Menachem Yedidah was the son in law of the Rebbe Yeshai Shapira, who descended from the Hasidic dynasty of Rebbe Yisroel Hopsztajn, the Maggid of Kozhnitz. His wife, my grandmother, was called Rayzele, she was known for her wisdom and piety.

The Rebbe Menachem Yedidah had many Hasidim followers from all over Poland who came to hear his teachings and interpretations. They were amazed by his wisdom in responding to their questions. They came by the hundreds from Warsaw, Lodz and other cities and towns. Large crowds arrived during the High Holidays. The Rebbe's court was filled all year round with people who saw him as a source of comfort, hope and spiritual awakening.

Many Hasidim would find lodging in the Rebbe's house. These were the lucky ones. Others had to stay in various hostels like the Stoskovski, Kuba, Eygele and others. Many found a place to stay in private homes and with friends.

The Rebbe's wife, my grandmother Rayzele, was a woman of valor. Following a custom, every Hasid who came for Yom Kippur brought his own fowl for the sacrificial ceremony. It was cooked in the Rebbe's house, supervised by his wife. She also prepared fish and baked *challah* and pastries. At the end of Yom Kippur people sat at the table until late at night. The Hasidim were anxious to take home some baked goodies for their families. The Rebbe's wife had a smile for everyone and made sure that they went home happy. She was loved by all the Hasidim.

My grandfather Rebbe Menachem Yedidah's court consisted of a spacious comfortable house and a large and a small *beit hamidrash*. They prayed in the small *beit hamidrash* throughout the year. The large *beit hamidrash* was reserved for the High Holidays, the Days of Awe, when hundreds of people arrived. The Rebbe was known as a great Torah reader. Sydney Berman, a Zychliner living in New York, told me that the Hasidim in America had offered the Rebbe a large amount of money to visit them for one holiday of prayers. He turned them down, saying that his place was in Zychlin together with the local Jews.

The Rebbe would lead the prayers on Yom Kippur - Kol Nidre, Musaf and Neillah. He would also blow the shofar and give a sermon. His praying was filled with devotion. He was covered with sweat and tears. The morning and afternoon prayers were led by my dear father, Reb Shmuel Avraham Abba. The already mentioned Sydney Berman told me that, when my father prayed, it sounded like a female voice from heaven. There was such a large crowd that they had to study Torah in five or six rooms. It is worth mentioning that on the eve of Yom Kippur the Jews form our town, Hasidim and non- Hasidim, would come to the Rebbe with a *kwitel* (request for a blessing). The Rebbe had a kind word for everyone and wished all of them a good year.

Many Hasidim would come on the second day of Kislev for the anniversary of the passing of Rebbe Moshe Natanel and the 25th of Elul for the anniversary of the death of Rebbe Shmuel Abba. The Hasidim would go to their graves and pray there, crying and asking God to protect all the Jewish people.

The Rebbe Menachem Yedidah sat day and night and studied. He did not even know the differences between coins, which showed how far removed he was from daily life.

The Rebbe's family consisted of two sons, my father Reb Shmuel Avraham Abba, my uncle Reb Yitzhak Yaakov Tuvyia and my aunt Chaja Rachel Dwora, may they all rest in peace.

The Rebbe was also loved by the Christian population. He enjoyed walking through the fields, especially during the harvest, and the gentiles showed him great respect. This is how things were until the big tragedy, when the Germans, may their names be blotted out, entered our town and confined all the Jews of Zychlin to the ghetto. In one swoop all the holiness and traditions were destroyed. The Rebbe continued his rabbinic duties for the local Jews from his hiding place, comforting them with better times and predicting salvation. He tied his beard with a handkerchief and would not allow it to be cut. One day an SS came into my grandfather's house and found him sitting and studying... with a beard. He flew into a rage and ordered me to bring scissors to cut my grandfather's beard. The Rebbe lifted his hands as if to protect himself and the scissors fell from the SS man's hands. Apparently he got spooked and left without causing any harm.

The Rebbe Menachem Yedidah,
who died in Zychlin ghetto.

Rebbe Menachem Yedidah's grief was great when he had to witness the Jewish suffering and tragedy. This shortened his life and he passed away during the interim days of Passover. The Hasidim managed to bury him in the family burial plot. Right after the burial, while still in the cemetery, the Hasidim crowned my father Reb Shmuel Avraham Abba as their Rebbe. He took over the leadership and continued this work in the ghetto.

Meanwhile the nightmares, persecutions and tortures were increasing. The Nazi murderers ordered all the Jews to cut off their beards but, like Rebbe Menachem Yedidah, my father risked his life refusing to carry out this humiliating order.

The situation of the people in the ghetto became intolerable. A few days before Purim in 1941 they learned that the Germans were preparing to liquidate the ghetto and all the Jews would be sent to Krosniewice. On top of that, each Jew had to pay a large sum of money for the transport.

I was told that my father, the last Zychlin Rebbe, told his Hasidim that his father Menachem Yedidah came to him in a dream and told him that terrible days were approaching for the Jewish people and all the Gates of Mercy in heaven were locked. He told them to repent, fast, and pray, begging the Master of the Universe to undo the punishment he was inflicting. They also told me that on the Fast of Esther the Nazi murderers took my father and all the other Jews and sent them to Krosniewice, where they were locked up in the church. Later they were sent to be gassed and burned at Chelmno.

My father, the holy Rebbe Shmuel Avraham Abba of blessed memory was the last heir of the Zychlin dynasty. He was fifty years old when he was murdered by the Nazi beasts. My father was the son in law of Reb Eliezer Weisblum from Staszow, who descended from the great Rebbe Elimelech Weisblum of Lizhensk. The tragic fate of all the Jews from Zychlin also included my dear mother, the Rebbe's wife Dwoyrele, my two brothers Avigdor and Bezalel Asher, my grandmother, the old Rayzele and my father's brother Reb Yitzhak Yaakov Tuvyia. At that time I was together with my eldest brother Reb Mordechai Afrin of blessed memory and his family in Lask. On the 26th of August 1942 he and his family were deported and died in Chelmno and I was sent to the Lodz ghetto.

Such was the tragic end of what was a bright page in the history of our unforgettable town Zychlin and, more generally, in the history of the Hasidim and all the Polish Jews.

A Jewish "Mother Town"

This is what life in our town was like

by Yosef Rozengarten

Translated by Leon Zamosc

[Original book: pages 39-43 Hebrew section, 181-186 Yiddish section]

The Jewish community of Zychlin was not large, but it had rabbis, *dayanim*, Torah scholars, public personalities and activists of political parties. There were several *heders*, a large synagogue, a *beit hamidrash*, and *shtiebels*. The courtyard of Rabbi Menachem was used for *minyanim* and for the meetings of the Linat Tzedek society.

Interesting things happened in the *shtiebels*. For example: after Shabbat prayer, they would hide the prayer shawls of those who did not pay their dues or their share of the rent. The idea was to force them to pay and redeem them, otherwise they would not have a tassel to wrap themselves in on the following Shabbat. (The Hasidim had two prayer shawls: one for weekdays and the other for Shabbat and the holidays).

On Friday afternoon, as Shabbat approached, there was a lot of movement in the streets of Zychlin as the Jews rushed to the *mikveh* to prepare themselves for the reception of Shabbat.

Before Shabbat began, the *shulklapper* Avrahamele would go around with a small wooden hammer and knock three times on every Jewish door to announce the beginning of Shabbat. And the Jews hastened - some to the synagogue, some to the *beit hamidrash*, and some to the *minyanim* and *shtiebels* for Shabbat.

Most of the craftsmen, small merchants, owners of carts and the common folk prayed in the *beit hamidrash*. The *dayan*, Rabbi Aharon Yehuda, a pious and righteous man, stood before the ark on Shabbat, the regular holidays, and the High Holidays. On Saturday afternoon, he studied the Torah portion of the week with the common people, who listened intently to his every word.

The *dayan* fasted twice a week, on Mondays and Thursdays. He only ate to strengthen his slender body and soul, so that he would be able to serve the creator of the world. His voice was weak, but he sounded loud. The Jews respected and adored him.

The synagogue and the *beit hamidrash* were adjacent to each other, but were different in their external and internal appearance. With the *mikveh*, which was

34

also nearby, they formed a kind of triangle. The rabbi's house bordered the *beit hamidrash*, whose door faced the entrance to the *beit din*. There was an ancient well in the middle of the space between both buildings. The people of the town had always drawn water from the well, until it was replaced by a "modern" pump.

There were four main streets in Zychlin: Budzyner, Buszkower, Pasieka and Podwal. They framed the market square. Separated by the square, Budzyner street faced Podwal street, and Pasieka street faced Buszkower street. In addition to these main streets there were, of course, side streets and alleys.

The main entrance to the town was from the Pniewo train station, three kilometers south of the town. The other entrance was from the direction of the neighboring town Gombin, whose only access to the train was through Zychlin.

Pniewo train station, 1915.
[Not in the original book. Image source: Żychlin Historia]

Horse-drawn carts and carriages connected the train station with the town. The owners of the carts competed for passengers, which often led to quarrels.

Before the war, there were about 650 Jewish families in Zychlin, mainly craftsmen, petty traders, peddlers and laborers. Few Jews were affluent, except for Moshe Mendel Wojdeslawski, who was certainly rich. There were some who made a decent living, but most of the residents had humble livelihoods and many were poor. The Jewish shops were mostly concentrated in the market square, while the Jewish butchers were located near the church.

Once a week, on Thursdays, there was a local fair and twice a year, a regional fair. The noise and commotion began the day before the fair, with the arrival of merchants who came from afar to compete with the local merchants. They would all set up stalls for their goods and very often things did not go smoothly. Just as out-of-town merchants came to the Zychlin fair, so did the Zychlin merchants go to fairs in other towns. For everybody, the days of the fair provided the main source of income. Farmers from all over the area came to sell eggs, chickens, butter, and potatoes. Cattle and horses were also traded. After selling their produce, the farmers spent their money buying goods and groceries. .

After a day of toil, the Jews would go to evening prayers at the *beit hamidrash* and, occasionally, to hear a *maggid* who happened to be visiting the town. They would "swallow" every word that came out of his mouth. We, the children of the *heders* and the *yeshivas*, gathered on the stairs that led to the ark in order to watch the *maggid* up close and hear his words of wisdom. There were always volunteers at the door of the *beit hamidrash* collecting donations for the *maggid*, and care was taken to invite him to a hot meal and a place to stay overnight.

After the death of Rabbi Itche Meir Zachil at the young age of 40, the Ger Hasidim succeeded in crowning Rabbi Mordechai Alter, another rabbi from the Ger dynasty. Inspired by him, the Ger Hasidim tried to impose their authority on the community and especially on religious Judaism in our town. However, they met the vigorous opposition from the vast majority of the popular groups and even from some of the religious Jews. The opposition was headed by Rabbi Menachem Mendel Meir Rozenblum, who had been a committed Zionist since the beginning of the movement. There had always been confrontations between these two factions, and more than once it had been necessary to summon great rabbis to settle their disputes.

Until the First World War, the town's Jewish children and boys were educated in heders and yeshivas. The people of Talmud Torah made sure that nobody was excluded for lack of means. There were yeshiva students from other towns studying with us, especially youngsters from poor families. They were fed by residents of our town who also took care of their accommodation.

The charitable institutions in the town included the Linat Tzedek Society, Bikur Cholim, Knesset Kala, and Talmud Torah. There were also anonymous donations.

At the end of the First World War, the good news about the Balfour Declaration, announced on November 2 1917, was heard all over Poland. The whole town awoke from the slumber of the war years. There were heated debates in Zionist and non-Zionist circles. The orthodox religious Jews painted the Zionists as unbelievers who were pushing things despite the fact that people were not ready for the coming of the Messiah. But most of our townspeople received the news enthusiastically, and the day of the Balfour Declaration became a holiday.

A public meeting was convened by the Bnai Zion Association in the hall of the Polish elementary school on Pasieka street, in front of the houses and flour-mills of Moshe Mendel Wojdeslawski. Crowds flocked to the assembly dressed in holiday clothes. The hall was too small to accommodate everybody. Veteran Zionist teacher David Steinberger (Shamir), wearing a tuxedo and beaming with joy, was the only speaker. He explained the meaning of the Balfour Declaration. The large audience occasionally interrupted him with stormy applause, and the gathering ended singing the Hatikva anthem with elation.

Public life became vibrant. A democratic community committee was elected with representation of most of the Zionist parties. Avraham Yitzhak Rozenfeld, the chairman of the Bnai Zion Association, was elected as head of the community committee. The secretary was David Steinberger, who also served as secretary of the Bnai Zion Association.

Zychlin's Jewish population was overwhelmingly Zionist. All the Zionist parties had branches in our town: General Zionists, Mizrahi and Hapoel Mizrahi, the Folkist party, Tzeirei Zion (later the Zionist Socialist Party, which united with Poalei Zion Right), Poaeli Zion Left, Hashomer Hatzair, etc. These groups were active everywhere and excelled in fundraising for the Zionist foundations: Keren Kayemet, the Jewish National Fund, Keren Hayesod, Torah and Avodah, and even held a fundraiser for the benefit of academics from the minority groups in Poland. There was also a small group of the Bund party, but it did not have significant influence. The members of Agudat Israel were zealous defenders of religion.

Another novelty after the end of the First World War was the opening of the Tarbut school under the direction of Zionist teacher and activist David Steinberger. He brought pedagogical innovators from Warsaw, including his brother Yosef Steinberger, and also organized Hebrew, bible and Jewish history evening classes. During the national holidays, there were readings and dancing and singing performances by the school's students.

Freiheit (Dror), youth movement of the Zionist-Socialist party
Poalei Zion in Zychlin.

Three dramatic theater circles were also active. One of them, run by the Bnai Zion Association and led by David Steinberger presented, among others, the play "Mentschn" by Shalom Aleichem. The Tzeirei Zion group, led by Israel Zafran, presented "Der Dorfs Jung" by Leon Kobrin, "Uriel da Costa" by Karl Gutzkow, and other plays. The third circle belonged to Poalei Zion Left, which brought in an outside director whose name was Hermelin.

Occasionally, drama groups from other towns visited Zychlin. As an avid teenager I loved to go to the theater. However, I did not have money for the tickets and I had to do it in secret due to my parents' misgivings. Eventually, I took advantage of a request from the theater staff. They needed typical Hasidic clothing items (like fur hats, silk capes, etc.) for the presentations. So I "stole" the stuff from our closet and, as a reward, I got free access to the plays.

There were two libraries in our town, one of the Bnai Zion Association and the other run by the Poalei Zion Left. We also had a sports association, which conducted an extensive operation under the guidance of the teacher Zayde. The festival they held in 1918 gained a reputation throughout Poland. We also had a soccer team, under the auspices of Tzeirei Zion and Poalei Zion.

Very famous speakers visited our town. Before the First World War, Rabbi Hillel Zeitlin came to Zychlin. Among the people who loved culture, his visit made such a big impression that it became a local holiday.

Zychliners emigrated to Eretz Israel participating in all the *aliyahs*, starting with the second aliyah. The name of the first emigrant was Fenigshtein. Today, there are about 150 families from Zychlin in Israel, living in cities, towns, *moshavim* and *kibbutzim*. Some of them occupy prominent places in various public and party institutions.

There was a wonderful, motivated, lively and fresh youth in Zychlin. There were sparks in the youth groups that, were it not for the Holocaust and the destruction, would have ignited into torches and large luminaries.

Zychlin was a Mother of Israel town. Jewish craftsmen, small merchants, peddlers, laborers, water-pumps and lumberjacks, Jews all year round, Jews of Shabbat and worldly Jews. Unfortunately for all of us, they are no more.

In 1925 I emigrated to Eretz Israel. Those who came after me or went to other countries, especially Holocaust survivors, will add to the story of life in our beloved town, because the more it is told, the better.

Some of the first Zychliner emigrants to Eretz Israel. From right: M. Lajzerowicz, Y. Kelmer, Moshe Kelmer, Y. Wojdeslawski, L. Olsztyn, Y. Rozenberg.

A Town full of Yiddishkeit

by Santze and Rashe Berman

Translated by Leon Zamosc

[Original book: pages 48-48 Hebrew section, 192-193 Yiddish section]

I was sixteen when I left Zychlin but I cannot forget the town. Everything is in front of my eyes: the long Budzyner street, Pasieka street, the market, Podwal street, the river, the bridge, the sugar factory, the businesses of the Jews, the few "gentlemen" of the nobility, the poverty, the landlords, the Hasidic followers and their opponents, the honest craftsmen, the rabbi, the synagogue, the *beit hamidrash*, the *mikveh*, the well, the water-pump, Shimshon the baker (his fresh pastries radiated exquisite aromas that stopped the breath of everyone who passed-by), Mendel Meir the Zionist butcher (the Hasidim did not eat from his slaughter), the tzaddik Rabbi Aharon Yehuda of blessed memory (who was thin because of his many fasts, and perhaps due to lack of food in his house), the Rebbe of Zichlin, whose followers came from near and far to receive his blessing...

Everything had a special charm: the organizations and institutions, the youth movements and their enthusiasm for deeds. The town had a special character, wanting to be active in everything that had to do with Jews and Judaism.

For hundreds of years there was a Jewish settlement in Zychlin. With blood and sweat our ancestors built the town. Despite the rejections, decrees and disturbances they remained loyal to the Jewish tradition for generations. Jewish Zychlin could be proud of its honest, idealistic activists, who preferred the public good over their own private interests. It was the privilege of Zychlin to bring forth faithful sons of the people of Israel, Torah scholars and famous personalities. The town could be proud of its vibrant, multi-talented youngsters.

With their own money, which came from hard and arduous labor, the Jews of Zychlin built a synagogue of splendor, houses of religious learning and lay education, institutions for charity and kindness. And all of that, the institutions and their builders, the leaders and the masses of the people, old and young, were so brutally destroyed.

Our house was for its own name, and our martyrs do not have monuments. Their ashes are scattered across the death camps, the ghettos, the forests and the fields.

On the religious ways

by Yosef Ben-Yehoshua

Translated by Janie Respitz
Edited by Leon Zamosc

[Original book: pages 248-253 Yiddish section]

The *beit hamidrash*

From the outside our *beit hamidrash* looked very poor, but inside it possessed spiritual content. It was a homey, folksy house of worship, always filled with people praying, the majority common folk from the poor social class such as craftsmen, retailers, butchers, coachmen and village peddlers who held their heads high despite their bent shoulders, and kept their high spirits despite their broken bodies. They were soulful Jews with earnestness and great virtues. For those Jews, the *beit hamidrash* was the best place to display their spiritualty.

Even before dawn the first "idlers" arrived to recite psalms. The other worshipers showed up as soon as day broke, particularly the coachmen who had to time themselves to avoid missing the morning and evening prayers as they went back and forth between Zychlin and the train station Pniewo.

At dawn the *beit hamidrash* was opened by Zalmenke the Beadle, a poor Jew who lived in destitution and poverty and waited for Hannukah so he could go from house to house collecting Hannukah *gelt* (money). He had a side "business" selling beef fat to poor people who used it to season their potato soup or their beans with *farfalle*. They didn't even dream of a piece of meat. They were happy with a piece of fat.

In that situation of insecurity and constant worry about earning a living, the Jews of our town wanted to warm their souls. They found this when they prayed in the *beit hamidrash*, recited psalms, read a chapter in the Talmud or listened to a preacher. These common folk received great spiritual pleasure from the most righteous man of their generation, the old *dayan* Reb Aron Yehuda, a regular at the *beit hamidrash*. His spot was to the left of the Holy Ark, while the Rabbi stood on the right. He was small in stature, but large in spiritual and religious devotion. He came to the *beit hamidrash* with a heavy bag with his prayer shawl, which weighed more than him. Jews and gentiles had great respect for Reb Aron Yehuda. He fasted every Monday and Thursday and, on the days when he did eat, he had his meal at lunchtime like a bird, not for enjoyment but to keep himself alive to serve the Master of the Universe.

On the Sabbath in the afternoon after a nap, he studied the weekly Torah portion with the worshippers. During the week he taught and offered explanations on the psalms and other prayers. Even the wealthier Jews would occasionally drop in to the *beit hamidrash* to study with him. The sound of prayer and Torah did not stop all day and continued until late at night.

The Days of Awe

On the first day of the month of Elul, hearing the sound of the Shofar, a feeling of dread fell upon our brothers, the children of Israel, especially during the days of repentance. Avreymele the *Shulklapper* would walk with his little hammer in his hand and knock three times on the doors of Jewish homes calling: "Jews, wake up for the prayers of repentance"! During this month the old *dayan* Reb Aron Yehuda prepared the worshipers to "repent, pray, and give charity".

On the first day of Rosh Hashanah, after evening prayers, all the worshippers pushed toward the door to wish the Rabbi to be inscribed in the Book of Life. The worshippers brought memorial candles to the afternoon prayers before Kol Nidre on the eve of Yom Kippur. The biggest enemies have forgiven one another and wish each other to be inscribed in the Book of Life. Some people returned to those they forgave the day before after the final Neilah prayers and ask for things to remain the same.

The old *dayan* Reb Aron Yehuda led the morning prayers from the lectern on the High Holidays. Musaf, the supplementary prayers, were always led by Reb Feyvish the Shochet. His voice was weak but, as the worshippers said, his prayers reached all the way to heaven.

Sukkot and Simchat Torah

As soon as Yom Kippur was over pious Jews hammered in the first poles of the *sukkah*. The gentiles brought the branches to cover it.

On Simchat Torah children would come with their parents carrying little flags in their hands decorated with a red apple and a candle stuck inside. Class distinction could be determined by the flags: rich children came with flags made of boards artistically decorated and with printed words. In the centre of the flag there was a Holy Ark with a Torah Scroll. The poor children came with paper flags which were torn by the slightest wind gust. There were such blatant differences between rich and poor… The rich were referred to as "beautiful" Jews.

The following morning when the Torah was read, the scene was the same: much greater honours were bestowed upon the rich while the poor were given three lines to read. All the boys who were preparing for Bar Mitzvah were called up together to recite a blessing.

The prayer for rain

This prayer had a different meaning for the poor people. They were afraid of the upcoming winter: they did not have enough coal, wood or potatoes. They lacked warm clothing and shoes for their children. In one word, no livelihood. They sang a folk song in town which characterized the situation:

> *Summer is quickly departing,*
> *Winter is approaching,*
> *The roof is broken,*
> *The pelt is worn out*
> *And there is no money".*

This song was sung to the same melody as the prayer for rain.

Hannukah

The days of Hannukah brought a special joy for the school boys. It was a big deal because they did not have to go to *heder* at night. They would go to the *beit hamidrash* for afternoon and evening prayers and lighted Hannukah candles. They shoved their way to the table under the window where the Hannukah menorah stood. They wanted to see it and hear the blessings. After the blessing everyone would break out in song singing Moaz Tsur and then there would be a stampede to parents and family to ask for Hannukah *gelt* and eat *latkes*. The boys also loved to play *dreidel* (spinning top).

Purim

There is a folk expression which says "Purim is not a holiday and malaria is not a disease". However, in reality, particularly in Eretz Israel, Purim is a holiday and malaria "was" a disease. The Jews of our town ran to the *beit hamidrash* to hear the reading of the Scroll of Esther by the regular Torah reader, Chaimke Melamed the Dumpling. He always mispronounced Queen Esther's name. The Scroll of Esther was also read by women in their homes.

My father of blessed memory was very good at leading prayers and reading Torah. Women would gather in our home to hear him read the Scroll of Esther. When he was done my mother of blessed memory served *hamentashen* to our guests, who wished my parents to live another year so they could return again to hear my father read the Scroll of Esther.

In the afternoon, a group of boys in disguise, headed by Shaul the Pigeon Catcher and Chaim Leib the Medic's Son, went through town on horseback. The younger boys from the *heders,* who waited all year to go from house to house and earn a bit of money delivering Purim gifts, would receive a coin in every house.

In the evening's Purim feast, Purim players from the *beit hamidrash* went from house to house performing a Purim play. Their last song was "practical":

> *"Hey Mr. Strong as Iron,*
> *Give money, give money,*
> *I must continue on my travels".*

They used to tell a story about a matchmaker who disguised himself as a wealthy prospective groom and announced how much money he earned in one day. It turns out that the day the matchmaker was referring to was Purim and his earnings were due to the delivery of Purim gifts.

Passover

On Hannukah they would already begin to prepare for Passover, rendering goose fat for Passover. While cooking, our mothers removed bits of crackling goose skin and give it to the children. These goose fat cracklings also served as seasoning for the potato soup and other dishes. After Purim they began to prepare the potatoes and whitewash the houses. Poor people earned some money for Passover helping the bakers bake *matzah.* They perforated the *matzah.* Those who ate *matzah* made under the strictest kosher supervision made it themselves taking water from the pump and carrying it to the bakers to be exact and ensuring that there would not be the slightest flaw. My father of blessed memory ate this strictly supervised *matzah.* From one "pot" of flour he baked 24 little *matzahs* for the entire period of Passover. He only ate *matzah* balls on the last day of Passover.

Women would begin to cook a week before Passover, placing beets in a keg for the meat borscht. The women who did not do this bought it from Ratze the Borscht Lady. They also made wine from raisins for the four cups. Wealthy Jews brought wine from Lodz or Warsaw for the four cups.

There was a rumour circulating in town that Reb Yitzhak received wine from Rishon Letzion in Eretz Israel. This news made a great impression on the Jews of Zychlin and everyone was jealous of him.

On the Sabbath before Passover (Shabbat Gadol) our rabbi delivered a sermon in the *beit hamidrash* about keeping strictly kosher.

On Lag Ba'omer school boys went out with bows and arrows. The Zionist youth organized outings outside of town where they enjoyed the fresh air, pitched tents, lit bonfires and cooked their own food. This helped to prepare them for immigration to the Land of Israel.

The Holiday of Receiving the Torah

On this holiday we remembered the story when Jews were in the Land of Israel, worked their fields and delivered their first fruits. In our town we symbolically marked this holiday with "glitter", which we bought from the gentiles and spread around in our houses.

When we read the Book of Ruth we longed for the Land of Israel even more.

Tisha B'Av

When we read Lamentations Jews cried over the destruction of the Holy Temple. There was a custom in the *beit hamidrash* to throw slippers.

The *yeshiva*

There was a *yeshiva* in the *beit hamidrash*. The head of the *yeshiva* was the great scholar and Talmudic genius Reb Reuven Mordechai Skrobek. Not only boys from Zychlin studied in this *yeshiva*, but boys from other towns as well, especially from Lecyca. They were given room and board in the homes of the wealthier Jews. Sometimes one of these young men would be taken as a groom for the host's daughter. For the young generation the *yeshiva* was like a university. The boys immersed themselves in the study of Talmud and other holy texts. Occasionally, some of these boys got their hands on secular books such as Shomer's novels (Shomer was the pseudonym of Yiddish author Nahum Meir Schaikewitz), Mendele Mocher Sforim's "The Mare" as well as Zionist pamphlets. By the way, Sholem Asch studied in the Zychlin *yeshiva*.

* * * *

All this was all obliterated by the murderous Hitler gangs, may their names be blotted out. Nothing remains of the Zychlin Jews, no graves and no one to recite the Kaddish prayer for the dead. Let my words serve as a memorial monument for our murdered parents, brothers, sisters and families as well as all of our holy martyrs.

Elijah the Prophet at Chaimke's doorstep

by Yosef Rozengarten

Translated by Leon Zamosc

[Original book: pages 204-205 Yiddish section]

I heard this story when I was small child.

Saul "the dove-catcher" was the son of the *feldsher* Chaim Leib. He and his friends had accounts to settle with Chaimke the teacher since they had studied with him in the *heder*. So they decided to pull a prank on him. On Passover *seder* night, they brought a tied goat to Chaimke's doorstep and waited until he opened the door to welcome Elijah the Prophet and recite Shefoch Chamatcha.[2] When that happened, they let loose the rope and ... in went the goat!

One can imagine the fright and the screams of Chaimke and his wife when they saw the goat. Saul "the dove-catcher" and his mates, who had been hiding behind the stairs, burst into laughter and fled away.

After calming down, the couple decided that it was not an ordinary goat, but Elijah the Prophet in the flesh, simply disguised as a goat. They regretted that, in their bafflement, they had not properly honored him with the glass of wine they had prepared for him.

In the morning the town went on a rampage. The event was the main topic of discussion in the prayer houses and especially in the *beit hamidrash* where Chaimke used to pray. Everybody envied him for the privilege of being visited by Elijah the Prophet during the *seder*... He was honored with a special *aliyah* to the Torah and, drinking after the prayers, someone toasted his health: "Just as you were blessed by the visit of Elijah the Prophet, may you also be able to hear the trumpets of the Messiah!" All the worshipers answered, "Amen, amen!" Later, the rabbi's wife Chana and the women of the Ezrat Nashim charitable society pushed themselves to wish Chaimke a happy new year.

Watching from a distance Saul "the dove-catcher" could not stop laughing...

---

[2] Translator's note: Near the end of the Passover seder, the door of the house is opened for Elijah the Prophet, harbinger of salvation. Traditionally this is coupled with the recitation of Shefoch Chamatcha (pour your wrath) - biblical verses invoking God's anger upon those who oppress and torment the Jewish people.

Hasidic wars in Zychlin

by Avraham Razon

Translated by Leon Zamosc

[Original book: pages 271-274 Yiddish section]

Shmuel Abba Zychlinski was born in Piatek and later he came to Zychlin. He was a very intelligent fellow who in his younger years was already engaged in spiritual work, writing songs dedicated to Eretz Israel. He was one of the first maskilim in Poland.

Shmuel Abba was a great admirer of nature. He had a beautiful garden in his yard, with all kinds of trees and fruits. There was a water well and a *beit hamidrash* for prayer on holidays. The garden was surrounded by a high fence.

Shmuel Abba excelled in music, loved to sing and listen to singing. He knew a great deal and spread knowledge among the intelligentsia of the region, as well as among the common people. It was not that easy -- the people were primitive and held him to no standards. He, however, did not panic. He liked to go to the Oporow forest every other day and give his thoughts there. On the way to the forest he greeted all the people he met, and would come back from his walks refreshed and full of hope. People were already waiting in his house to receive a blessing from his holy lips. Many of them slept in his garden,

Shmuel Abba was a powerful speaker who knew how to win an audience. Every Friday afternoon he would speak, in different tongues. The *yeshiva* students of the area used to come to hear his Hebrew. He was able to talk, without interruption, for six hours. Even Nahum Sokolov came from Wyszogród to hear him speak Hebrew.

His teachings began to spread and he talked more and more to the youth about the return to Zion. Against this were the Kotzker Hasidim, followers of Rabbi Simcha Binem Bornstein, the Zychliner rabbi. And the fighting began. Two camps were formed in Zychlin – the disciples of Rebbe Shmuel Abba and the Kotzker adherents.

Then Shmuel Abba started fighting for his ideas, which included creating a more modern *yeshiva*, where one could also learn Hebrew. His main followers were Leibl the scribe, Hersch Kasha and Esther the wife of the *gabbai*.

On one occasion during Rosh Hashanah, when Shmuel Abba's followers had gathered around the well to pray, their opponents tried to interrupt them. But the Rebbe continued the prayer and said with pain: "Dear God, I submit to you the whole matter and I ask you to judge who is right - and you should judge justly." His followers began to fight with the Kotzkers and there was a public outcry. The Kotzkers accused Rebbe Shmuel Abba of writing books against Czar Nicholas II Romanov, the last Emperor of Russia.

Then came Shavuot. The Rebbe was walking in the garden and his followers were coming to pray in the *beit hamidrash*. The place was full of people, also outside. Suddenly three policemen approached the Rebbe when he was starting the Shavuot prayer. They wanted to arrest him for writing against the Czar. There was pandemonium.

In those days there was a law that allowed someone else to temporarily substitute for an offender. Rabbi Hersch Kasha, one of the most devoted followers, told the police chief that the Rebbe could not go to prison on holy Shavuot, forged in chains. "I'm going to sit in for our holy rabbi", he said. He was chained and taken to prison, where he spent two weeks.

The episode was a major scandal, but the whole matter was eventually clarified. It was demonstrated that the Rebbe's poems and writings were in the spirit of the Torah and not against the Czar, and that he called the Jews to go to their home, to the Holy Land - the Land of Israel. Rabbi Hersch Kasha was released. The Rebbe entered the small *beit hamidrash* and the congregation was full of pride about the great victory. There was rejoicing and a lot of talk about the righteous man's triumph in the town. In his garden, the great teacher said nothing - he just looked at the trees and went back to study.

After the High Holidays the Rebbe opened the roof of his *sukkah*, so that more air could enter. He went again to the Oporow forest. On the way, he blessed the reapers in the fields and his heart sang a song about the Jews harvesting their own fields in Eretz Israel.

When he returned from the forest, he wrote a poem and hid it in a bookcase. After the Holocaust, when Leibl the scribe was preparing to go to Palestine, he told him: "I know that you are going to Eretz Israel and I will give you a blessing with a poem that I have dedicated to our holy land. You will put it in the synagogue among the books of our prophets."

Leibl traveled to Eretz Israel carrying the poem and the blessing. When he arrived in Jerusalem, he went straight to the Western Wall. Not far away stood the old synagogue. He approached the Holy Ark, placed the Rebbe's poem and the blessing among the books, and said: "In the name of the holy righteous,

Shmuel Abba of Zychlin, I ask you Holy God, to pay heed to the troubles of my people and bring them back to their land, their fields, where they want to live and work, because they have not forgotten anything." When he received Leibl's letter about this, the Rebbe was very happy.

Not long after that, the Rebbe passed away. His son Moshe became a rabbi in Zychlin. He did not interfere in any matters. He was a great learner and always kept busy. Rabbi Hersch Kasha also passed away .

A new life began in Zychlin. Rabbi Simcha Binem became the spokesman. Although he was not a Kotzker Hasid, he was a supporter of the Kotzker dynasty. He did not have many disciples studying with him. The rabbi was very clever, had a distant look. His students were part of a theatrical group. For Purim, they performed the play "Ahasuerus," once with Rabbi Simcha Binem and the second time with Israel Yitzhak Helmer. Mordechai Ber Weiden, who was a very delicate man, played Queen Esther.

Later on, a Hanukkah society was formed, headed by Binem Kilbert. The richer people of Zychlin used to go to the village of Tretki where they celebrated the holiday. Binem Kilbert led the way. They ate and drank, using wine from their own garden for the *kiddush* ceremony. They went on Sunday to the village and would come home by Friday, rejoiced and pleased with the Hanukkah holiday, as if it were an "Olympics." The participants included Israel Yitzhak Helmer, Binem Kraut, Avraham Helmer, Avraham Lenchinski, Ferber, Chlawny, Moshe Rozenberg and Rabbi Simcha Binem. At the end of the holiday, the rabbi used to give a speech about the Maccabee heroes and the miracles of Hanukkah. They sang Hanukkah songs and celebrated Hanukkah with latkes and donuts, like all the Jews of the small towns.

Some time later, a war broke out over *shechita* and *hazanut.* Shlomo Zebulun was a beautiful singer and a butcher. The Kotzker Hasidim were against him and there was a fight between Avraham Helmer and Zebulun. Avraham Helmer was a respectable *baal tefillah* who led the prayers with his five sons. Shlomo Zebulun had a beautiful voice and you loved him. Their war lasted a long time.

In the meantime, Rabbi Simcha Binem died. He was succeeded by his uncle Itche Meir Zachil, who was not a Ger Hasid and faced strong opposition from Moshe Chelmski. In any case, Itche Meir did not serve as rabbi of Zychlin for long because he soon passed away as well.

But the war was bound to continue. In the next chapter, the Ger Hasidim would confront the *dayan* Aaron Yehuda of Mszczonow, one of the most righteous men of our generation.

A joyous Purim

by Yaakov Ben-Binah

Translated by Leon Zamosc

[Original book: pages 56-56 Hebrew section, 205-206 Yiddish section]

The Ger Hasidim controlled the life of the community in Zychlin. They were led by Reb Moshe Chelmski, who had ruled for such a long time that it seemed as if he had been anointed for it. After the uprising in Russia and Poland against the oppressive regime of the Czar, demanding democratic rights, the people of Zychlin also organized in order to end the rule of the Ger dynasty. And they succeeded in doing it. For the first time a candidate of the people, Reb Yehoshua Fayvel Kelmer, was elected to replace Reb Moshe Chelmski.

The results of the election were announced in the month of Adar, which is a joyous time. One of the activists involved in the revolt was Reb Aharon Berman. He was so happy that he decided to celebrate the victory in a unique way. He brought two musicians at his expense and placed them in front of Reb Moshe Chelmski's shop. When they started playing, and the sound of the drum, cymbals and trumpet resonated throughout the town, the crowds flocked and gathered around. To everyone's delight, Reb Aharon Berman raised the hem of the capote and danced to the music.

For the Jews of Zichlin, there was dance, joy and gladness celebrating the people's victory and the defeat of the Ger Hasidim and Reb Moshe Chelmski personally.

The holiday of Purim turned out to be the most joyful that the Jews of Zychlin had seen in years.

Traditional and modern

by Ben-Nachum

Translated by Leon Zamosc

[Original book: pages 54-56 Hebrew section, 202-204 Yiddish section]

Esther Malka Zyger was a well-known figure in the town. After the death of her husband Shmuel Zyger, she had to take care of five children, three of her own and two from Shmuel's previous marriage. Despite her economic troubles, she was gifted with a social sense and devoted to others. Her best friend was Chaya Rachel Helmer, the wife of the late Reb Yehoshua Helmer, who perished in the Holocaust.

Esther Malka Zyger

Noah Zyger, an older son of Esther Malka's husband Shmuel's first marriage, was one of the students of the *beit hamidrash* (most of whom were old enough to stand on their own, and yet remained "close to their parents' table"), It was natural that they would socialize together (this was in the mid-1910s), and they would meet in the house of Noah, who lived with his father's first wife in a room and a kitchen. Esther Malka did not resent the fact that these relations disturbed the normal order of her family's life. On the contrary, she accepted it with sympathy, as if they were all members of her own family. She shared herself in their dilemmas and problems.

And there was one problem that was "hot" in those days. Young people were expected to fulfill the sacred principle of honoring father and mother. In traditional homes, any deviation from that norm involved mental anguish, both for the parents and the sons. Now, the usual Jewish dress at the time was long clothes, and a round hat with a hard brim. But we wanted to move from that to a more modern attire: a short garment and a hat with a soft brim and indented crown.

Traditional people: Members of Torah and Avodah in Zychlin

We could not buy one of the new garments because, being dependent on our parents, we did not have our own money. So we took a torn Shabbat garment and asked the tailor to fix it. The tailor, who sympathized with us, changed it into a short garment. This would typically take several weeks and was done in secret. In the meantime, we would try to get a modern hat, which we then kept secure in some hidden place. Until the long-awaited Shabbat came and in which we would show up at home dressed as a "gentile".

Disgrace and shame cannot be described in words. Such a Shabbat was tantamount to Tisha B'Av – a sad day of mourning. One must remember the kind of dogmatism that prevailed in those times in order to understand the courage that was required to change one's attire. It was not just a change in dress, but a challenge to tradition.

Modern people: group of friends in Zychlin, 1930. From right: Aharon Hanoch Kutnovski, Noach Plonski, Yosef Wolkowicz, Yosef Chelmski, Yitzhak Kelmer, Eliahu Ryster, Noah Zyger. Second row: Yaakov Noy (Neufeld), Avraham Foiershtein, Moshe Zyger.

Even the irregularities in the form of wearing the old traditional Jewish hat would often involve harsh condemnation. In Zychlin there was a study room where, in cycles of three-four years, students prepared to continue later in the study of Gemara, Perush (Rashi) and Tosafot. The nickname of the Rebbe of the room was Reb Lakish.[3] He once saw one of his former students wearing the traditional hat leaning to the side of his ear and the forehead down. Said Reb Lakish in Yiddish: "Der ying vet oysgein tzu tarbut rah" (this guy will go down the wrong path). And indeed, that same guy emigrated to America, studied dentistry and developed new medicines that to this day are used worldwide. His name was Nahum Opatow, son of Shlomo Opatowski.

---

[3] Translator's note: Rish Lakish or Rabbi Shimon ben Lakish was one of the greatest second generation Amoraim (scholars of the period from about 200 to 500 CE in Eretz Israel). He worked in Tiberias during the second half of the third century CE.

Esther Malka was among those who did not see a future for their family in Zychlin. In the early 1930s, with the help of relatives who had emigrated to Australia, she and her family left the town and went to live in Melbourne, where they died in good health.

May her memory be blessed.

Our little town

by Miriam Jacobi (Mania Olsztyn)

Translated by Leon Zamosc

[Original book: pages 45-47 Hebrew section, 188-192 Yiddish section]

Although Zychlin was a small town, it was big and wonderful in its spirit. It had everything - everything needed for a developed and cultured town. The Polish population was economically established, but the bulk of the town's soul was the Jewish community.

The Jews of Zychlin, seemingly simple people, also worked. They were honest and good. They were active in a variety of occupations and in commerce, and some of the merchants had dealings with their Gentile neighbors.

There was usually peace between us and the town's Gentiles, but anti-Semitism was also present in Zychlin. Like the rest of the Jews in the Diaspora, we often heard the hostile remark: "Go back to Palestine!". The anti-Semites did not know it, but that was precisely our greatest dream...

We were free to develop our social and cultural aspirations. Among us, there were Jews who were completely free and there were Jews who were ultra-Orthodox, traditionalist and meticulous in their fulfillment of the *mitzvot*. We were organized and united, big and small together, as one large family. Together we suffered and together we rejoiced. And one great ambition beat in the hearts of us all: to go and live in the Land of Israel.

Here I would like to mention some of our wonderful people, such as the late Yitzhak Kelmer. He was the living spirit of the General Zionists in Zychlin. If I am not mistaken, at some point he was the chairman of the Jewish community. But Yitzhak never waited to be elected to public office. For all the people of the town, he was a faithful and devoted father, someone who dedicated his life to helping others. In our hearts, he will never be forgotten.

We once asked Yitzhak: "when will you go to Eretz Israel?". He replied with a wide smile: "There is a lot of work I still have to do. First I must make sure that all the town's Jews are able to go - then I will start thinking about myself." But he would not be able to make it: when the Nazi oppressors arrived in Zychlin, Yitzhak was among the first to be murdered.

I also want to say something about our Zionist home, about my mother and my dear brother Leibush (Aryeh), who are no longer with us. My parents were dedicated Zionists in heart and soul and all our ambition was to live in Eretz Israel. Our economic situation was good, we lacked nothing. Yet we dreamed about going to Palestine. My father and the boys were tinsmiths who worked in the villages of the landowners, and my mother had a shop of kitchen utensils. When it became known that we were preparing to leave, some of the Gentile friends tried to convince my mother that Jews like us should not leave Poland: "You are good, dedicated people and we love you. Please stay with us. Here you make a good living, but Palestine is a land of deserts where you will suffer hunger and poverty".

My late mother, wonderful in her pride, stood before them holding her head high and replied: "Yes, it is good for us with you, but we are in a foreign country. We want to live on our land, in our homeland, where our people are waiting for us, in our place, and it is better for us to eat dry bread in the Land of Israel than to stay here". I was in the store with my mother and, hearing her wonderful words, I burst into tears of excitement.

And indeed, we were the first entire family of Zychliners who returned to Eretz Israel. Many of the older boys and girls had already left Zychlin. My brother Leibush and my older sisters were among the first pioneers. It was them who attracted the whole family.

I was a girl when we came to Israel, and it is difficult for me to remember all the people of Zychlin. But it is even more difficult to forget the place where you are born, and especially a place where you spent the gorgeous days of the dawn of life, your youthful days. We had a beautiful youth. Zychlin's youngsters were the most animated youngsters of the region. They took good care of us. We had schools with good teachers from Warsaw, evening lessons in Hebrew, and a library. We read a lot and attended cultural classes, drama classes, art, reading, recitation... And all of that we did on our own. There were youth movements in the town: Hashomer Hatzair, Tzeirei Zion, General Zionists and others. There was a mandolin orchestra and there were choirs. My brother Leibush participated in all these activities. He had a great talent for art and poetry. But he passed away when he was only 52 years old. Our consolation is that he died a natural death and is buried in the holy land of Jerusalem. May his memory be blessed,

The town itself was beautiful. Extensive green fields, miles of tall grain crops in the summer, plenty of fruit orchards, ornamental gardens, a small bridge sloping over a water pond, a train passing by... I loved walking around the town, and spent my youth in the fields. I enjoyed going out to the train station from time to time. I would sit there, looking at passengers waving their hands, not knowing who these people were. There was a childhood joy in that. The town also had flour mills and a large sugar factory. They belonged to the Gentiles, but we enjoyed watching the movements of the people who worked there. The sound of the sirens marking the lunch breaks and the beginning and end of the working day added a touch to our childhood experiences.

I spent my youthful days in Zychlin and I loved the town. I enjoyed everything! I was sorry when I had to move to the big city of Lodz and work to continue to study and stand on my own. It was a completely different way of life. I spent two years in Lodz, far from what was most precious to me, until I fulfilled my dream and came to Israel with my whole family on the Hanukkah of 1926.

The first year in the country was tough, we endured real hunger, but we were not disappointed. My late mother was the living force among us. She saw that the situation was difficult, but her spirit did not fall. She said: "Children, we will all roll up our sleeves and start working so that we can live with dignity."

She was sick for most of her years in Palestine, but she never despaired or longed for the life of exile. She was happy to live and die in Eretz Israel.

We had no relatives left in Zychlin, but we thought often about the friends and acquaintances we left behind, especially when the persecution of the Jews and the mass killings began.

Our small and beloved town is gone, with all those people who did not get to come to us. In their bitter fate, their aspirations and holy lives were sacrificed, along with those of millions of Jews, on the altar of evil. Our hearts bleed when we are reminded of that horror. Pure, good, and honest Jews, who did their work in peace and with integrity, blameless people... victims of terrible burning and killing.

A crime that will live in infamy.

May their memory be blessed.

The cradle of Zionism

by Bracha Yair (Olsztyn)

Translated by Leon Zamosc

[Original book: pages 51-52 Hebrew section, 198-200 Yiddish section]

Bracha Olsztyn

Many years have passed since I left Zychlin. Many changes have taken place in the world and in our country, but I have not forgotten the foundations of Zionism in my town. Frequently the image arises before my eyes. Zychlin in all its forms: the humble life of exile, the hostility that surrounded us for many generations, the eternal fear of hatred against the Jews. Even so, we had a wonderful, vibrant youth. That was the honor and glory of our town.

I remember my childhood days, when we learned to love our land through the holidays and traditions at home. Every holiday was related to Zion and the celebration and redemption of the people. The prayers were imbued with hope and supplications for the return to Zion: "and we thought of Zion and we were like dreamers." I remember the deep sorrow and mourning on Tisha B'Av. Shadows hovering around and on the walls, projected by the candle flashing in the corner. Mother sits on the floor, reads the book and weeps over the destruction of the Temple, the glory of our country and our people in the past. As the prophet Jeremiah put it: "How lonely lies the city that was once full of people!" It is hard to describe the mystical emotion that I felt. I began to dream about returning to Eretz Israel.

Part of my childhood connection with Zionism had to do with the beloved Rozenfeld family. It was a family blessed with many children and poverty often knocked on their door. The late Avraham Rozenfeld, a watchmaker, was one of the founders of Zionism in Zychlin. He was an educated man whose very presence inspired respect, and his house was home to the most enlightened men in town. He attentively followed what was happening in the world at large and especially in the Zionist movement. I was friends with one of his daughters and, when Rosenfeld and his comrades discussed some subject, we would hide in a corner of the house and listen to everything that was said. The conversations were about Zionist congresses, about the great leader Teodor Herzl, about the pogroms in Romania and the blood libels in Russia, about the expulsions of Jews and so on.

In 1915 the Germans invaded Poland and introduced some progress and culture. We were allowed to engage in sports and open libraries and schools in Hebrew. The youth got organized with the formation of groups of scouts and pioneers. With incredible joy and vigor, we got involved in public activism. We were thirsty for knowledge and education. The Bnai Zion Association was created by Pinchas Getzel, Rivka Chelmski, Riva Rozenberg. David Steinberger (Shamir), Aharon Kanarek, Avraham Rozenfeld, Yitzhak Kelmer, Meir Helmer, Yehezkel Helmer, and others.

I remember the day I registered as a member of Bnei Zion. How proud and happy I was to be part of the Zionist movement and to be able to work for the realization of the noble Zionist ideal. The founding members engaged in the sacred work, opened libraries, and organized evening classes. My late brother Leibush (Aryeh) Olsztyn, with other friends from Poalei Zion, founded a dramatic circle and I participated in performances. We sent all the proceeds to the organization's main office in Warsaw, which donated the funds to the Keren Kayemet and Keren Hayesod.

One of the activists was my friend Chava Najdorf, whom I deeply loved and whose image stays in my heart to this day. She was an educated and noble girl with a strong will to overcome all the difficulties of life. Her personality illuminated everything around her. We studied Hebrew together and she was familiar with every cultural subject.

The personality of the late David Steinberger (Shamir) looms large in my memory. He was one of the founders of Bnai Tzion. He came to Zychlin from the big outside world, equipped with a great deal of knowledge. He had a blessed influence on the Zionist youth in the town. He instilled in us his love for the Hebrew language and every lesson with him was an unforgettable experience.

When the third *aliyah* began, many members of our organization came to Palestine. I arrived with other friends in 1926. Each one of us laid a stone for the building and progress of the country. We raised a new generation that would continue the sacred work after us. Our families are extensive and involved in the life of the country, which is a source of satisfaction and happiness for all of us.

The heart aches for those who were not able to fulfill their ideal and see the resurrection of our people in their land. Their work and memory will be blessed forever.

A bundle of memories

by M. Koren

Translated by Leon Zamosc

[Original book: pages 44-45 Hebrew section, 186-188 Yiddish section]

I remember Zychlin as I saw it at the dawn of my childhood. Dark in every way. A town without any lighting. I remember my fears when I ran home at night from the *heder* through the market, which was full of fools. I also remember when the town was "modernized" and a chandelier was installed at the synagogue. We were very proud of Zychlin then. In the evenings the lamp moved back and forth and cast a red light around it. I think that my fears grew more then than before it was installed. Now there was also lighting inside the houses, but enlightened public activity did not exist. The Russian authorities did not allow the Jews to organize any institutions except the *heders* and a *beit hamidrash*.

Under the cover of darkness and distress, however, there was a strong yearning for a free public cultural life. A change took place in this respect in our town, and in the whole of Poland, during the First World War, when the Germans occupied the country in 1914. We must not and cannot forget what Hitler's barbarians would do to us later, but at that time, when we were under the yoke of the Russians and Poles, the arrival of the Germans spurred an awakening in the town. For their own political reasons, they allowed the establishment of social, cultural and sports organizations, as well as the functioning of political parties of all shades. In this respect, I should note that public and cultural life in Zychlin was more developed than in other towns, including some that were larger than ours.

Today, with the hindsight of time, I must say that there were mistakes in the way we conducted the activities of the political parties at the time. But I prefer to abstain from mentioning the names of those who repeated seven times a day the phrase "Next year in Jerusalem" or those who opposed the idea of establishing the State of Israel. We were active in Zionist parties whose main goal was the foundation of a Jewish state, but each party had a different political and ideological approach. We were torn and divided. Nevertheless, our hopes were fulfilled. It cost a lot of sacrifices and blood, but the State of Israel exists and the people of Israel is alive.

I remember well a characteristic episode from Zychlin's cultural life. The members of the Jewish Drama Circle of neighboring Kutno had offered us to come to town and present a play that they had prepared and adapted for the stage. We rented the hall for the show and started selling tickets. On Saturday night, the group of actors from Kutno showed up. We had announced that the show would start at exactly 8:30 in the evening. However, the preparations continued until about ten o'clock. I do not really remember whether the show turned out to be as good as our friends from Kutno had promised, but I do remember that when it was supposed to finally start the lights went out. We brought an electrician, who tried to fix the breakdown. By midnight, the hall was still shrouded in darkness. A few people in the audience demanded their money back, but all the others sat patiently waiting for the show to begin. All this happened in the middle of the summer, when the sun rises early. And as the first rays of light appeared on the horizon, the actors finally took the stage and the play began ...

The town of my childhood

by Helena Bodek (Tzinamon)

Translated by Leon Zamosc

[Original book: pages 52-54 Hebrew section, 200-201 Yiddish section]

Helena Bodek (Tzinamon)

Zychlin - the town of my childhood, the world of a little girl who could not imagine life beyond its limited confines.

Now, from the distance of time, after all the suffering we endured during and after the war, I see Zychlin in a more sober light: a scanty, poor little town, and yet so close to my heart.

I evoke the image of the main square, dominated by the towering church. Every week on Sunday, the sounds of the organ and the chants of the faithful rose and resounded from there. Crowds of Gentiles wearing their best clothes for the holiday - peasants, clerks, burghers, all the local "aristocracy" flocking to the church from all sides of the town. On that day, the Jews disappeared from view, locked in their small, stuffy apartments, behind their dark shops. Shabbat, on the other hand, was the day of the Jews. The main streets were crowded with people, well-dressed boys and girls, noisy adults and children, loud conversations in Yiddish interwoven with Polish words.

On weekdays, the Jews stood out in the town. Their shops and workshops provided the population with groceries and goods, especially on market days. Bustle, bargaining, quarrels over attracting customers, especially among the farmers who gathered in the market with their carts laden with dairy products and agricultural produce. In the market in the center of town, the residents stocked up on groceries for the entire week, from vegetables and fruits to fattened geese, which Jewish housewives used to buy for the Shabbat celebrations.

Zychlin market square.
[Not in the original book. Image source: Żychlin Historia]

On Fridays the town rested peacefully as the sun went down. In their homes, the Jews were preparing for Shabbat. The candles gleamed in polished candlesticks, on tables covered with white tablecloths, spreading their light on the *kiddush* wine, the glasses, and the *challah* covered with an embroidered napkin. The table was set for the reception of the worshipers returning from the synagogues and the Shabbat meal.

In the packed Synagogalna and Zdrova alleys, where the synagogue and the offices of the Jewish community were located, there was a lot of activity. Men with beards and *payot*, some with fur hats and others wearing regular caps, hurried to the synagogue, individually or in groups. More than once, an insolent young Pole, seeing a bearded Jew, would throw a stone at him. In general, there were passable relations between Polish and Jewish residents. There was tolerance, but it was not devoid of a copious dose of mutual derision.

There was a group of Polish youth in the town who were under the influence of the antisemitic party Endecja (National Democracy), but they did not pose much danger to the Jews. Anti-Semitism was prevalent mainly in the lower strata of the Polish populace and was rooted in religious hostility. On certain Christian holidays, for example Corpus Christi, it was not advisable for a Jew to be seen on the street during the procession. However, Christians usually treated "their" Jews properly and became accustomed to them - until the Nazis arrived. The Jews had their own cultural life – their *heders*, schools, libraries, and charitable and public institutions. Their impact on the general life of the town was very significant. Their temperament, vivacity, and industriousness gave the town a special character. Therefore, when the Jews of Zychlin were brutally annihilated, the town also died out. True, a place called Zychlin still exists, but it is no longer Zychlin, the town of my childhood.

Remembering the shtetl on the eve of Yom Kippur

by Bracha Berman-Kroshinski

Translated by Leon Zamosc

[Original book: pages 49-50 Hebrew section, 193-197 Yiddish section]

A market square with a water pump in the center of town, framed by four streets. That is all. Around the square stood the church, many Jewish shops, the *shtiebel* of the Ger Hasidim, and the "Izba" - the meeting place of the Hashomer Hatzair youth, the library, and the Zionist organizations. On Budzyner, the street that faced south, one would find the town's only pharmacy, a hotel and several shops, two of which sold candy and ice cream. On that street lived the Zychlin Rebbe, which used to be visited by his followers during the holidays. From there the road led to the Pniewo train station, passing through the Brown-Boveri factory (electrical motors and transformers) and the sugar factory in Dobrzelin. Many residents of the town and the surrounding villages made their living working at these factories.

The opposite street, known as Podwal, turned north, leading on its left to the town's park. In the summer, acacia and jasmine trees bloomed in the park, which had a promenade and was the favorite meeting place for the youth. Further on to the right, the road led to the forests that stretched as far as the nearby town of Gombin, where people used to make frequent excursions.

To the east was Buszkower street, smaller than the others, which led to the cemetery. Wanting to increase its importance, the municipality had located the post office, the telegraph, and the savings bank on that street

Along Pasieka street, which led west, were the schools, the municipality, and the flour mill, which belonged to Moshe Mendel Wojdeslawski, the richest man in the town.

Near Budzyner street there was a small alley. The carriages that took people to and from the train station used to park there. Located between that alley and Pasieka street were the municipal school, the *mikveh* and the residence of the town's rabbi, who was a relative of the Ger Hasidim's Rebbe Avraham Mordechai Alter.

On holidays and Saturdays everything changed. On Friday evening the shops closed, the Jews dressed for Shabbat and they went to pray - some to the synagogue, some to the *beit hamidrash*, and some to the *shtiebel* of the Hasidim. All the worries of the week vanished - Shabbat came, rest came.

Zychliners knew each other well. They educated their children in practical *mitzvot* and were always ready to help the needy. Sick or lonely people did not feel abandoned. They knew that the others were concerned about them and would extend a helping hand when it was needed.

There was a *yeshiva* in Zychlin, and there was not a single Jewish child who did not study in the *yeshiva*, the *heders*, or at home with a private teacher. The Jewish families made every effort to instill in their children the spiritual values of previous generations.

The young were inspired by Zionist ideals, and their ambition to return to the Land of Israel was strong. In the days after the First World War, the ideals of self-liberation and taking matters into one's own hands were very strong. The Zionist movement expanded in all its variants: Poalei Zion Right and Left, Mizrahi, Tzeirei Zion, Hashomer Hatzair, and Agudat Israel. There was also no shortage of young Jewish communists at the time, which was a source of concern for their parents.

It was not easy for the children of Hasidic parents to fulfill their desire to learn Hebrew, go to summer camp, or attend vocational training courses in preparation for *aliyah*. For their parents, it was like a stain in the family's reputation. There were heated arguments between husbands and wives on how to curb the urges of their children, among party members on how to lead and win elections, and within the Zionist youth movements on how to speed up emigration.

If it was not possible to get a visa for Palestine, the youngsters would in the meantime go to a big city, Warsaw or Lodz, to attend a public high school or a university, to get to know the world and expand their horizons. They dreamed of a better, more beautiful world, as envisaged by our prophets. Inspired by humanist and socialist ideas, they went out into the wide world, rejecting the traditional values of the small town. Their sentiments were deeply human and sincere.

The town they left behind was brutally destroyed. Its Jews were murdered and every sign of its old Jewish life and culture was erased. Geographically Zychlin still exists. In the spring, the lilac, acacia and jasmine trees bloom again, but the Jews are no longer there. Gone are *shtiebel* of the Ger Hasidim, the "Izba", the arguments about the Rambam, and the discussions about Marx. We no longer hear the melody of the Gemara or the Hatikvah. All that remains is the deep pain, and the *mitzvah* to never forget.

The town is no more. Went up in smoke and flames, wiped out by the cruel hands of the Nazis. In the fires shaded by fire, only memories remain, which accompany us, the survivors, in our wanderings across seas and continents: torn in our souls and torn in our hearts, thrown into other lands. It is as if a plant, after being uprooted from the ground, is replanted in soil covered with shade.

On the eve of Yom Kippur

The Jewish town, bloodied, crushed and destroyed, was filled with Jewish virtues that had been passed down from generation to generation. It still illuminates the life of an entire week with a Sabbath of kindness and love, thus creating the specificity of Jewish uniqueness. The day of Yom Kippur is indeed a brighter light in the soul of every Jew in exile - and he asks himself: "Where is the power to forgive so many evils?"

When the world, with its beautiful promises, disappoints, we remain alone and seek the power that elevates the offended and crushed to holiness.

The light of the town where we sang the Sabbath hymns and camp songs celebrating our great ideals, the light that brightened our melodies of *"Lecha Dodi"* and *"Tachezakhna"* has not been extinguished. And when we hear them again, somewhere in a place of Jewish exile, our thoughts go back to the town. We take the candle again and go to the synagogue...

It is getting dark in the autumn. The day still warmed by the sun, smiling and smiling with the satisfaction that it is a day on this sinful world when people forgive all the little quarrels, shake hands and wish each other a "good signature" for a new year which, written in heaven, shall be sealed for good.

All the shops in the market and surrounding streets have long been closed. From afar one can hear the weeping voice of a mother wishing the children a happy new year. A trembling voice of a father blessing the children.

You enter Shiloh - the biblical place of Ancient Israel. Men stalk in long capotes, soft boots with white socks and fur hats on their heads. Women in wigs or velvet head wraps, with guipure collars or white silk scarves, walking with candles in their hands. Their frightened eyes looking into the distance,

The synagogue is crowded, full of people and lit candles, the air is hot. A woman is sobbing quietly in a corner. Her heart is full of sorrow. Where is her son? Her Yosele, for whom the town had become too narrow and who had decided to go out to the wider world. Here it is so cozy, so close to God... And there everything must be so strange... Even for God it is too far away. Who knows if his prayers will be heard there? And maybe he won't go to school at all... But in his heart he will certainly miss the town, where everything is so simple and sincere.

The sun has already set, leaving a reddish-brown line of clouds in the sky on the west. From the distance, where the old synagogue is located, the melody of Kol Nidre.

Is it just a prayer of remorse for bad deeds and a statement to improve oneself, or a collective expression of a desire to do something better? The melody is the same, the words the same, the difference is just the place. From a small town to a metropolis.

Is this an expression of mental reckoning? Does this Jewish collective expression of remorse convey the desire for something better for us, for our children, for our people? Or is it a "routine" prayer that is just recited to pay a debt to God before going back to life as usual?

No! Our prophets have said that such "routine" prayers are not heard in heaven. Let's keep that light in our souls and continue to lovingly build our Jewish continuity.

Only then our prayers will be truly authentic.

Community organizations and parties

The committee of the Jewish community

by Yaakov Neufeld (Noi)

Translated by Leon Zamosc

[Original book: pages 90-91 Hebrew section, 244-247 Yiddish section]

When Poland was part of the Russian Empire, it was customary for the Jewish communities to have overseers. They were typically appointed by only a handful of the town's Jewish residents, but they were generally respected by the members of the community and recognized as the local Jewish leaders by the government. In those times, they were considered omnipotent in the running of all aspects of Jewish religious life, including the synagogues, houses of study, *mikvehs* and slaughterhouses.

The first open elections for the Jewish community committee took place during the First World War, under the supervision of the German occupation authorities. All the heads of families who paid dues to the Jewish community were qualified to participate in the ballot. In Zychlin there were two lists of candidates: Agudat Israel, which included the followers of the Ger Hasidim; and a coalition of the General Zionists and the religious Zionists of the Mizrahi party. With the support of a majority of the Jewish residents who until then had not been able to participate in the management of community affairs, the Zionist coalition won the election. However, while they were still in the process of getting organized as the new authority of the Jewish community, the withdrawal of the Germans from Poland left them without legal basis.

With the end of the First World War and the restoration of Polish independence, a special department for the affairs of Jewish communities was established at the Ministry of the Interior. The constitution and subsequent legislation defined new rules for the internal governance of the Jewish communities, which had to be based on democratic elections in which the community's committee members would be chosen by all those who paid dues to the community.

The Zionist movements were determined to gain control of the towns' Jewish community committees. In Zychlin, however, the majority of the voters were not members of parties. Instead, they tended to follow and support different personalities. As a result, only one of the members of the committee elected in 1919 was a candidate of a political party - Aharon Oberman, from the Agudat

Israel list. The other elected members were Zalman Morgentaler (as chairman), Wolf Dorn (a shoemaker who represented the artisans), Shalom Kilbert, Yitzhak Kelmer, and Michael Kozisovitz. The activist of Hashomer Hatzair Bunim Steinberger (Shamir) was appointed as secretary.

Shalom Kilbert, Yitzhak Kelmer, and Michael Kozisovitz were the most active members of the council, the living spirit of the institution. Kelmer was a tireless promoter of Zionism, fighting to get subsidies from the committee for Keren Kayemet, Keren Hayesod and the Zionist youth organizations. He served as deputy mayor and played important roles in the general development of the town. Kozisovitz had settled in Zychlin because his wife came to work in the town as a dentist. He was very knowledgeable, fully devoted to social work, and interested in the religious affairs of the community.

The center of Jewish religious life in Zychlin as depicted in a drawing by W. Reszelbach. Surrounding the square and the water pump, from left to right, the *beit hamisdrash*, the synagogue, and the *mikveh.*

The town's Jewish religious institutions were concentrated in a large area in the shape of the Hebrew letter Het (ח). On the east side was the *beit hamisdrash*, on the west side the *mikveh*, and on the south side the synagogue. In the middle of the square there was a well that was considered the best water source in the town. The synagogue was a spacious building whose foundations reached down into the depths of the earth, with many steps leading down, recalling the biblical verse "From the depths I have called thee." In a large fenced yard, next to the *mikveh*, was the building of a poultry slaughterhouse, where the blood used to flow in open canals under poor sanitary conditions. At Kozisovitz's initiative, and with the help of experts from Warsaw, a sewer was installed and a pit was dug to treat the waste according to modern techniques. People were amazed that clean water came out of the pit... Other improvements included a new wooden floor in the synagogue and the renovation of the neglected *mikveh* with the installation of baths and a roof over the bins.

All this was possible because the religious services and their maintenance were now the responsibility of the community's committee, which collected membership dues from all the Jewish families and operated according to an annual budget that had to be inspected and approved by the Jewish Communities' office of the Polish Ministry of the Interior. In the past, the slaughterers had depended on payments from the butchers and the rabbis had to make a living from several different sources. In the new system everyone received a monthly salary, each according to his position, and all the income from the religious services went into the community's fund.

Board of the Gemilat Hesed in Zychlin, with visitors from Warsaw and America.

Next to the office of the community committee operated the Gemilat Hesed fund, which offered interest-free loans to the poorer Jewish craftsmen and small merchants. The capital for this fund was provided by the American Joint Distribution Committee and the loans were repaid in weekly installments.

Needless to say, there was a good dose of friction between the rabbi and the community committee. One example was the dispute over the rabbi's salary. The rabbi's supporters, who were followers of the Ger Hasidim, were worried that there was not enough difference between his salary and the slaughterers' salary. Another example was the committee's decision to open a door on the south wall of the *beit hamidrash* in order to facilitate the entry and exit of worshipers. Since the adjacent courtyard was shared by the rabbi's apartment, his supporters saw it as trespass and filed an appeal with the authorities. In the end, the appeal was rejected and the community committee was allowed to complete the door's installation.

In the same courtyard, a Talmud Torah was later established for the children of impoverished families.

In 1942, Hitler's henchmen deported all the Jews of the Zychlin ghetto to their deaths at Chelmno extermination camp. Since then, there have been no Jews in the town. This book will serve as a memorial for future generations. May the memory of those who perished be blessed.

In the name of the common people

by Yehoshua Wojdeslawski

Translated by Leon Zamosc

[Original book: pages 79-81 Hebrew section, 230-233 Yiddish section]

More than anything else, the livelihood of the Jewish families of Zychlin depended on small-scale commerce and the crafts. The craftsmen, mostly tailors and shoemakers, made their living selling their artisanal products to the urban population, while the retail merchants, who made up the majority of the Jewish population, bought and sold a variety of merchandise in the town and in the surrounding villages. Once a week, on market day in Zychlin, the small merchants would put their goods up for sale and the peasants from the villages would bring in their agricultural produce. It was a day of lively trade between them.

Zychlin had a municipal council of 24 members, including Jews and non-Jews. Given the composition of the town's population (60 percent Jews and 40 percent non-Jews), the Jewish members of the council should have been in the majority, but the Starosta (district governor) artificially reduced the Jewish representation in the municipality by including Christian rural villages from the surrounding area within the town's boundaries.

The Jewish political parties played a very important, active role in public life. There were three active branches of parties in our town: Poalei Zion Yemin, Poalei Zion Left and Agudat Bnai Zion. I do not mention the Socialist Bund, because it did not really have a working branch in Zychlin. In terms of their level of activism, the two Poalei Zion groups were by far the most important parties. Particularly noteworthy was the activity of their representatives in the municipality, where they did much for the town's residents in the area of taxes and the cost of health care and hospitalization, which was a heavy burden on the Jewish population.

The work of a Jewish member in the municipal council was not easy, especially when he represented a party that defended the interests of the common people. Everyday their work of advocacy met with objections and appeals. I, however, did my best to fulfill the promises I had made when I ran for election. Proof of it was the fact that, when I ran again in the next election, the number of votes for my candidacy doubled.

It is especially important to say some words about our work in the Zychlin Jewish community. Before we gained representation in the community committee, its main job was to raise funds for the salaries of the "holy vessels": the rabbi, the slaughterers, the cantor, etc. When we run for election to the committee, we promised that we would work for a more "modern" community and that we would promote the *aliyah* to Eretz Israel, giving material support to the Jewish pioneers who lacked financial means to emigrate to Palestine and raising funds for the Keren Kayemet and the Keren Hayesod.

It is praiseworthy that the Jews of Zychlin, who were always sympathetic to the ideals of socialist Zionism, made their contribution to establish its foundations, and massively participated in the lectures that we offered on political and literary subjects. Among the speakers who came to town, I remember the writer and historian Yitzhak Schipper, M. Naishtat, Dov Ber Malkin, Israel Ritov and others, including Avraham Morawski, who gave a lecture on Yiddish theater.

Members of Freiheit, the youth organization of Poalei Zion in Zychlin.

The members of Freiheit, the youth organization of Poalei Zion, were wonderful people in terms of their physical and spiritual development. The movement was active in the professional and cultural field, organizing joint meetings with the youth of the Polish Socialist Party. On May 1st, our youngsters would demonstrate with them on the streets of Zychlin (a daring feat that not even the Bundists of Kutno were ever able to achieve).

It is very painful to think about all those Jews who were active in the socialist Zionist work and were murdered through no fault of their own. They left a huge empty space behind. They cared for the poor Jewish population, they stood at the forefront of the social and public life in Zychlin, they worked for the Keren Kayemet, the Keren Hayesod and other national institutions. In sorrow and pain I remember them and the members of all the other movements with whom I frequently worked in our public activities. Thanks to the Zychliner organization in Tel Aviv, I have been able to recall the memories of those tragic days on various occasions.

Polish Jewry, which was so rich in its creative forces and so accomplished in the fields of literature, science and Zionist activism, no longer exists. An immense human pool of Jews, Zionists and pioneers has disappeared as if it had never existed. The Nazi beast plunged into the heart of Judaism and consistently carried out its murderous plan. First it destroyed the Jewish intelligentsia, the academics, the people in the liberal professions, the public activists, and then the starving masses, which were crushed to submission and led like sheep to the slaughter. It was the end of Polish Jewry and, with it, the end of the Jewish community of Zychlin.

Founders and activists of the Bnai Zion Association

by Rivka Kanarek

Translated by Leon Zamosc

[Original book: pages 87-89 Hebrew section, 241-244 Yiddish section]

From my youth, I remember Zychlin as a town with a long Zionist tradition that went back to the days of the Hovevei Zion movement. Already in the late 19th and early 20th centuries, there were families that had special coin boxes to collect money for Eretz Israel. With great love and affection for Zion, they run fundraising campaigns among the Jewish residents, encouraging them to follow in their footsteps and do the same. Among those families I remember the following: Rozenfeld, Zhukhovski, Farber, Mendel-Meir Rozenbaum, Avraham Katz, Berish Adler, as well as the family of my father and teacher, Mordechai Mendel Adler, their memory is blessed.

By the standards of that period, their activity was so effective that it succeeded in motivating the younger generation, arousing among them a national awakening and a deep disposition to love Eretz Israel and work for it. From the dawn of their youth they harnessed themselves to far-reaching actions, organizing groups for education and culture, and all this despite the fact that the way in which they began to walk was still uncertain.

The youngsters who were first active in the Zionist movement in Zychlin were unique figures. They included Riva Rozenberg, a noble daughter of a Gur Hasid, Pinchas Getzel, Fischel Lesman, Meir Kilbert, Goldbfarb, Aaron Kanarek, Meir Helmer, Bracha Olsztyn and myself (I was known as Altaleh in Zychlin). There were of course others who are not mentioned here.

In 1916 or 1917, these young people founded the Bnai Zion Association in the town. In those days the group did not have a clearly defined ideology and was not affiliated with any political party. Often in the evenings and sometimes early in the morning, the activists consulted among themselves about the activities that the group should undertake. Initially, there was no one to provide guidance to them. External instructors or lecturers could not be invited to come to Zychlin because of the lack of resources. But those limitations did not last long. Help came in the form of a gifted and talented man who elevated the Bnai Zion group to the King's Road - David Steinberger (Shamir).

Here I should mention the Biderman family of Zychlin. The head of the family, Shmelke, was looking for a groom of all virtues for Tova, his eldest daughter. He indeed succeeded in finding a good boy from an ultra-Orthodox, noble Hasidic family. The young man, David Steinberger, was a Torah scholar, a prodigy who was also proficient in secular studies. During the week he wore a low cape, while on Saturdays and holidays he wore a silk cape and a *shtreimel.* But it did not take long for David to change his traditional clothing to a modern style. Then he joined the Bnai Zion group and, to our delight, we discovered that we had been blessed with the kind of leader that our group needed. The tasks he undertook on his own were all-encompassing. He gave talks about Zionism and organized evening classes in Hebrew, the Bible, and Jewish history. He was fluent in Hebrew. Within a short time, the Tarbut school, which provided Hebrew instruction, was established in Zychlin under his leadership. The school was affiliated with the nationwide Tarbut organization, which had a central office in Warsaw. The Jewish youth of the town, thirsty for knowledge and education, quickly filled the classes. It should be noted that, until the opening of the Tarbut Hebrew school, there had not been a single school in Zychlin that deserved to bear that name and where Jewish children could receive a decent secular education.

Students in the Hebrew evening classes, taught by Rivka Kanarek. First row: Lederman, Sara Rubin, R.Kanarek, R. Koren, R. Landshnaider. Second row: unknown, Feiga Kelmer, teacher Rivka Kanarek, Nomi Landshnaider, Koren. Third row: Zelda Klinger, Malka Rubin.

One day we were informed that the Keren Hayesod had established WIZO, a world organization of Zionist women. Their role was to organize fundraisers that were considered especially appropriate for women, such as the Gold Fund campaign, which was mainly about collecting rings and jewels among Jewish women as a contribution to the Keren Hayesod. The headquarters of the organization sent iron rings to the Zionist organizations all over Poland, to give to each woman as a gift in recognition of her donation. Such rings also reached the Bnai Zion in our town.

The Bnai Zion group in Zychlin maintained its unity, and the female members remained as loyal to it as before the founding of WIZO, but they participated vigorously and passionately in the Gold Fund campaign. When we went out in pairs to all the districts of the town to collect donations, the doors of all the Jewish homes were opened to us. We explained the purpose of our mission and got a very favorable response. The campaign was a great success. Not only did the women remove the wedding rings from their fingers, but they also added other gold rings, earrings, necklaces, brooches and watches. Our success became known in many other towns and cities, some much larger than Zychlin. They followed our example and were also successful.

Sadly, many activists did not fulfill their aspiration to emigrate to Eretz Israel. Before their own *aliyah*, they felt that they had to stay as long as possible to fulfill the important goal of training other pioneers and assist their emigration to Palestine. So they postponed from one day to the next, fearing that nobody would fill the empty space that they would leave behind.

Nevertheless, some of the Bnai Zion activists did manage to reach Palestine in the mid-1920s, including David Steinberger (Shamir) and his wife Tova, Yehuda Jakubowicz, Meir Helmer, Bracha Olsztyn, Aaron Kanarek, and myself. They got to see that the families they established in Eretz Israel were among the founders and builders of the Jewish state.

The Bnai Zion activists who stayed behind were interrupted In the midst of their blessed activity. They were working with supreme fidelity when calamity descended upon them. The Nazis murdered them, along with our other brothers and sisters, men and women, elders and children.

We will never forget them.

The General Zionists – Bnai Zion Association

by R. Yosef

Translated by Leon Zamosc

[Original book: pages 61-62 Hebrew section, 209-210 Yiddish section]

After the Hovevei Zion held the Katowice Conference in 1884, the Zionist idea gained traction in the Diaspora, especially among the Jews of Eastern Europe. The General Zionist Organization was the first Zionist political party in Poland and in our own town, where the name of the party's local branch was Bnai Zion Association.

Under the Czarist regime, all political activities were prohibited. Being illegal, the Zionist movement had to function underground. However, with the German occupation of Poland during the First World War, the Zionist activists were able to work openly, launching extensive operations throughout the country.

The founding members of the Bnai Zion Association in Zychlin were Avraham Yitzhak Rozenfeld (first chairman, died in the United States), David Steinberger (Shamir) (first secretary), Aharon Kanarek, Avraham Getzel, Rivka Rozenbaum and the late Berish Adler, who passed away in Israel. Yitzhak Kelmer, Fischel Lesman, Pinchas and Hinda Getzel, Yosef Zislender, Riva Rozenberg, Rivka and Yosef Chelmski and Chava Najdorf, of blessed memory, perished in the Holocaust. Distinguished for their good lives in Israel were also Yehezkel Helmer, Meir Helmer, Altale Kanarek, Bracha Olsztyn and Shoshana Kelmer.

The Balfour Declaration of November 2 1917 had a spectacular impact on the Jews of Zychlin. I remember the solemn assembly at the elementary school on Pasieka street. There was a huge crowd and David Steinberger's speech was impressive. The meeting ended with everybody singing Hatikvah in a tremendous expression of hope.

After the defeat of the Germans and the reestablishment of Poland's independence in 1918, the activities of the Bnai Zion Association led to considerable achievements for the town's residents and the Zionist cause. Particularly important was the effort to organize a Jewish defense for fear of pogroms by the Gentile population, with the possible assistance of the Polish army. All the political parties in our town participated in the defense initiative.

Extensive social and cultural activities were organized by a club that functioned in the house of Moshe Mendel Wojdeslawski on Pasieka street, and later in the house of Icze Opatowski on Market street. There were balls and celebrations for the national holidays. The holiday festivals and the plays of the dramatic circle gained a reputation, attracting people from all the other towns in the region to the performances in Zychlin. The main force behind all of that was the great teacher and Zionist activist David Steinberger, who took the initiative for the activities and had a decisive role in their implementation.

It is worthwhile to mention the activities of the Bnai Zion Association, which distributed the Zionist shekel and raised funds for Keren Hayesod, Keren Kayemet, and the Jewish National Fund. The association held a special fundraiser for the benefit of Jewish academics in Poland and it also distributed the weekly Hebrew newspaper HaTzfira in Zychlin. All these efforts were led by the devoted Zionist activist Yitzhak Kelmer.

A special chapter was the struggle for control of the Jewish community. In 1908, there had been a succession conflict following the death of Rabbi Itche Meir Zachil. On that occasion, the orthodox Jews of Agudat Israel had managed to beat back a challenge of the Zionists, crowning Rabbi Mordechai Alter, a Ger Hasid, as the new rabbi of Zychlin.

But in the first community elections that were held after the First World War, the General Zionists beat Agudat Israel by a decisive majority. Avraham Yitzhak Rozenfeld and David Steinberger, the leaders of the Bnai Zion Association, were elected as chairman and secretary of the Zychlin Jewish community.

In the 1920s, the rifts that took place in the Polish Zionist movement also affected the General Zionists in Zychlin. The majority tended to support the Al-HaMishmar faction, which had been founded by Yitzhak Gruenbaum.

The General Zionists did not invest the efforts that were required to make sure that the youth would stay within their organization and take responsibility for its further development. The result was that the youth, for the most part, left the Bnai Zion Association and joined the more radical organization Tzeirei Zion.

The Turen Farein sports association

by Y. Gil

Translated by Leon Zamosc

[Original book: pages 63-65 Hebrew section, 211-213 Yiddish section]

Among the refugees who came to Zychlin at the outbreak of the First World War was Gombinski. He had been an active athlete in the Turen Farein movement in Lodz and was determined to establish a branch of that sports organization in Zychlin.

To accomplish this task, he called for a meeting that was attended by people from all the movements and political parties. Attended the meeting. David Steinberger (Shamir), Meir Helmer, Yehoshua Zyger, Getzel, Zaiderman, Ettinger, Bielawski, and the author of these lines. Gombinski lectured on the program under the slogan "A healthy mind in a healthy body", and the participants responded enthusiastically to the idea of establishing a sports organization in the town. I was chosen as secretary and all those who were present undertook to obtain the first necessary financial means.

Not long after, we received a license from the German occupation authorities allowing us to establish the Turen Farein branch under the name Association of Jewish Athletes and Gymnasts in Zychlin. We invited Mr. Zaida, a sports teacher from Lodz and purchased the necessary equipments. We leased an open lot on Podwal street, which used to be a lumberyard and was surrounded by a fence.

The registration of members for the Turen Farein sports association aroused great interest in the town. Soon more than a hundred members of all movements were recruited - active athletes and fans. The activists were divided into groups, and a special youth department was established. In the summer we exercised on the field and in the winter in the town hall. The official uniform was: white trousers, a white shirt and a white hat with a blue stripe around it. The flag was blue and white with the gold emblem of the Turen Farein association. At the beginning, the teacher used German terminology. After much debate, it was decided to use Hebrew terminology in the performances and German in the exercises.

The Jewish Turen Farein association in Zychlin, 1917.

The first general meeting of the Sports Association was held in early 1917. The following people were elected as members of the committee: Gombinski, Ettinger, Steinberger, Bol, Bielawski, Getzel, Chlawny, Zaiderman, Rozenkopf, Meir Helmer and me. The functions of the committee were assigned as follows: Gombinski as chairman, Ettinger as treasurer, and me as secretary. The meetings were held in the hall of the general library.

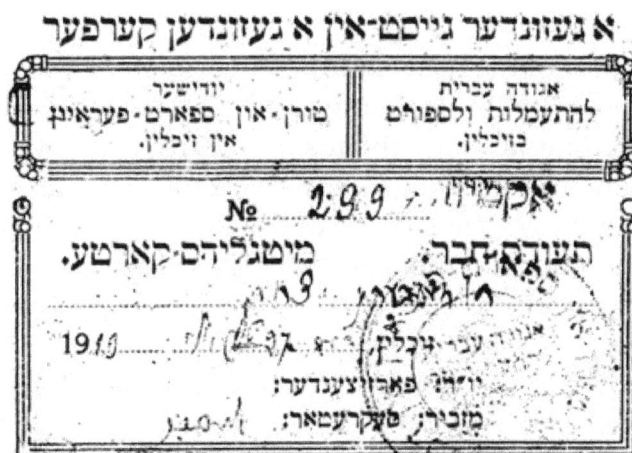

Turen Farein membership card of Yitzhak Rozenberg.
On top of the card, the slogan: A healthy spirit in a healthy body.

The Turen Farein's committee with the first group of gymnasts. Standing from
right: Leibush (Aryeh) Olsztyn, Noah Zyger, Pantzer, H. Kelmer, M.
Schwartzberg, W. Reszelbach. Seating from right: Moshe Davidovitz, A.
Davidovitz, W. Bielawski, Gombinski, Y. Lemberg, Aaron Lemberg, Zyger.
Below: Meir Rozenberg, Yitzhak Rozenberg, Gleider.

During the first year of the association, a sports show was held in the yard of
the Wideslawski flour mill, arousing an enthusiastic response from the
spectators. The participants were athletes from Kutno, Gombin and Gostynin. In
the second year there was another impressive performance: there was a festive
atmosphere in the town and the sounds of the Kutno orchestra accompanied the
athletes as they marched to the sports field. David Steinberger opened the
celebration and welcomed the guests. The first group performed exercises with
the help of sports equipment, the guests performed some other exercises, and
then there was a show of mass gymnastics. Acrobatic human pyramid formations
were finally presented to the sound of the orchestra, with the spectators holding
their breath in trepidation. The Sports Association become the general athletics
organization for the Jewish youth of Zychlin. It also made appearances in sports
festivals and tournaments that were held in the neighboring towns.

The third and final sports festival took place in 1918. There was a larger number of athletes and the performances included really difficult exercises. This time, a youth group also participated in the shows. Later on the same year 1918, the association held its second general meeting, electing a new committee that included Bol, Bielawski, Aaron Lemberg, Yehoshua Zyger, A. Schwartzberg, Reszelbach, Noah Zyger, Leybush Olsztyn, Moshe Davidovitz and me. No one was elected from the Bnai Zion Association because they only had a few members in the Turen Farein association.

At the end of that year Poland regained its independence and by the beginning of 1919 it issued an order for general conscription into the Polish army. A large part of the youth was drafted into the army and many others left Zychlin. By the summer, the heyday of the Sports Association was over.

Soccer team of the Turen Farein association in Zychlin.

In 1922, the activists of Poalei Zion made an attempt to resume the association's activities under the leadership of Moshe Davidovitz. A soccer team was established, but it did not last long. In 1924, the group of Poalei Zion Right organized another soccer team that also dispersed after a short time,

In 1927, Poalei Zion Right, together with Hashomer Hatzair, renewed the activities of the Turen Farein sports association under the leadership of Hirsch Kelmer. They organized a soccer team called Hapoel, with Yosef Gostynski as captain. The team played in competitions with the local Polish team and with

Jewish and Polish teams in the nearby towns. On Saturday evenings, ballrooms were held in the sports hall.

The association was active until the outbreak of the Second World War. The arrival of the German Nazis marked the end of the Turen Farein association and all the other social activities of the Jewish community in the town.

Hashomer Hatzair in Zychlin

by Bunim Steinberger (Shamir)

Translated by Leon Zamosc

[Original book: pages 67-75 Hebrew section, 214-222 Yiddish section]

The first group of scouts, from which Hashomer Hatzair would later grow, was founded in Zychlin in 1917 by Avraham Toroncyk, a student from Lodz, who came to the town during the First World War and stayed with us for several years.

In those days there was unemployment and shortage of foodstuffs in the large cities. Many people returned to the small towns, where at least a modest subsistence was possible thanks to the food supplies provided by the peasants from neighboring villages.

Zychlin was one of those "happy" small towns where life was relatively normal. During that war, it received many temporary residents, who came from the "big world" to stay with their relatives during the economic crisis. Among them were educated young people who made a considerable contribution to the enrichment of the town's public and spiritual life. One of them was the student Toroncyk, who was hosted by members of his family. He was the one who brought the idea of initiating a youth movement to the town and, thanks to his initiatives, branches of Jewish scouts organizations were established in Zychlin and in neighboring Kutno.

It was a time of great anticipation and expectation. After the Balfour Declaration, which heralded a new era in the life of our people, and after the October Revolution, which seemed to offer a new direction to the development of all mankind, there were hopes that a large immigration from the Diaspora would lead to the rapid construction of the new Jewish homeland in Eretz Israel. It seemed that we were on the threshold of a new period in history, that the First World War would be the last war and that, from then on, humanity would take decisive steps to abolish exploitation, oppression and discrimination and establish a society founded on equality, justice and freedom.

Poland, which had gained its independence after years of enslavement, was experiencing a wave of rising anti-Semitism. There were pogroms and the beards of the Jews were being ripped off in the open air, on trains and in public squares, in cities and towns.

This was the background for the development of the Jewish youth movement Hashomer Hatzair, which was inspired by the Hashomer organization that had been established by young pioneers in Palestine. The Hashomer youth fulfilled the sacred role of protecting the new Jewish settlements from harassment and were ready for any sacrifices to achieve that goal. From its earliest days, and as it matured over the years, the Hashomer Hatzair movement served as a creative home for idealistic, dreamy and warrior youngsters who carried in their hearts a deep longing for the national and social liberation of the Jews in their homeland.

In those days, the Jewish community of Zychlin numbered 600 families with approximately 3,000 souls. Like the vast majority of the Jews in Poland, most of them lived a life of deprivation. It was a period of great awakening leading to the development of a turbulent public life among the Polish Jews. A vibrant, ramified public life flourished among those 600 Jewish families in Zychlin. Branches of all the parties and organizations that existed on the Jewish street operated in the town, including the General Zionists, the right and left-wing factions of Poalei Zion, Agudat Israel, Mizrachi, the Bund, Hechalutz, and even a small cell of the Folkist party. A Hebrew school was established and evening Hebrew classes for adults were organized. Libraries were opened, a gymnastics association was founded, and a dramatic circle routinely performed a variety of plays. Balls, lectures and roundtables were held. Despite the material scarcity, the town had a rich civic and cultural life.

The first group of scouts in Zychlin, 1917. From right: Avraham Zhukhovski, Aaron Kanarek, Avraham Wrontzberg, Kalman Kizelsztein, Yaakov Zhukhovski, Eliyahu Rosenfeld, Yaakov Lemberg (leader).

This was the background of the founding and operation of the Hashomer Hatzair movement in town. I will mention the members of the first group of scouts that provided the basis for the subsequent establishment of the Zychlin branch of Hashomer Hatzair. That group included seven members: Yaakov Lemberg (the leader), Yaakov Zhukhovski. Avraham Zhukhovski, Eliyahu Rozenfeld, Avraham Wrontzberg, Aaron Kanarek and Kalman Kizelsztein. When he arrived in Palestine, Avraham Zhukhovski joined a kibbutz of Hashomer Hatzair and to this day he continues as part of the movement. The other members of the group left to Palestine as they grew up and followed different individual paths. That first group served as a kind of match that lit the flame.

I should also mention that when the Hashomer Hatzair branch was established, it had the patronage of a group of veteran Zionists who monitored its activities and took care of its needs. The group included David Steinberger (Shamir), Avraham Rozenfeld and Meir Helmer.

The youth that huddled in the small clubhouse of Hashomer Hatzair at the time did not have external temptations. What they had was a rich and meaningful inner life. In those two rooms they spent a couple of hours a day. The rest of the time they were busy in other ordinary activities. And yet, that couple of hours became the center of their lives. Outwardly, it may have seemed like a children's game, but the game was serious: they were part of a movement and they had a goal.

Today the youth seems to have an aversion to social movements and pre-determined patterns. The deep desire is not to identify too much with a trend and to maintain full individual freedom. But the fact is that the Hashomer Hatzair "trend" and its stubborn concentration around a conscious goal forged the character, refined the mind, and trained the youngsters for the task of building a country and establishing a new society. It prepared them for self-fulfillment, pioneering, *aliyah*, and life in the *kibbutz*. It was a bright light shining in the darkness of an oppressive reality of Jewish poverty and anti-Semitism.

Anti-Semitism was a weighty factor in shaping the Jewish youth's national consciousness and the aspiration to a homeland of their own, where they would be able to live a fully independent national life, free from harassment and persecution. Life in Zychlin, where Jews made up about a third of the population, was rife with numerous anti-Semitic manifestations. Every gathering of Jewish children, every meeting of Jewish youth could trigger a bout of stone-throwing by Polish boys, with the encouragement and blessing of their parents and most of the older Polish population. When we organized our activities it was necessary to take into account the threat of such attacks. More than once they would organize in gangs and stalk our boys and girls when they were out for walks, with the malicious intent of striking at the Jews and preventing them from spending time together in nature, which would apparently preserve the "purity" of the Polish countryside.

From the very beginning, Hashomer Hatzair had to take vigorous steps to deal with harassment and protect its members, especially the youngest who were children below the age of ten. Self-defense, the need for constant vigilance, and the perpetual confrontation with Polish anti-Semitism became an integral part of the movement's operation. They forged the spirit and character of our youngsters and taught them to stand up for themselves in front of hostile foes that sometimes were stronger than them. Indeed, we never suspended our excursions, games and activities for fear of the threats. We were always prepared to defend our right to exist and our freedom of movement. When necessary, we were also ready to return blows in that hair-raising war.

Group of Hashomer Hatzair in the 1920s. From right: R. Landshnaider, Kalski, Kanarek, Zylberberg, M. Olsztyn, N. Landshnaider, Tzvi Lemberg (instructor)

In accordance with the tradition of the Hashomer Hatzair movement, our work focused on scouting, the cultivation of a "healthy body" culture, and an extensive array of activities designed to foster the intellectual, educational and ideological development of our young people. Scoutism had the effect of straightening the bent backs of the Jewish youth and taking them out of the confined walls of life in exile. It brought them into the bosom of nature, strengthened their muscles, developed their orientation in the field, and increased their agility and resistance to difficulties. Therefore, a substantial part of the activities of our educational units consisted of order exercises, gymnastics, camping, scout games and trips. Every summer, our groups would spend about two weeks in scouting camps that were organized on a regional level, with participation of hundreds of young people from all the shtetls in the area.

In Zychlin, we carried out our scouting activities in what we called the "Hashomer field". It was an open pasture area that stretched along the side of Pasieka road outside the town. Our groups, companies, and battalions would gather there on Saturday mornings and sometimes on weekday evenings, spending hours in various scouting and sporting activities. The battles with the Polish boys were often fought there, as they tried to attack the guards that we posted around the field.

Our main efforts, however, were invested in enriching the intellectual, educational and ideological capabilities of the youth. There was no high school in Zychlin, the only school for post-primary study was the Commercial School, which offered the equivalent of a sixth-grade secondary education. The number of Jewish students in this school was small - only a few members of Hashomer Hatzair received their education there. Therefore, among other things, our movement had to serve as a substitute for school, in order to fill as far as possible the gaps of our members' education in the areas of general and Jewish knowledge. The majority of our instructors did not have a high school education either. What they knew they had learned on their own, as self-educated people, taking advantage of every free hour of the day and night for reading and study. They had to deal with books that, due to a lack of thorough education, were not easy for them to digest. Nonetheless, they did important educational work with their groups and, in the process of preparing for lectures and conversations on various topics, they expanded their own education. What they acquired for themselves and then passed on to the boys and girls in their groups, came from their hearts. This is how our young people learned about general and Jewish history, literature, biology, economics, social and political history, psychology, the Jewish national question, anti-Semitism, and other things. This is how they acquired the foundations for articulating a worldview of their own. They did not obtain a formal high school education, but they overcame their intellectual poverty and became enlightened people, seeking their way through society and the world through their own tireless mental and spiritual effort.

A lot of time was devoted to the Hebrew language, the Bible, and Hebrew literature. Some of the older groups were even able to switch from Yiddish and conduct all their activities using the Hebrew language. Equally important was the effort to educate our members about Eretz Israel. The older instructors, who were familiar with the Hebrew language, did their best to gain as much knowledge as possible about what was happening in Palestine, the struggles of the working class, the experiments being conducted by the *kibbutz* movement in general, and the views in the *kibbutzim* that belonged to Hashomer Hatzair in particular. They regularly read "Davar", the newspaper of the Jewish workers in Palestine, and the magazines "Ketuvim" and "Torim", which reflected trends in the young Hebrew literature produced in Eretz Israel. Any new book, in fiction or poetry, that came from Palestine, and especially those that discussed the realities of life in the country, would serve as a topic for conversation and exchange of views. The songs that were popular in Eretz Israel were sung at our assemblies, talks and parties. They were brought to us from the summer camps and from meetings with delegates or visitors from Palestine. Thus, Hashomer Hatzair was like an enclave of Eretz Israel in the midst of the gray reality of our life in exile. The atmosphere was "Palestine" in every way. "There" was more important than "here." Our life "here" was considered a temporary life, the whole purpose of which was to prepare the young for their future lives "there".

At this point it is worth mentioning the dedicated action of the members of Hashomer Hatzair on behalf of the Keren Kayemet. They were always on the first line of every effort to raise funds, participating in "Flower Day" festivals, "Blue Box" campaigns, and in the organization of banquets and lotteries whose proceeds went to the Keren Kayemet.

The heyday of the Zychlin branch of Hashomer Hatzair was the period between the end of the First World War and the mid-1930s. During that period we did not have competitors – we were the only branch of a Zionist youth movement in the town. Our educational units were full and the size of the organization depended solely on the number of available instructors. As stated, back then we had about one hundred and twenty members, sometimes we had even more. We were considered one of the best and most active branches in the region, and in the years 1927-1928 we were given responsibility for managing the regional office of Hashomer Hatzair for the entire area of Kutno-Wloclawek. I had the honor of serving as regional secretary during that period.

In the late 1920s, when the leadership of Hashomer Hatzair made final decisions about the duty of individual self-fulfillment and about the pioneering and *kibbutz*-oriented character of the movement, our older comrades began to go out for *aliyah* training. Among them, the first to emigrate to Palestine were members of the Olsztyn family - Meir, Miriam and Sarah, who, together with their entire family, settled in Jerusalem. They were followed by Chaya Kelmer, Chaya Tuszynski, Hanna Zyger and Malka Rubin.

The "Revival Company" of Hashomer Hatzair in Zychlin.

With the British Mandatory government's reduction in the number of immigrant visas, the movement sought and found indirect ways of reaching Palestine. That was the case, in early 1932, of a group that included Avraham Helmer, Zelda Klinger, Feiga Kelmer, Yehuda Zyger and Bunim Steinberger (Shamir). They got tourist visas for a visit to Palestine on the occasion of the first Maccabiah Games that were held in Tel Aviv. Once they were there, they stayed in the country as illegal immigrants. Rivka Kanarek, Pinchas Kanarek and Hannah Feldman also managed to reach Palestine in the early 1930s.

With the *aliyah* of those who for many years had been running the organization, there was a generational change in the movement. The younger cohort took over the reins and continued the activities. Thus, in accordance with the tradition of Hashomer Hatzair, the chain of activism continued and one generation passed on to another generation the educational and ideological legacy of the movement. In time, the members of the younger cohort also began to go for training and the *aliyah* continued, despite the fact that, due to the

British growing restrictions to immigration, the drizzle was thin and only a few members were able to break the siege. Two of them were Chava Rubin (Shamir) and Eliezer Kanarek, who arrived in 1934-35.

According to the comrades who stayed longer in Zychlin, Hashomer Hatzair declined rapidly during the second half of the 1930s. The reasons were both objective and subjective. The effects of the world economic crisis caught up with the town, impoverishing people and reducing the chances of employment. Jewish youths rambled around, without jobs and without prospects. Because of the barriers to immigration into Palestine, thousands of pioneers were bottled up in the preparation for *aliyah*, sitting in training camps for years. Many began to despair, hopelessly returning to their cities and towns. Those who returned to Zychlin no longer had the option to stay within the organization and they left it. In general, young people were less likely to go to training under these conditions. The movement, which was built on the duty of self-fulfillment, training and *aliyah*, was halted in its development. There was no anvil for the hammer.

The general atmosphere changed and there were profound changes among the youth. With the unopposed rise of Hitler to power, the suppression of the forces of revolution in Spain, and the political trials in the Soviet Union, the bright hopes of the 1920s vanished. The cloud of uncertainty replaced the clear perspective of the paved road. These conditions severely affected the members of Hashomer Hatzair. As the Second World War and the Shoah approached, the number of members and the level of instruction went sharply down, despite the efforts of the activists who were in charge. That group included Israel Lenchinski (who managed to flee to the Soviet Union during the war), Yechiel Zyger, Grunam Opatowski, Hannah Liebfreund and Rivkah Borowski.

It is difficult to obtain verified details about what happened in Zychlin during the Shoah. Very few people remain alive and some of them are outside Israel. The information we have is that the social activities in the town came to an end with the outbreak of the war and the occupation by Hitler's armies. There were furtive meetings of Jews, but there was no organized public life. Among the people who had been active in Hashomer Hatzair, we know that Fela Michalska, Belchia Cohen and Melah Rubin were involved in assisting the sick and the needy.

In 1940, the Jews were confined into a ghetto. The Germans liquidated the ghetto in 1942, sending all the remaining Zychlin Jews to their deaths at Chelmno extermination camp.

Thus came to an end the existence of the Jewish community of Zychlin, with its material poverty and the richness of its inner life. As in other Jewish communities, its younger generations had been involved in a revival movement that was interrupted by the annihilation – a movement whose members did their best to contribute to the gathering and rebirth of the Jewish people in its homeland.

We carry in our hearts the memory of our shtetl and of our ancestors' efforts to sustain their communal life for hundreds of years despite persecution, suffering and destitution. It encourages us to continue our struggle for the full liberation of our people in the restored national state of the Jews.

The workers' movement – Poalei Zion Left

by Moshe Zyger

Translated by Leon Zamosc

[Original book: pages 75-79 Hebrew section, 223-230 Yiddish section]

Until the second half of the 1920s, neighborly relations between the Polish and Jewish populations were fairly normal in Zychlin. In the 1930s, however, things changed as a result of the strident anti-Semitic propaganda campaigns that were being conducted by the right-wing party National Democracy and by some circles in president's Jozef Pilsudski's coalition. The venom of hatred against the Jews was increasingly felt in the town. Against that context, the Jewish labor movement of Zychlin, which excelled in the intensity of its social activism, stood at the forefront of the struggle for the defense of the cultural and political interests of the Jewish population.

To understand the background of the Jewish workers' movement in Zychlin, we must go back to the beginning of the 20th century, when the construction of the railway from Warsaw to Lodz and towards the German border spurred the development of industry throughout western Poland. The effects of industrialization were also felt in Zychlin, which was located at a distance of 25 km from the Pniewo train station. A large foundry was built on Podwal street, and a smaller foundry on Budzyner street. Moshe Mendel Wojdeslawski opened his steam-powered flour mill on Pasieka street and two sugar factories were also established oustide the town, one in Dobrzelin and the smaller Kronenberg-Bloch factory in Budzyn. These factories employed dozens and, during the sugar production season, hundreds of workers.

These economic changes stimulated an increase in the number of Jewish merchants and craftsmen. The socks and weaving workshops received orders from traders in Lodz. A large number of people were engaged in the so-called "Jewish crafts": tailors, shoemakers, seamstresses, makers of hats and caps, tinsmiths, who toiled 12-14 hours a day for a meager income.

The difficult economic and social conditions of the laborers served as a fitting background for the establishment of branches of Jewish socialist parties in Zychlin. The first of them was the Bund, which was founded in 1903 by Yitche Getzel, brother of Pinhas and Avraham Getzel, who later emigrated to the United

States. They were joined, among others, by Eliezer Skrobek, brother of Shimon Skrobek.

In 1905, a branch of the Zionist-Socialist party was opened in town by Shimon Skrobek, an excellent orator, and my cousin Moshe Zyger. The Zionist-Socialists, who called themselves S.S. by their Russian initials, favored the idea of Jewish territorial autonomy, but rejected the mainstream Zionist movement idea that the Jewish national home had to be built in Palestine. In Zychlin, the organization existed until the end of 1907. The local shopkeepers referred to them as the "Union Boys" because they called for the unionization of the wage laborers. The Zionist-Socialists conducted an outreach campaign among the workers and fought for improvements in their economic situation. As a result, wages were raised and working hours were cut.

In addition to workers, the Bundists and the Zionist-Socialists also attracted the middle class youth. But their successes were short-lived. After containing the 1905 revolution, the Czarist regime cracked down on the activists, which led to the emigration of the leaders. The Socialists ceased all public activity in Zychlin and the previous achievements of the workers were abolished.

The more progressive youth in town, however, did not put up with the stagnation in public activity. They looked for ways to change the situation and came up with the idea of establishing a Jewish library. To promote the idea, they invited the well-known author Hillel Zeitlin from Warsaw to deliver a Purim lecture on the subject of "Assyria, Jerusalem and Rome". The speaker was late and the lecture began at ten o'clock in the evening, but the municipal theater hall was filled to capacity and the audience received the lecturer warmly. Eventually, though, the Czsarist authorities refused to grant the license and the goal of establishing the library could not be fulfilled. After Yaakov Zaiderman and my brother Yehoshua returned to the town, they took steps, together with Shlomo Zeiber, Yechiel Bicz and David Skrobek, to revive the idea of opening the library. They requested permission to invite Y. L. Peretz and Sholem Aleichem to give lectures, but again they encountered many difficulties on the part of the authorities. In the end, the initiative to open the library had to be dropped.

With the outbreak of the First World War in August 1914, economic life came to a standstill. The two sugar factories stopped working and the flour mill reduced its activity to a minimum. This caused the impoverishment not only of the workers, but also the craftsmen and shopkeepers. The German occupiers, wanting to gain sympathies among the locals, pursued a liberal policy towards the Jewish community.

Under the new political conditions, Yehoshua Zyger, Yaakov Zaiderman and the son-in-law of Moshe Mendel Wojdeslawski finally obtained the official permission to open a library with an adjacent reading room. The new library, which was inaugurated in October 1915, was supported by a circle of youngsters who worked to expand its literary and artistic activities. In 1916, the library staged a musical concert with works of the Jewish composer Mattathias Bensman in the municipal theater hall. It also organized an extensive program of literary evenings inviting lecturers such as Meir Weissenberg, D. Ben-Tzipor and S. Stopnitzki.

The economic conditions in the big cities had worsened as a result of the war. Many people moved to the country towns, where it was easier to get food. Among those who came from Lodz, there were some who went into public work and helped enrich the social and cultural life of the Zychlin Jews. In 1916, the library's management expanded to include, in addition to its founders, David Steinberger (Shamir), Yechiel Bicz, Pinhas Getzel, Gombinski and Yechiel Landshnaider. An organization for gymnastics and sports was also established, attracting dozens of members who trained under the guidance of the Zayde brothers.

There were efforts to reactivate the labor movement too. The temporarily arrivals included the Zolty family, whose son, Wave Zolty, had been a weaving worker in Lodz. He took the initiative to reestablish the branch of the Bund in Zychlin and succeeding in recruiting many workers into the ranks of the party.

In 1914, my cousin Moshe Zyger returned from Switzerland and founded the Zychlin branch of the Poalei Zion party. He reached an agreement with the Bund to cooperate in the establishment of a youth cultural association under the name of Tsukunft (Yiddish for "future"). The association attracted a large number of youngsters, organizing readings from the classics of Yiddish literature twice a week. The readings were accompanied by debates about the content of the works and there were also lectures on various cultural topics. But this idyllic cooperation did not last long. The Bund's pressure to impose their party's ideology on Tsukunft led to conflicts and scandals. Eventually, the German authorities closed the association.

The Poalei Zion organization expanded its activities and its influence on the workers increased. In 1917 they brought one of their national leaders from Warsaw, Briskman, who gave a lecture in the library's reading hall about the ideology of Poalei Zion. Motivated by the event, Yaakov Zaiderman, Yehoshua Zyger and Shimon Majdat became activists of the organization. Together with

Katz from Kutno, they organized classes to study cultural history and the teachings of Karl Marx and Dov Ber Borochov.

The committee of Poalei Zion Left in Zychlin, on the occasion of Moshe Zyger's departure to Palestine.

At the time, the Poalei Zion party in Poland split into two factions, left and right. At the founding meeting of Poalei Zion Left, which took place at the end of 1917 in the residence of the Hebrew teacher Maizel, a new committee was elected. It included Moshe Zyger, Yaakov Zeiderman, Yehoshua Zinner, Shimon Majdat and a few others whose names I do not remember. In the summer of 1918, Poalei Zion Left obtained a license from the German occupation government to open an office in the town. They rented a four-room apartment on Pasieka street and their activities were expanded in all areas. They held lectures and evenings of questions and answers on political and cultural issues, with local speakers and outside guests. They also organized a dramatic circle that presented many plays in the town. Other initiatives of Poalei Zion Left included the establishment of a youth department and a trade union that fought for higher wages and shorter working hours for textile and leather workers.

In 1918, immediately following the establishment of the independent state of Poland, we heard about preparations made by anti-Semitic extremists to riot against the Jews of Zychlin. Poalei Zion Left convened a meeting of all the Jewish political organizations in which it was decided to organize a self-defense group. Some small arms were purchased as part of the preparations. However, things did not get to that point, as the supposed threat turned out to be just a rumor.

The Polish Socialist Party conducted extensive activities among the Polish population of the town. As in other cities and towns of Poland, a joint Labor Council of Polish and Jewish workers was established in Zychlin in 1919. In the elections for the Labor Council's committee, Poalei Zion Left won the largest number of representatives from the Jewish population. It should be also mentioned that Poalei Zion Left established a consumer cooperative that only existed for a short time. The managers of the cooperative were Moshe Avraham Shwartzberg, David Schwartz, and Israel Wolf Lemberg.

In the elections for the Polish parliament, Poalei Zion Left received 40% of the votes of the Jewish population. They were represented in the municipal council and also in the Jewish community board until the outbreak of the Second World War.

After the end of the Polish-Soviet War of 1919-21, the emigration of teenagers from the town began, and many of those who had left Zychlin during the war did not return. This caused a temporary reduction in the activity of Poalei Zion Left. Also, there were some activists, led by Shimon Majdat, who abandoned the organization to join the Communists, as well as a second group that moved to Poalei Zion Right. Still, in spite of these defections, Poalei Zion Left remained the most influential Jewish party in Zychlin. The activists who emigrated or went to other parties were replaced by new members who, together with the remaining veteran activists, continued to work in all areas – economic, cultural and political.

Following a Poalei Zion Left initiative, a central office was established for all the trade unions. In 1924, it successfully organized a strike of all Jewish and Polish bakers, which led to an increase in their wages.

During the Polish-Soviet conflict, the Polish government had closed the Bund's cultural center Arbeter Heim (Workers' Home). To fill the gap, Poalei Zion Left established a Society for Evening Classes and organized a sports and gymnastics department that was headed by Moshe Davidovitz until his departure for the United States. The general meeting of the library members decided to attach the library to the Society for Evening Classes. Also at the initiative of Poalei Zion Left, a branch of Poland's Central Organization of Jewish Schools was established in the town. In all these activities there was participation of members of the other Jewish parties, including the Bund, the Folkists and the non-partisans.

When I visited Zychlin in late 1937, I found that the institutions were continuing their work, albeit without much enthusiasm.

In March 1942, the Jews of Zychlin were exterminated by the Nazis in the gas vans of the death camp at Chelmno. The town's Jewish community was wiped off the face of the earth. May its memory stay engraved in our hearts.

An active political life - Poalei Zion Right

by Michael Schwartzberg

Translated by Leon Zamosc

[Original book: pages 81-86 Hebrew section, 234-241 Yiddish section]

As in a kaleidoscope, thirty years of my life in Zychlin pass before my eyes – the years of my childhood and youth before I left the town forever. It is hard to believe that all those Jews, from the youngest to the oldest, were still alive; that all the cultural, political and religious institutions that they created have disappeared from the face of the earth.

Zychlin, like many other country towns, excelled in its public and cultural vitality and in the diversity of its political orientations, which ran the gamut from the religious orthodoxy of Agudat Israel to extreme Communist views. Most of the town's youngsters, however, were inspired by the national spirit and identified themselves as Zionists.

My father's house

My father, Yitzhak Ben-Yaakov, had eight children and toiled hard along with the workers that he employed. Still, despite his preoccupations about livelihood concerns, he did everything he could to make sure that his children received a national-religious education. He was also active in public social work and in the Zionist movement. His house was open to all visitors. Many Jews would show up every day to read the newspaper, because not everyone could afford the "luxury" of spending money on a subscription. Two or three times a week, people from all walks of life would gather with us to read the news, chat, and argue about what was going on in the world. In one way or another, the debates always ended up focusing on the same critical issues: Palestine, Zionism and the Bund. Among the regular visitors, I remember Yosef Rozengarten, Yehezkel Crook, and Itche Zeifert. But they were only a few of the many visitors that regularly came to our house.

Even though I was young at the time, I would listen to the conversations and arguments with great interest. My father was very pleased and, seeing that I liked the debates on political issues, he would often take me with him to the Zionist clubhouse. I remember well a particular evening in which my father and I attended a session dedicated to Theodor Herzl, the visionary of the Jewish state. On the way back home, my father proudly told me that the first Zionist organization in our town had been established as early as 1901.

First sorrows

In 1920, while still a *yeshiva* student, I joined the Zionist movement through the youth ranks of Poalei Zion. In those days, after the revolution in Russia, many of the town's youngsters were fascinated by the new winds blowing from the east of Poland. I, however, under the influence of my father, did not follow the current. I remained in the movement, which brought the Jewish people to a life of freedom in its independent state.

Yaakov Zaiderman introduced me to the youth of Poalei Zion. He was then called "the father of the youngsters." Sometimes he would have conversations with us about current issues, Jewish literature, and the value that literature for the Zionist movement and socialism. We were organized into different circles, according to our topics of interest.

In August 1920, at the Poalei Zion World Conference that was held in Vienna, the party was divided into "right" and "left". The Poalei Zion Right movement joined the World Zionist Organization and participated in its congresses. The Poalei Zion Left had opened negotiations with Moscow over their admission to the Third International, but those negotiations ended in failure because they did not want to give up the name Poalei Zion. In our town, as in other places, a fierce propaganda campaign was launched by the two Poalei Zion factions against each other. In Zychlin, the members of the party formally decided to stay with Poalei Zion Left. I should note that the younger activists were not allowed to attend the meeting in which the decision was made.

At that meeting, there were two members who opposed the majority decision: Yaakov Moshe Berman and Pinchas Davidovitz, who began, on their own initiative, a broad advocacy campaign supporting the principles of Poalei Zion Right. This led to the formation of the first nucleus of the Poalei Zion Right youngsters in Zychlin. I participated in that group, which in 1921 also included, in addition to Berman and Davidovitz, other activists like Noah Rozengarten, Bunim Bornstein, Avraham Hodes, Michael Schwartzberg, Moshe Iatzkovski, H.V. Zandberg and Leibl Rozenberg. We had to conduct our work in secret because it was contrary to the official position of the party in the town. At one point, however, Tzeirei Zion gave us some *shekels* for the Twelfth Zionist Congress, which we began selling in the town. When the party heard about this, we were expelled from its ranks, which left us with no alternative except declaring ourselves as members of the Poalei Zion Right party.

Youth organization of Poalei Zion right in Zychlin.

That same year we invited A. Sh. Yuris, a well-known Poalei Zion Right activist from Warsaw, to visit us in Zychlin. His lecture was a great success and motivated us to continue working. We were also in contact with the Poalei Zion Right activists in Wloclawek. One of them, Yosef Horn, visited us frequently for long conversations that helped us develop our lines of work in Zychlin.

On that same year, the first Poalei Zion Right conference was held in Warsaw. We sent Y. Zyger as our own delegate to the conference. Since we did not have a place of our own and the Tzeirei Zion organization (which was theoretically aligned with Poalei Zion Left) did not have enough members, they informally allowed us to conduct our activities in their clubhouse, which allowed us to recruit more youngsters for our organization.

The unification

In 1923, an official negotiation took place on the unification of Poalei Zion Right and Tzeirei Zion. We already had an ongoing "cooperation" and, since we did not have major ideological differences, we decided to merge and informed our party's central office in Warsaw, which expressed its satisfaction. We were the first to reunify the two Zionist parties (at the national level, the reunification took place in 1924). This step was good for us. It allowed us to grow numerically and attracted experienced activists like Yosef Rozengarten, Yaakov Lemberg, and Yehoshua Wojdeslawski. That same year we were visited by Berl Locker, who was already known as one of the world leaders of our movement. After the lecture, he sat with us until dawn, chatting like friends and offering orientation for the continuation of our work.

Election failure and its lessons

Our confrontation with the other parties in the city sharpened in 1924, when we decided to run in the elections to the Zychlin municipal council. Since all of us were below the minimum age that was required to run for office (25 years old), we knew that we could not submit a candidate from within our ranks. So we decided to present the candidacy of Mr. Zafran, who was a supporter of our party. This step surprised the other parties and helped us a bit. In the end, our candidate was not elected, although the difference in votes between him and the winner was small.

Members of Poelei Zion Right, bidding farewell to Yosef Rozengarten and his wife Bracha as they emigrate to Eretz Israel, October 4, 1925.

We learned the lesson from the election and decided to work harder. The work with the youth was handled by Yaacov Lemberg, whose initiatives and organizational abilities brought an increase in the number of party members. The day-to-day party work was in the hands of Yosef Rozengarten, who did the job with dedication and success until the day of his departure to Palestine in 1925. He was followed by our youth leader Yaacov Lemberg, who also emigrated to Eretz Israel in 1926. After that, the new chairman of our party was Yehoshua Wjodeslawski.

We made steady progress in our work. We became an active force in the Zionist movement and, more generally, in Zychlin's political life. We developed contacts with the local branch of the Polish Socialist Party and they agreed to our proposal to hold a joint demonstration on Workers Day. Our cooperation and the joint activities lasted until the outbreak of the Second World War in 1939.

Youth committee of the Poalei Zion Right party, on occasion of the departure of Yaakov Ben-Binah (Lemberg) to Palestine. From right: L. Szenowski, Yaakov Moshe Berman and Avraham Hodes (Rozen). Below: P. Zik and Yaakov Ben-Binah (Lemberg).

We approached the next elections to the Zychlin municipal council, which took place in 1928, with more experience in the field of communication. Our candidate was the chairman of the party, Yehoshua Wjodeslawski. The bulk of our struggle was against the activists of Poalei Zion Left, who tried to obstruct and disperse our election rallies. But they did not succeed. Thanks to our door-to-door campaign, our party won its first seat in the municipal council. Wjodeslawski's work as a councilman was of great value. He staunchly defended the interests of the poor Jews in Zychlin.

A puzzling event

In 1928, there were two events that, by today's standards, may seem strange to us, but at that time they were important "focal points" in the public debates of the Polish Jews. On that year, the first conference of the League of Workers of Eretz Israel was held in Warsaw. The political parties represented at the conference were Poalei Zion Right, Gordonia, Hashomer Hatzair, Ahdut HaAvoda, and the General Zionists of Yitzhak Gruenbaum. At the opening session, when the chairman of the Tarbut movement M. Gordon presented his greeting in Hebrew, he was booed and jeered by the delegates of Poalei Zion, who demanded that the speaker speak Yiddish. Yitzhak Gruenbaum, who was also the vice-chairman of Tarbut, called them to order, arguing that the League of Workers of Eretz Israel was as important for Tarbut as it was for Poalei Zion. In response, the activists of Poalei Zion angrily left the hall, and they only returned after Mr. Gordon finished delivering his greeting in Hebrew.

The second weird incident took place later in the year at the next conference of the League, which had a special festive atmosphere because it was attended by more than 200 delegates and important visitors like Yitzhak Ben-Tzvi and Yosef Sprinzak as special envoys from Eretz Israel. Emile Vandervelde, a Socialist politician of worldwide-fame (at the time, he was serving as Belgian Foreign Minister and chairman of the Second International) was also present with his wife at the conference's opening session.

After the high-ranking guests left the hall, some of the Poalei Zion delegates made noise, and protested against the hoisting of the blue-and-white flag. Sprinzak tried to convince them of their mistake, but his words were lost in the midst of the commotion. So Yitzhak Ben-Zvi stood up, waited for the clatter to subside, and sharply condemned the protesters, saying that the blue-and-white flag was our national flag, the same flag that was waved and honored at all the events of the World Zionist Organization. He demanded an immediate end to the protests. As Ben-Zvi spoke, a young man waved a red flag and things finally calmed down.

The establishment of Hechalutz

Avraham Helmer, the head of Hashomer Hatzair in our region, approached us to launch a joint effort to establish a branch of the Hechalutz youth movement in Zychlin. After a lot of hard work, we were able to convene the founding meeting of the new organization.

The Hehalutz organization in Zychlin.

Hechalutz was run by a committee chaired by Helmer, who fulfilled his role with great devotion until he emigrated to Eretz Israel. At that point I was chosen to replace him. Over the next few years the movement expanded with the recruitment of many teenagers that were sent for training and preparation for *aliyah.* Over time, Hechalutz became the largest youth organization in Zychlin.

The training

The Poalei Zion organization continued to grow in Zychlin. By 1932, we were able to establish our own training base. We reached an agreement with the Kibbutz Borochov in Lodz and they began sending their groups for training with us. We took care of their accommodation and all their instruction, coaching and preparation for their *aliyah* and future work in Palestine.

In 1933, Yehoshua Wjodeslawski, the leader of our party and our first representative in the town's municipal council , emigrated to Eretz Israel. Pinhas

Davidovitz became chairman of our party. On that same year, our representative Yaakov Moshe Berman won a seat in the elections for the Jewish community committee.

When the British Mandatory authorities drastically reduced the number of immigration visas for Palestine, the few available certificates were reserved for pioneers who had done the training and preparation for *aliyah*. The advice that we gave to those who wanted to go to Eretz Israel was: "you must go to training and preparation". With Meir Helmer, we went to training in the town of Kolo during the year 1934. After a few weeks, Meir Helmer decided to take a shortcut: he left the training camp and eventually succeeded in reaching Palestine as an illegal immigrant.

Zychliners in the United States

Adapted by Y. B.

Translated by Janie Respitz
Edited by Leon Zamosc

[Original book: pages 259-266 Yiddish section]

In 1905 when strikes, demonstrations and street battles broke out throughout the Russian Empire against the Czarist regime, a significant sector of the Jewish population participated in the events. The enlightened youth and the conscientious workers threw themselves into the active struggle with the hope and belief that bringing down the Czar would bring equality and renewal to the Jewish masses. Unfortunately this beautiful dream ended in failed revolution, a general crackdown against the rebels, and agitation and pogroms against the Jews. It was the weak and oppressed who paid the price of this rebellion.

In Zychlin, as in other places, the Jewish youth, disappointed, repressed and despondent began to look for a practical solution. There were no prospects in the town. They began to leave, some to larger cities and others across the ocean. They dreamed about the "Golden Land", America, where one could breathe freely, earn a living, and in time, bring the rest of the family.

The First Steps

However, being an immigrant in a strange land, without the language or a profession, without family or friends, proved to be very difficult. In addition, there was much longing for the wives and children, parents, brothers and sisters who had been left behind. It was particularly sad on the Sabbath and holidays when one remembered how everything was celebrated in Zychlin with family and friends, gathering for celebrations or simply for a glass of tea. All that was gone!

Still, nobody wanted to return home because the bottom line was that there was nothing to go back for.

In time, the number of immigrants from Zychlin increased. By 1910-1914 there were already entire Jewish families from Zychlin living in New York. People helped each other in the process of leaving the town and coming to the United States. It was then that the idea emerged to establish an organized landsmen's society in order to help the new immigrants and keep the people from Zychlin closer together in a foreign unfamiliar country. The initiators were: Aaron Berman, Shmerl Berman, Avraham Makover, Sam Zaiderman and Meir Kelmer.

With the outbreak of the First World War in August 1914 the earnings of the Zychlin Jews in America were improving and they began to think about helping their brothers back home. This idea was transformed into action. They really helped, particularly when the war ended and the economic life of the Jews in independent Poland was completely ruined. Antisemitism and boycotts were rampant throughout the country and also reached Zychlin.

The Official Founding of the Society

Our landsmen's society was officially founded in November 1923 under the name Zychlin Young Mens' Society. The meeting took place in the home of Avraham Makover. The following were elected to the executive committee: Avraham Makover, Shmerl (Sam) Berman, Israel Lemberg, Sam Zaiderman and Sidney Berman.

It is worthwhile mentioning a few of the first important decisions:

- Each member would pay an annual membership fee to cover ongoing expenses.

- The executive committee would hold meetings every two weeks.

- A Gemilat Hesed Kasse fund for interest free loans would be created in Zychlin with our support (Avraham Elye Berman donated money on the spot for this fund).

- Land would be purchased to have our own cemetery.

- A fund would be created to provide Passover assistance to the poor in Zychlin, sending the money every year on the eve of Passover.

Of course we did not refuse individual aid. When we got a letter from the Zychlin rabbi about his difficult situation and the fact that he was not receiving anything from the funds we sent on Passover, we immediately sent aid to his address.

At the same time, we had to take care of our landsmen in New York. To achieve this we established the following:

- A benefit for the sick to help our members and their families with aid for medications and hospitalization.

- A relief fund to help our members in emergency situations.

- An interest free loan fund to give loans in comfortable conditions.

We also worked out the bylaws for the organization, stipulating an annual general meeting in which the president and treasurer would present a report of activities. We also agreed that the executive committee would include the following positions: president, vicepresident, treasurer and manager of the cemetery. Besides these, there were three members who were responsible for the medical assistance to our membership.

In 1938 we sent one thousand dollars to Zychlin for the Gemilat Hesed Kasse and also arranged for the Society of Polish Jews in America to send 600 dollars from their fund. On that same year we also sent 110 dollars to Zychlin for the sick.

During the Second World War

When the Second World War broke out in September 1939 and Zychlin was occupied by the Germans, all contact was lost with our hometown. In 1941, we sent through Spain, with the help of the Red Cross, 16 packages of food with the hope of alleviating the suffering of our unfortunate brothers. Unfortunately those packages never arrived in Zychlin.

The executive of the Zychlin Society in the United States. Standing from right to left: M. Kovent, T. Leibowitch, A. Kirshtein, M. Helmer, M. Waitzberg, and G. Makover. Seated: S. Berman, L. Lasky, S. Kubski, and G. Gorki.

While waiting for Hitler's defeat, we prepared to help the Jews from our old town. We provided collection boxes to every Zychliner home in New York in order to have money ready for the Zychlin Jewish children after the war. When the German army was defeated on all fronts and the Third Reich ceased to exist our joy was disturbed by the horrific news about the extermination of Jews in Europe and especially about the scale of the destruction in Poland. It appeared we did not have many Jewish children from Zychlin to help...

However there were survivors that needed assistance to get back on their feet. The material help provided by our townspeople in America was exceptional, but the moral help was no less important. We had to encourage those who had survived that great national catastrophe. We sent out this appeal from the president of the Zychlin Society in New York, Nat Opatow written in 1944:

"Let us help those who hope to be able to help themselves some day!"

To all landsmen from Zychlin,

As you know we are living through the worst and most inhuman period in human history. Never, in the history of Jewish suffering (and we Jews have suffered a lot) have we had an enemy as brutal and horrifying as Hitler, who with his bloody rule tried to annihilate the Jews from the entire world, and to a certain extent, satisfied his thirst for Jewish blood.

He has already killed millions of our sisters and brothers in Europe and who knows how many more millions will be killed. To solve the Jewish problem is the obligation of the whole world, but saving our unfortunate brothers and sisters in Zychlin is our task.

We must not forget for one moment, that we, the Zychliner Jews of America are their only hope. We must not disappoint or abandon them.

Therefore the Zychlin Relief Committee of New York is appealing to you with the cry of those who cannot speak for themselves: Fulfill your obligation!

This appeal is aimed directly at all Zychliners, including those who do not live in New York. This is the first time that we, the Zychlin landsmen of New York are asking you to help the relief effort. We do not need to tell you that collecting funds for Zychlin is not new in New York, but at this present moment, when the need for rescue is far

115

greater than ever, we must turn to you to help us out. Get to work and join a committee with other landsmen in your city and explain to them the importance of sending help for Zychliners. We hope to receive donations from everyone, as you deem appropriate for this sacred objective.

We are calling a meeting of all Jews from Zychlin in New York. However to all of you who live in other cities in the United States, we are appealing in writing.

Help is needed now. Do not put it off to tomorrow. People's hopes depend on you. Give more than you can. Be generous, we are dealing with a great tragedy.

The money received will be deposited in the bank until the moment we can send the aid to Zychlin.

Zychlin Relief Committee, Nat Opatow, Chairman.

This appeal was warmly received and the Jews from Zychlin living outside New York joined the effort to help the survivors.

After Liberation

Right after liberation in 1945 we sent 20 packages with food and clothing to Zychlin because we hoped that many who had survived would benefit. Sadly, there was no one there to receive that help.

Subsequently a member of our executive, Sam Berman, sent letters to all the Displaced Persons camps in Germany asking about survivors from Zychlin that we could help. At the same time a special fund was set up to bring Zychlin survivors to America. Thanks to this, we were able to help them to find work, place a roof over their heads and more importantly, stand on their own two feet with the financial and moral support from our association.

After the war we also sent packages of food and clothing to Palestine for the needs of the Zychliner surivivors who were getting there.

On May 15th 1948 the establishment of the State of Israel was declared. The Zychlin Jews in America were very excited. We decided to actively raise funds for all the campaigns for the State of Israel. Every year on Israel's Independence Day we organize a party for our members and their families with tables covered with tablecloths. There is a holiday mood and atmosphere. Our hearts beat in rhythm with the hearts of all the Jews in the world who are happy about the existence of our independent Jewish state.

Of course, we do not forget our holy martyrs. Every year we organize a memorial evening to remember those who perished.

Zychlin House in Israel

In 1951 the chairman of the Zychlin Society in New York, Zechariah Targovnik, travelled to Israel with his wife. He proposed to the Israeli Zychliner organization to build a memorial house to perpetuate the memory of Jewish Zychlin. The idea was approved and the Zychlin society in New York quickly collected a respectable amount of money to achieve this goal. Land was bought in Holon, but in 1953 Sam Berman visited Israel and realized that Holon was not an appropriate place to erect the Zychlin House. The lot was sold and, through the joint efforts of our landsmen in America and Israel, two old buildings were purchased on Bograshov street in the centre of Tel Aviv.

Three active members of the Zychlin Society in New York. From right: Nat Opatow, Sidney Berman and Sam Berman.

Ten years later, when Sam returned to Israel in 1963 bringing ten thousand dollars to build the house, there was no agreement between him and the Israeli committee regarding the character and function of the Zychlin memorial house. The realization of the project was postponed.

In July 1965, Nat Opatow arrived in Israel with full authorization from the New York committee to resolve the differences with the Israeli committee. The newly elected committee in Israel quickly reached agreement with their guest from America and, on September 6th that same year, they laid the cornerstone for the Zychlin House in the presence of Nat Opatow. The building now stands proudly in Tel Aviv bearing the name "House of the organization of Zychliners in Israel and America". There is a synagogue in the building dedicated to the holy martyrs of Zychlin.

Nat Opatow with the Committee of the Zychliner Organization in Israel.

The house serves as a reunion place for the Zychlin Jews living in Israel and as a welcome center for landsmen from abroad who come as tourists to Israel.

It is regrettable that our dear members Sam Berman and Nathan Opatow, who dedicated so much energy and devotion to the idea of Zychlin House, did not live to see the fruits of their efforts. May their memories be blessed.

The Zychliners of America intend to continue their activity for our people in Israel, the United States, and wherever our landsmen are living today.

Nat Opatow and Yaakov Ben-Binah at the Zychlin House
cornerstone laying ceremony in Tel Aviv.

Sam Berman AND Yaakov Ben-Binah installing the remembrance
plaque for the Zychlin martyrs in Martef HaShoah, Jerusalem.

The Zychliner Organization in Israel

by Yehoshua Wojdeslawski

Translated by Leon Zamosc

[Original book: pages 92-96 Hebrew section, 254-259 Yiddish section]

Until the outbreak of the Second World War, the Zychlin Jews who had left for Palestine did not feel the need to establish a landsmen's organization. Each one of us had their own attitudes on social and political matters and their own private circle of personal acquaintances. We were not immigrants in a foreign country. Every Zychliner who came to the Eretz Israel was received with open arms by the previous settlers. Some of the immigrants joined kibbutzim and the rest settled in cities and towns. They would socialize with their friends in their homes, or in the clubs of the political parties to which they belonged.

When we began to hear about the criminal acts of the German murderers in the occupied lands, we became anxious about the fate of our friends and relatives who had stayed back in Zychlin. But we could not imagine that the disaster was so horrendous. In those days, the idea was born to organize ourselves as Zychlin landsmen in order to be ready, when the war was over, to help the survivors who would be coming to Eretz Israel. To this end, several activists gathered at the home of Reb Mendel Meir Rozenblum, who had been an activist of the religious Zionist party Mizrahi in Zychlin. The meeting was attended by Yosef Rozenberg, Yosef Rozengarten, Yehezkel Helmer, Leibush Opatowski, Yitzhak Rozenberg, Shlomo Wojdeslawski, Yaakov Neufeld, David Steinberger and Yechiel Plotzker. We discussed the tragic situation of the Zychlin Jews and decided to establish an organization that would include all the Zychliners who were living in Eretz Israel. A temporary committee was elected and charged with the task of preparing the organization's bylaws.

On May 13, 1944, the founding meeting was held at Yitzhak Rozenberg's home. It was attended by 40 members. As elected chairman, Moshe Kelmer lectured on the organization's goals, read the bylaws and proposed the immediate establishment of a charity fund. Yaakov Neufeld was elected as treasurer. Those who were present at the meeting made donations on the spot. Five members were elected to the executive committee: Yosef Rozenberg, Yaakov Neufeld, Yehezkel Helmer, Yitzhak Rozenberg and Aryeh Szenowski. The audit committee included

Yosef Zolty, Yosef Rozengarten and Moshe Helmer. There was also a membership committee that included Mendel Meir Rozenblum, Bunim Boim and Leibush Opatowski.

The war came to an end. Of the four thousand Jews living in Zychlin, only a few dozen had miraculously survived the Shoah. Some of them tried to resettle in Zychlin, but they could not endure it. Very soon, they left the town. Zychlin became a "Judenrein" place.

In 1952 we were visited by Sam Berman, the most engaged activist in the organization of Zychliner landsmen in America. We received him with a large meeting that was attended by veteran Zychliner residents from all over Israel and by the first group of Zychliner survivors. After a report on the organization's activities in Israel, the survivors described the heartbreaking loss of our relatives and friends. We learned that on Purim 1942, the Jews of Zychlin were taken to be gassed at the Chelmno extermination camp.

At the meeting, we made a decision to commemorate the holy victims and to establish a permanent home for the activities of the organization in Israel. Sam Berman promised to work with all his might to achieve this goal. A new committee was elected including Yehoshua Wojdeslawski, Yosef Rozenberg, Zechariah Targovnik, Yitzhak Helmer, Shmuel Jakubowicz and Yehoshua Kowent (among the new immigrants).

Zechariah Targovnik's proposal to buy a small residence for the organization was also adopted. Thanks to the joint effort of the Zychliners in Israel and the United States, two small houses were purchased at 88 Bograshov Street in Tel Aviv. One of the small houses was dedicated as a memorial synagogue for the Shoah victims of Zychlin and the other was designated for the meetings and activities of the organization. The Zychlin House became the permanent memorial for the Jewish community of Zychlin in the State of Israel.

As the activities expanded we realized that the small house was insufficient for the needs of the organization. On Sam Berman's second visit to Israel in 1962, the committee discussed with him the building of a larger house for the organization. He supported the proposal and promised his assistance. But the opinions were divided and the matter was not pursued.

A new committee was elected at the 1964 annual meeting. It included Aryeh Opatowski, Yaakov Ben-Binah (Lemberg), Yaakov Noy (Neufeld), Shmuel Jakubowicz, Yitzhak Kelmer, Yitzhak Rozenberg, Meir Helmer, Avraham Zigelman and Yehoshua Kowent. The committee pushed forward the plan for the construction of the house. They again contacted the Zychliner landsmen's organization in the United States, which sent to Israel the activist Nat Opatow, with whom we found a common language. We hired a contractor and on September 5, 1965, we laid the cornerstone for the new Zychlin House. In an uplifted mood, the committee appealed to all Zychliner landsmen in Israel and abroad for help. With those joint efforts, the new Zychlin House was finally completed with a hall that can accommodate three hundred people. At the synagogue, which was also rebuilt, regular prayers are held on Saturdays and holidays.

House of the Zychiner Organization in Tel Aviv.

Our meetings and celebrations are held in the large hall. We welcome our guests from abroad and facilitate their meetings with relatives and friends. We also use the hall to observe Holocaust Day with memorials and celebrate Israel's Independence Day. Friends from all over the country come to the Zychlin House to participate in all these events.

Our committee decided to publish a memorial book in order to commemorate the social, economic, cultural and political achievements of the Jews of Zychlin, our ancestral town.

בס"ד

5 לספטמבר 1965

אור ליום ח' באלול ה'תשכ"ה

נירתה אבן הפנה
לבית ארגון יוצאי – זיחלין
ישראל אמריקא
להנצחת זכרם של קדושי עירנו
אשר נספו בשיאה ע"י קלגסי היטלר ימ"ש :

הועד הישראלי   הועד האמריקני

יעקב בן-בינה	נתן אפטוב
יעקב נוי	גודל גירקי
יהודה אפטבסקי	סם ירמן
מאיר הלמר	סידני ורמן
אברהם זיגלמן	יוסף למברג
שמואל יעקובוביץ	ישראל למברג
יצחק קלמר	סידני קיסקי
יהושע קובנט	מש"ה.ה.למר
יצחק רוזנברג	לאיס לסכי
	דוד לזרוס

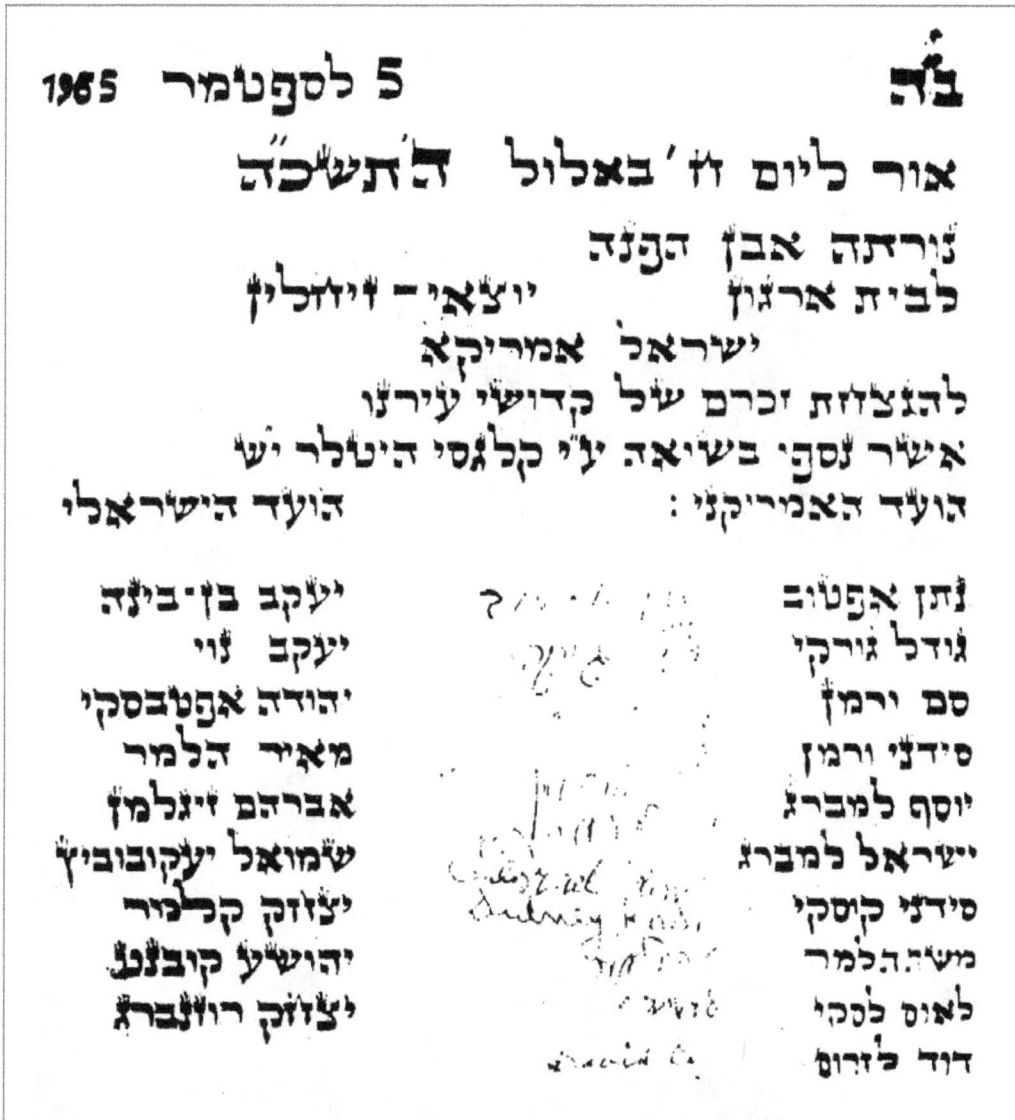

Foundation Document for the Zychlin House cornerstone laying ceremony in Tel Aviv, 1965. The document reads: On this day, 5 September 1965, we laid the cornerstone for the House of the Zychiner Organizations in Israel and America, dedicated to the remembrance of our town's martyrs who perished in the Shoah. The American committee: Nat Opatow, Godel Gorki, Sam Berman, Sidney Berman, Yosef Lemberg, Israel Lemberg, Sidney Kujawski, Louis Laski, Moshe Helmer, David Lazarus. The Israeli committee: Yaakov Ben-Binah, Yaakov Noy (Neufeld), Yehuda Opatowski, Meir Helmer, Avraham Zigelman, Shmuel Jakubowicz, Yitzhak Kelmer, Yehoshua Kowent, Yitzhak Rozenberg.

Laying the cornerstone for the Zychlin House in Tel Aviv, 1965.

Exchange between Yaakov Ben-Binah and Sam Berman from New York,
on the design of the Zychlin House.

Yaakov Ben-Binah reads the Foundation Document at the Zychlin
House cornerstone laying ceremony.

Zychlin House cornerstone laying ceremony in Tel Aviv. From right Yosef
Zolty, Yitzhak Kelmer, Nat Opatow (holding the Foundation Document),
Zechariah Targovnik, Yaakov Ben-Binah, Levkovitz, Yitzhak Rozenberg,
Yaakov Noy (Neufeld).

Zychliners at the installation of the remembrance plaque for the Zychlin
martyrs at Martef HaShoah, Jerusalem.

Personalities

The righteous Reb Aharon Yehuda

by Yaakov Ben-Binah

Translated by David Goren

[Original book: pages 99-100 Hebrew section, 269-271 Yiddish section]

Reb Aharon Yehuda, the *dayan* (religious judge) of Zychlin, was a great *tzadik* who feared God, avoided sin, and was extremely knowledgeable of both the revealed and the hidden. His day began very early in the morning. With the first light he went to the *beit hamidrash* to do the work of the creator. He carried a bag that was full to the point of overflowing with his prayer shawl, two pairs of *tefillin*, books, and food and water for the whole day. It was difficult to fathom how this Jew, small and weak, all his body skin and bones, could manage to carry such a large and heavy load, other than accepting the fact that Reb Aharon Yehudah was not actually walking on the ground – he was rather floating between heaven and the earth.

When he walked to the *beit hamidrash*, he did not look to the right or the left to avoid, God forbid, to seem distracted, though that was not his heart's intent. All those who were in the *beit hamidrash* would look at him and be filled with joy, as he washed and immersed, whether in the summer or the cold of winter, in order to be worthy of doing his holy work. By the scant light of a candle (we did not have electricity in the town) he started to study and pray and went on almost until the afternoon. Like Rabbi Hanina ben Dosa, he was satisfied with a "dry morsel", eating a roll and drinking a glass of milk in order to fulfill the *mitzvot* of Hamotzi and Birkat hamazon (blessing on bread before and after). People brought him his minimal daily serving with the hope that by doing this they would go to heaven.

In addition to the prescribed fasting days, Reb Aharon Yehuda fasted on Mondays and Thursdays. He was small, but his eyes radiated tenderness and affection. He delivered a sermon on the bible and commentaries on Shabbat and every other day of the week before afternoon and evening prayers. Everyone was ecstatic absorbing his teachings. When he was asked about the *kashrut* of a chicken, he did not rush to decide. He looked for ways to make things easy and avoid leaving a family, God forbid, without meat for Shabbat. He was modest and humble, innocent and honest. Above all, he was spiritual - he did not know the shape of a coin. He was full of love for his fellow human beings and the people of Israel. When people approached him with problems, he would listen with great

128

mercy, trying to find the most reasonable solutions. He never turned the Torah into an ax for digging.

The righteous Reb Aharon Yehuda
of Mszczonow.

During the days of awe, he would pass before the ark of the *beit hamidrash* or the great synagogue begging and sobbing before the merciful God – not for himself, but for his holy congregation and for the Jewish people. Despite the fact that his voice was weak, it could be heard throughout the building, even raising to the women's section.

During the holiday of Sukkot, he fulfilled the commandment to spend eight days in the *sukkah* and stayed there to sleep. He was sensitive to the truth, a glorious trait. Whenever he thought that something was wrong, he did not shy away from those in power. He would express his opinion explicitly and impartially. Reb Aharon Yehuda died at a good old age. During his funeral, all work and trade ceased. The entire town accompanied him on his last way with great sorrow.

Avreymele Gelach

by Yaakov Ben-Binah

Translated by Janie Respitz
Edited by Leon Zamosc

[Original book: pages 57-58 Hebrew section, 302-304 Yiddish section]

In our town there was a wagon driver who was called Avreymele Gelach. In Yiddish, "Gelach" was one the words used to refer to a Catholic priest or bishop. Nobody knew why he got this nickname, just like no one knew his family name. He himself did not know. He never signed a promissory note or a cheque, because he did not know how to write either.

His work place was in the market beside the well. He stood there with his horse and wagon, day after day, summer and winter. His mare was blind in both eyes. He stood and waited until he had something to transport or was asked to bring merchandise from the train arriving from Warsaw. Neither he nor his mare ever ate to their fill. From all his hard work he barely had enough for some potato soup and a piece of dry bread. But on the Sabbath he allowed himself to buy a piece of meat.

Avreymele's destitution did not affect his gentle character. He was honest and kind. He never complained about his situation because he believed this was his fate, God's will. He was happy with what he had and did not ask anyone for anything.

His mare was his best friend. They understood each other. He never whipped her. In fact he did not even have a whip. He had a rod without a strap.

If the mare had difficulty pulling the wagon he harnessed himself to her and spoke to her like a kind brother and promised her that if they returned home safely, with God's help, he would give her a double portion of hay. He did not promise her oats because he could not afford them. And so, with joined forces, they would pull the wagon with the load.

In the morning, after placing the horse and wagon in the designated spot, Avreymele ran to the *beit hamidrash* to pray. In the evening, after finishing his work, he unharnessed the mare who knew her way to the stall where her meal was waiting. Although he was hungry and tired, he would then hurry to the *beit hamidrash* for evening prayers. On the Sabbath he was the same as all other

130

Jews, a king. He would put on his Sabbath coat which he had used for many years.

In the *beit hamidrash* Avreymele did not stand by the eastern wall, but rather together with the common folk, behind the platform where the Torah is read. Perhaps once in a while he obtained the privilege of removing the Torah or lifting it up. On Simchat Torah he would take part in the traditional procession, without any special honours.

He was one of the regular listeners at the table in the *beit hamidrash* when Reb Aaron Yehuda read the Torah portion of the week for the common folk. It is hard to know how much he actually understood. In any case, he would listen attentively, not missing a word of what Reb Aaron Yehuda said.

This is how this simple, kind, honest, God fearing Jew lived.

Avreymele never complained, not to the Creator or to other people.

This was his fate. This was his luck. Apparently, this was how it should be…

The Shatin family

by Bar-Yosef

Translated by Janie Respitz
Edited by Leon Zamosc

[Original book: pages 301-302 Yiddish section]

At the end of the 19th century Reb Moshe Aron Shatin lived in Zychlin, a young Hasid, a great Talmudic scholar and a passionate follower of the Ger Hasidim.

Twice a year he would put aside his business, wife and children and leave town, freeing himself from all things material in order to travel to Gora Kalwaria and visit the Ger Rebbe. For weeks after coming back he would tell stories to the other Ger Hasidim in Zychlin about the Rebbe's family table, his teachings and behaviour.

His wife Roza was a woman of valor and a beautiful woman. She descended from a respected family of rabbis, Rebbes, and prosperous businessmen. Reb Moshe Aron Shatin died young leaving the widow Roza and six children, four sons and two daughters. His son Yosef Avraham married the pretty Soreh Layele, the daughter of Sholem Zyger. After their wedding they moved to Plock, where he ran a small sausage factory. He was a great scholar and also a follower of the Ger Hasidim. For years he was the manager of their prayer house in Plock.

Two of Reb Moishe Aron's sons, Menachem and Shmuel, left for England. Shmuel, who had settled in London, died there leaving a son.

Reb Yosef Avraham and his family in Plock were killed by the Nazis. The only survivor was Reb Yosef Avraham's son Moishe Aron, who has been living in Israel since 1934.

The fourth son of Reb Moshe Aron Shatin was Meir, who also perished in the Shoah with his wife Iteh and their children, Royzele and two boys whose names I never knew.

An artist in town - Israel Zafran

by Moshe Lemberg

Translated by Janie Respitz
Edited by Leon Zamosc

[original book: pages 123 Hebrew section, 301 Yiddish section]

It is with great reverence that I want to perpetuate the memory of Israel Zafran of blessed memory. With his artistic – theatrical talent he contributed a lot toward the cultural work in our small town, instilling joy amidst a difficult reality.

His was of short stature but his small body was filled with spirit. I left Zychlin in 1926 as a young man, but I will never forget the magnificent Friday artistic evenings of Poalei Zion Right, where he read monologues from the classical Yiddish repertoire.

The club was always packed. Young and old came to hear him and enjoyed his performances. It was a true recreational gathering in honour of the Sabbath.

Besides that, he founded a drama circle which from time to time performed under his direction with great success.

Those artistic evenings left a big impression on me. I remember how we impatiently awaited the Sabbath, when Zafran would perform. Even today I often recall the sheer enjoyment of it all.

Let his memory be honored.

My brother Yaakov Iashchemski

by Blumeh Iashchemski-Schwartzberg

Translated by Janie Respitz
Edited by Leon Zamosc

[Original book: pages 299-300 Yiddish section]

Yaakov Iashchemski

My brother Yaakov Iashchemski of blessed memory was born in 1913. When the Second World War broke out in 1939 he was participating in military exercises of the Polish army near the Lithuanian border. From there his regiment was sent west and he took part in the battle of Warsaw, where he was taken prisoner and sent to Germany.

In 1941 he returned to Zychlin. In 1942, a resident of Zychlin whose family name was Sloma was shot by the Germans while standing in line to buy some bread. The Germans ordered that the body be taken to the cemetery. They sent my brother Yaakov and his friend Avraham Glotzer to bury him. After they dug the grave the Germans ordered both of them to jump into the grave and they shot my brother and his friend.

My mother, Soreh Rivka Iashchemski was taken to an unknown place when they liquidated the ghetto in 1942 and killed.

A memorial candle for my father and family

by Yehoshua Wojdeslawski

Translated by Janie Respitz
Edited by Leon Zamosc

[Original book: pages 121 Hebrew section, 305 Yiddish section]

It is difficult, very difficult to take the pen and write about my parents, sisters and brothers who were killed in the Chelmno death camp.

We lived together for many years, connected like children to a father, and suddenly, everything was torn apart. I knocked on many doors of Poles in Zychlin. Later, I wrote to the mayor, who was then Edmond Dembowski, to find out who survived. But until now I have not received an answer about the fate of those closest to me. For me, it is clear that they are no longer among the living. They shared the fate of all the Jews who were in Zychlin in the moment of the deportation.

According to other information I received, my father Yaakov David Wojdeslawski and one of my brothers died on the same day. My mother Gitel of blessed memory as well.

My father worked as the head warehouse keeper at the mill of my grandfather Moshe Mendel Wojdeslawski. He belonged to the Piltz Hasidim (Piltz, Pilica in Polish, was a town near Zawiercie). Twice my father brought me to his Rebbe Mendele Piltzer of blessed memory. He wanted me to become a Hasid, but without success. I was attracted by the Zionist movement, especially because my closest friends Zhukhovski, Wrontzberg and Lemberg were the founders of Tzeirei Zion in Zychlin.

Thanks to my father, our home was always open to the poor and needy. Father was a kind hearted, fair man. My mother always gave her consent to his actions. Their memory is engraved deep in my heart.

My father, Anszel Tzinamon

by Helena Bodek (Tzinamon)

Translated by David Goren

[Original book: pages 120-121 Hebrew section, 295-296 Yiddish section]

My father, the teacher Anszel Tzinamon, was the first victim of the Nazis in our town. It happened a few months after the Germans occupied Zychlin. On April 14 1940 – the most tragic day of my life – I was awakened by loud ringing. Frightened, I opened the door. Three cursed policemen – an old gendarme and two Polish police. They confronted my father and ordered him to dress. My appeals and those of my mother were useless. Bourscheka, a Czech with a friendly face, explained that he had received an order to arrest my father and he was responsible that nothing bad would happen to him.

They took my father out to the street, I desperately ran after them. There was great panic in the town. Everywhere you looked, there were police dragging scared men. This was the mass arrest of the Polish intelligentsia: doctors, engineers, teachers and priests. Among them was my father and two other Jews. The teachers had submitted a request to the German authorities to re-open the schools and my father was in the list of those who signed the request. He had dedicated his life to educational work and could not accept the closure of the school that he had founded.

It was not easy to keep a Jewish private school going in Zychlin. It was a constant battle to balance the most modest budget. My father faced frequent problems and impediments posed by the principals of the Polish schools and the local government. He was thrilled with every accomplishment in purchasing educational materials, passing inspections, and recruiting new teachers. He founded the school in one small room, and through his persistence and stubbornness as the school's principal, he managed to acquire a modest building that was the property of the school. My father's life vocation was teaching. He loved all of his students equally, whether talented, diligent or slackers. The students also loved him and treated him with respect.

My father worked more than twenty years in teaching. He raised and educated three generations of students. He dedicated his free time - of which there was not much - to Jewish public service. In addition to being a member of the management of the Gmilat Hessed fund, he gave Polish language classes in the *heder* and financially supported the Zionist movement as much as he could. He had learned Gemara in his youth and was fluent in Hebrew. He was proud of all the Jewish accomplishments in Palestine and dreamt of visiting. Unfortunately, he could not witness the establishment of the State of Israel.

A short time after his arrest he was brutally murdered by the Nazis. The whole town of Zychlin deeply mourned his death.

Reb Itche Jakubowicz

by Shmuel Jakubowicz

Translated by David Goren

[Original book: pages 122-123 Hebrew section, 288-289 Yiddish section]

My father, Reb Itche Jakubowicz, was known in Zychlin as a man of noble spirit. People interacted with him politely and with respect. He was an observant, God-fearing Torah scholar, but he did not disqualify secular culture, from which he derived much insight. He had a broad, deep knowledge of classical literature and Jewish and general philosophy. And he was interested in the issues of the time.

In his youth, he attended the *beit hamidrash* and learned Torah from morning until night. After marrying he persisted in his learning. Earning a living was problematic in our home. My father tried his hand at trade but was not very successful. We found some livelihood supplying paper bags to the grocery stores. There were six children in the home and my father had trouble making ends meet. Despite that, when I decided to learn the sewing trade to help the family's finances, my father did not see it as a good thing.

My father supplied the whole town with flour for *shmurah matzah*, the four species for Sukkot and willows for Hoshana Rabbah. He was the *shamash* in the synagogue. He inherited this job from his father-in-law, Lipsh. He maintained the synagogue and distributed the honors of going up to the Torah on Shabbat and holidays without giving preference to wealthy Jews over poor Jews. He fulfilled this role with honor and dignity, never raising his voice. He respected others and they respected and appreciated him.

The writer, Shalom Asch, who was born in nearby Kutno, would visit Zychlin periodically, and when he was in town he visited my father and discuss literature and philosophy. The *yeshiva* boys who attended these meetings thought that they were discussing the Talmud when in fact they were dealing with general issues of study and thought.

My father did some writing as well. He authored lists and stories which he never revealed to others out of modesty. That secret remained with him.

He understood and made peace with our aspiration to leave the *beit hamidrash* and join the movements that were flourishing among the Jewish youth. He gave me his blessing when I became an activist of Hechalutz and went to training, and he was truly happy when I later left to Eretz Israel. He wanted my three sisters to join me, but the war broke out and they were murdered in the Shoah.

May his memory be blessed.

Three Zychliners

by David Steinberger (Shamir)

Translated by David Goren

[Original book: pages 112-114 Hebrew section, 285-288 Yiddish section]

Yitzhak Kelmer

Yitzhak Kelmer distinguished himself by his great imagination, inexhaustible knowledge about Zionism, and tireless disposition for public service. He was "one of the people", the child of a typical, simple family of Zychlin. He inherited from his father problems to solve and the responsibility of having to earn a living for his family. He took all those responsibilities as a matter of fact. He was a manufacturer, merchant and salesman but he lacked proficiency in the inner workings of Jewish trading. He was an honest man who could not cheat and as a result got into trouble, borrowing here and paying there, writing, erasing, positioning, eliminating, fluttering and treading water. For him, all those troubles were temporary and passing. He did everything with a strong sense of commitment, whether it was related to his work or to his service to the Jewish community and Zionism.

He was not discouraged by obstacles or lack of cash. We needed a more spacious place for the Zionist Association, which required a significant amount of money to modify the building. Even the optimists shrugged their shoulders – where will the money be found? Yitzhak said little, but his smile suggested that he had a plan. And when the moment came, he executed his plan quickly. I cannot remember how the miracle was accomplished, but there were many others. He illuminated the room, took care of culture, marketing, parties, visa certificates, and his greatest satisfaction came from accompanying someone to the train station and seeing him off to Eretz Israel. Then, happiness radiated from his face.

Yitzhak was single. Everybody wanted to change that, including his mother, his friends, and even himself. But his public service in general and his Zionist activities in particular were always expanding and he had no time for such personal matters...

-- Yitzhak, when will you go to Eretz Israel?

-- It is not my turn yet, I must first assist several friends to make *aliyah*... And by the way, who will we leave here to take care of things?

Riva and Rivtcha

Here was an inseparable pair, two girlfriends, like twin deer. I do not think anyone ever saw one without the other. Riva and Rivtcha were always together. They were both full of grace, from "nice Hasidic families" where the fathers fought our movement in every possible way. But the girls joined the movement with heart and soul despite their parents' objections.

Riva helped her aging parents at home and Rivtcha was the main salesperson in her parents' store, she practically managed the business. In the store, between one shopper and another, there were discussions on Zionism. Somehow, in addition to her work, Riva found time to help the town's poor, to listen to anyone who had difficulties, to help, lighten, comfort, calm... And despite all of this, she still had time to be with Rivtcha.

In the evenings, Riva and Rivtcha participated in meetings, lectures, activities... They collected donations and managed election campaigns. And if something was urgently needed during the day, they would made themselves available as if there were no home and no store. They were always ready to give their time to the cause of Zionism.

Rivtcha somehow managed to marry as well. Riva, however, could not waste time in such mundane things. "I simply don't have the patience", she would say... They were happy when they were busy with their activities, and the holy work had a way of always returning to glorify them and raise their souls.

Pinchas (Pintcha) Getzel

Pintcha was an out-and-out *yeshiva* boy and a baker by profession. He worked nights in his parents' bakery and relaxed during the day. He used to sit and snooze, stand and snooze, speak and snooze and even walk and snooze. In our organization, he was a member of many committees, and despite his hard work he never missed a meeting. He usually slept a few hours during the day, but if there was a Zionist activity, Pintcha did not hesitate to skip his nap. At the meetings he was wide awake, participating in all the discussions, arguments, and votes. But at work he occasionally fell asleep, which resulted in ruined baked goods that had to be trashed. When his parents reprimanded him he felt bad, but he did not change his ways - Zionism took priority over work and all personal matters.

Pintcha had a good demeanor. He would never yell or get angry. I would give a prize to any Zychliner who could testify they had seen Pintcha upset or heard him raise his voice. He would not begrudge or complain. He accepted everything with love. He treated all sad cases with extra tenderness. When someone refused to donate, Pintcha did not give up. He would make his case until he reached his goal.

I recall a lecture about "Love and Hate in Zionism." The lecturer opened the talk arguing that to love the goal of building a Jewish homeland, one must hate living in the diaspora. Pintcha opposed this idea saying that we did not need to hate our lives, and that if we wanted to change our lives we had to do it on the basis of a healthy foundation. I remember that I told him: "In fact, you identify with the lecturer's idea except that the word 'hate' bothers you... The concept is alien to your personal nature."

Time went by and I eventually caught him displaying anger. During the electoral campaign for the Polish parliament a speaker of the religious orthodox party Agudat Israel began badmouthing Zionism and Zionists. Pintcha heatedly said "I hate him as much as I hate an anti-Semite Gentile."

If you insulted Zionism – even Pintcha got angry.

[Published in "Yediot Zychliners in Israel" December 1944]

142

My grandfather, Reb Avraham Itche Boim

by Yaakov Neufeld (Noy)

Translated by David Goren

[Original book: pages 111 Hebrew section, 288-289 Yiddish section]

My grandfather Reb Avraham Itche Boim was a Mszczonow Hasid and student of the Torah, but he did not outwardly appear to be part of the group of Hasidim in the town. He stood out in the community, synagogue and *beit hamidrash* for the strength of his convictions and the personal example of his daily life. He was revered and respected in the Jewish community. As a regular subscriber of the Hebrew daily HaTzfira, he allowed other Hasidim to secretly come to marvel at the sight of a newspaper in the holy language. Despite the admonitions of the fanatics, they looked and discovered that no harm came to them. My grandfather contributed greatly to reducing the extreme religious dogmatism that prevailed in the town.

His son, Reb Bunim, was also an Mszczonow Hasid and student of the Torah. Contradicting the anti-Zionist stance of his peers, he decided that his place was in Eretz Israel. On Sundays, when the stores had to close by state regulation, some Hasidim would furtively come to the back door of his store to hear the news from Palestine and ask about the progress of his plans to make *aliyah*. They thought that he was hallucinating. It was like this for many years, until he fulfilled his dream. Several family members had already left before him, and in the mid-1930s he joined them with his wife and children. He died in Israel.

We will remember forever my father Reb Nachum Neufeld (son of Israel Shmuel); my mother Chawa, daughter of Reb Avraham Iche Boim; my sister Chana, her husband and their daughter; and my brother Aharon Leib, his wife and their daughter. They were all murdered in the Shoah by Hitler (may his name be erased) during the Second World War. May their memories be blessed.

The Lemberg family

by Yaakov Lemberg

Translated by David Goren

[Original book: pages 115-117 Hebrew section, 289-292 Yiddish section]

With deep respect for their memory, I want to share these notes on my grandfather and my parents, who were known in Zychlin for their noble spirits. My brother and I were blessed with parents who gave us a traditional and general education as well as freedom to develop, something that was not common in the old times.

Before I write about my parents, I would like to describe my grandfather Reb Eliezer Lipsh Lemberg, an honorable figure that inspired everybody's respect in the town. He was a scholarly and spiritual Jew who did not rule out general knowledge and culture. He had a thorough acquaintance with Jewish and general literature and was attentive to the problems of the time. Of naturally democratic and noble spirit, he understood my father's aspirations when he left the *beit hamidrash* and went on to learn a profession. My grandfather was not a Hasid and did not belong to the *shtiebel* of any Rebbe, which was unusual in that period. He was a natural contrarian.

In Zychlin, my grandfather was known as Reb Lipsh. Everyone simply referred to him in that way, without a family name or nickname. They did not even reference his job. He began his public involvement in communal life as supervisor of the construction of the great brick synagogue. When the synagogue was built, he became the *shamash*. In that role, he made sure the synagogue was maintained and the budget was balanced. He was also responsible for assigning the *aliyot* for reading the Torah on Shabbat and the holidays. When he distributed the honors, he never ignored a poor person or gave preference to the rich.

In addition to his role in the synagogue, Reb Lipsh was responsible for registering the Jewish residents of the town. Back then, the Zychlin Jewish community did not have an elected governing committee, and the registration was a government job. The registration book of the community had to be kept in the Russian language, and my grandfather had learned both Russian and Polish, verbal and written, on his own. He held another post in the Kutno recruitment office, where all men had to appear for medical exams before entering the army. His job was to confirm the identity of each recruit.

Reb Lipsh was the *kashrut* supervisor when wheat was ground into flour for *matzah*, and he supplied the flour for *shmurah matzah*. He was also responsible for raising money for Eretz Israel in our town. His house was decorated with the pictures he received from Eretz Israel depicting the Western Wall, Rabbi Meir Baal HaNes[4] and the Rambam. Every day he would come to us to read the newspaper that came from Warsaw, despite the fact that the paper was condemned by the Hasidim. I remember my father and grandfather breaking out in bitter tears when they read in the newspaper that Theodor Herzl had died. They considered rending (tearing) their garments as a sign of mourning. My grandfather declared that rending was not required, but they still took off their shoes and sat on low seats for the rest of the day. He was known as a smart, kind and honest person. Many would knock at his door for advice or ask him to resolve disagreements, choosing him as a single arbitrator. Both sides trusted his integrity, wisdom and judgement.

My grandfather Reb Lipsh requested that sand from Israel and the ribbon distinctions he had received for his social services be placed with him in his grave. When he passed away at age sixty-eight, there was sadness in the entire town, including the Christians. The mayor, the heads of the police and fire departments, and other senior Christian dignitaries visited our mourners' house. All of the town's youth participated in the funeral.

My father, Avraham Mordechai Lemberg, made his livelihood in the sewing business. He hired workers who were local and from outside the town. We also had a leather business managed by my mother Bina (nee Storczyk). She made a good living until the start of the First World War, but she passed away in 1917 at the age of thirty-eight.

Our home was a place of culture, daily newspapers and "external" books. We received both a traditional and secular education, as much as that was possible in Zychlin. The house was always open to all, and needy people who came for help did not leave empty-handed.

My father was also active in public service, assisting travelers to find a place to sleep and in the selection of the Jewish authorities. He had a common language with the workers he employed. "Revolutionary" meetings were held in our house and my father was involved in Zionist activities.

---

[4] Rabbi Meir Baal HaNes was a sage who lived in the time of the Mishna. He is considered one of the greatest Tannaim of the fourth generation.

I came to Eretz Israel in early 1926. My father also wanted to come, but the Mandate laws in Palestine did not allow him to get a visa certificate because he was too old to be independent and too young to be supported. His premature death put an end to our hope to see him arrive in Eretz Israel.

In 1929, when he heard that I had participated in the defense of Hulda, I received a short letter from him: "I am proud of you for fulfilling your duty to the motherland, if I had been there, I would have done the same..."

My father excelled in his deep love for the Land of Israel. He had a progressive world view that he passed on to us. Looking back, I view him mainly as a spiritual advisor and an honest person. He handed down his spirit to us, giving us his vision for feeling an integral part of society and participating in Tikkun Olam (repairing the world). A proper life is primarily based on fair relations among people and caring for others. He educated us to fulfill the commandment to "love thy neighbor as thyself".

Yitzhak Kelmer

by Yaakov Ben-Binah

Translated by Janie Respitz
Edited by Leon Zamosc

[Original book: pages 114-115 Hebrew section, 304-305 Yiddish section]

Yitzhak Kelmer

Yitzhak Kelmer was well known in our town. Old and young knew him. He was devoted to the Zionist ideal. He was not an ideologue or a party speaker and he did not push himself to the front, he only wanted to work for others. He belonged to the Bnai Zion Association, but was ready to help, without exception, other Zionist groups when they came to him for assistance.

Everybody in Zychlin loved Yitzhak. There was always a gentle smile on his face. He was blessed by God to be a community worker and he was around the Bnai Zion's clubhouse from the time it opened until it closed. Because of this, he neglected his family life. His main efforts were devoted to the Jewish Agency and the Jewish National Fund, for which he worked as the local agent.

Yitzhak would accompany every Zychliner who emigrated to Palestine to the train station. When people said that the whole town was "on his shoulders", it was not an exaggeration. He dreamed about going to Eretz Israel after achieving his goal of seeing that all the Jewish shops on Budzyner street had been closed and everyone had gone to Palestine. Unfortunately, his dream was not realized. He shared the bitter fate of the Zychlin Jews who were killed by the Nazi murderers, may their names be blotted out.

Yitzhak Kelmer had been elected as a member of the Jewish community committee as a candidate of the Bnai Zion list. Even in the ghetto, Yitzhak continued his Zionist activism. From time to time, as much as the conditions permitted, he organized gatherings and meetings.

His memory will always accompany us.

David Steinberger (Shamir)

by Yosef Rozengarten

Translated by David Goren

[Original book: pages 103-105 Hebrew section, 277-279 Yiddish section]

David Steinberger (Shamir)

David Steinberger was born in 1888 in the city of Mszczonów. Coming from a family of distinguished Torah sages, he attended a *yeshiva* and became a Jewish scholar. In 1907 he married Tova, the eldest daughter of Reb Shmuel Biderman from Zychlin. As was customary at the time, he was invited to live with his in-laws for a few years. Two years after the wedding, however, he reached a turning point, giving up his free accommodations, leaving Zychlin, and beginning an independent life in Lodz.

The occupation of Poland by the Germans during the First World War allowed all proscribed political organizations throughout Poland to come out to the open, including the Zionist movements and parties. In London, Chaim Weizmann was negotiating the Balfour declaration with the British government. David

Steinberger, who by then had returned to Zychlin, immediately joined the Zionist activities with great energy and dedication. He founded the Bnei Zion Association, organized the local youth and developed friendships with activists of all the different Zionist tendencies. Among other things, he founded a Zionist library, worked in the committees for Keren Hayesod and Keren Kayemet, and organized Jewish and Zionist literature gatherings on Friday evenings.

He instilled a love for Hebrew in the Zychlin youth by teaching the language in evening courses that also included classes on Torah, Jewish History and the Land of Israel. He was a superb lecturer and teacher, and his home served as a base for all the Zionist groups in the town, especially the young activists. Every Shabbat we, the youngsters of Zychlin, gathered at David's home and argued passionately about Zionist and literary topics. He charmed the audience with his passionate conversation and we thirstily absorbed his words.

Eventually, he initiated a daring project – to create a Jewish/Hebrew school in Zychlin. It was an idea that few believed was possible. He recruited the best pedagogical minds in various disciplines, including his brother Yosef, who had previously been a teacher in Warsaw. The school gained reputation in the district and its impact was felt in Poland at large, including among those who were heading the Tarbut school in Warsaw.

I remember well the day of the Balfour declaration, which became a big holiday in the town thanks to David's initiative. A big party was held in the hall of the school on Pasieka street, where he appeared dressed in his best holiday clothes. His face was shining from excitement and joy, reflecting the huge significance of that historical event.

David also served as teacher in the Hebrew schools of Kutno, Bialystok and other places. For a short time, he was also a writer for the Warshaver Togblat (Jewish Daily) by invitation of its editor A. D. Nomberg.

David Steinberger became David Shamir when he came to Palestine in 1925. During the first years he had difficulties finding employment – the typical problem of all the arriving pioneers. But he had always been very good at both asking for help and fulfilling requests. We were roommates and, as a union worker, I was able to help him get day jobs, though the work he did was not even close to matching his knowledge and capabilities. Still, he never refused the jobs that were offered to him – he was willing to do anything to support himself.

In 1926, David got a teaching job in Jeda, a new settlement in the Valley of Jezreel. From there he moved to Ramat Gan, where he was the pedagogical manager of a boarding school. Over the years, he taught at many schools and educational institutions, where he inspired in his students a great love for the land, language and nation of Israel. In the 1930's he opened LeOr, a boarding school of his own in Ramat Gan that he managed for more than 10 years.

After the War of Independence, already in his retirement age, David volunteered to teach in Beer Sheva, where he served as the first principal of a school for new immigrants. With unlimited energy and excitement, he devoted himself to educating children from diverse origins, especially Sephardim, with whom he shared his love of Israel as a nation and country.

In his last years, he worked in the construction sector of the Kibbutz Artzi movement. Despite his age, he did not want to give up work – he claimed that without work there was no point to life. David was a very conversational man who exceled in his depth of knowledge about literature, Torah, Judaism and many other aspects of life.

He was proud of his sons, daughters and grandchildren. His first son, Bunim Shamir, lived in kibbutz Shaar Hagolan and was a leader of Hashomer Hatzair and the Kibbutz Artzi movement. His second son, Ami Shamir, was a reporter and translator. His three daughters and their husbands were all members of the labor movement and educated their children in that spirit as well.

All who knew him, especially his thousands of students, were distraught with grief when he passed away. Many of them had come as pioneers to the Land of Israel as a direct result of his strength of conviction, education and spiritual inspiration. I am deeply saddened by the loss of my teacher, rabbi and good friend.

His memory will live in all those who knew him.

[Published in the newspaper Al HaMishmar, May 14, 1960].

Tova Steinberger (Shamir)

by Yosef Rozengarten

Translated by David Goren

[Original book: pages 105-106 Hebrew section, 279-280 Yiddish section]

Tova Steinberger (Shamir)

Tova Steinberger (later Shamir when she came to Eretz Israel) was raised in a traditional Jewish home of Zychlin. Her father, Reb Shmuel (Shmelka) Biderman, was an observant Jew who traded in wood, was a member of the Jewish community's committee, had strong opinions, and was very strict. Following the customary ways, Reb Shmuel insisted on leaving his mark on his children's education. His daughter Tova, however, was one of those young women who fought for a new, freer way. Her struggles paved the way for herself and her siblings, who also became committed Zionists when they matured,

During the first years of Tova's marriage with David Steinberger (who also came from a very traditional family) they stayed close to their parents' ways, but they quickly took distance and stood on their own. Their home in Zychlin became a center of Zionist activity and Hebrew literary discussions. It was always crowded with activists of the Zionist movement (young and old) and students of the Hebrew school.

Her life was not always easy. She was able to get through crises thanks to her personality, sense of responsibility and love for her family, all of which were reflected in her various activities.

She was full of life and pleasantness. From the depth of her heart she knew how to be truly happy and how to respond to the pain of those who were less fortunate. In Israel she was proud of her children and for good reason. Her first child, Bunim of kibbutz Shaar Hagolan, was a leader of Hashomer Hatzair and Mapam (the United Workers Party). Her second son Ami was a talented journalist and translator, and her three daughters and their husbands were people of the labor movement who raised their children in that spirit.

When you saw Tova exuding happiness on Passover's seder night, surrounded by her children and grandchildren, you saw the true happiness of a Jewish family.

A few months before celebrating her golden wedding anniversary, Tova fell sick and passed away. She was a true woman of valor, someone who epitomized the traditional role of the Jewish mother.

May her memory be blessed.

[Published in the newspaper Al HaMishmar, February 11, 1958].

My father-in-law, Reb Menachem Meir Rozenbaum

by Yaakov Neufeld (Noy)

Translated by David Goren

[Original book: pages 101-103 Hebrew section, 275-276 Yiddish section]

Reb Menachem Meir Rozenbaum

My father-in-law, Reb Menachem Meir Rozenbaum, was one of a kind in the town. He was the man that offered inspiration to all those *yeshiva* students who were seeking their way after the First World War, when new horizons were opening to the youth. Reb Menachem showed us the path to Zionism. Without disconnecting us from the traditional ways and Torah study, he taught us to prepare for personal fulfillment in Eretz Israel. The students of the *beit hamidrash* would huddle around him to absorb his words. He was a guiding light for an entire generation.

In those days, all the *yeshiva* students learned the oral and written scriptures, but there were two distinct groups among them. There were those who studied in the "shtibel" of the Ger Hasidim, who believed that the Jews had to reconcile with diaspora life until the arrival of the Messiah and not rush to redemption. The other group were the students of the *beit hamidrash*, who did not accept that narrow horizon of fate and sought to break the cycle of life in the diaspora. Reb Menachem Meir, who was a founder of the religious Zionist party Mizrahi, was the instructor and guide of these students at the *beit hamidrash.*

His inspiration was completely spiritual. He did not bother about life's practical things - his wife Leah dealt with those issues. But when it came to causes related to Eretz Israel, he would donate personally and generously. During the "socialist campaign" to establish the Histadrut (the workers' trade union central in Palestine), he was praised for his superb example of how to raise money.

Reb Menachem Meir devoted all his energy and strength to help the students of the *beit hamidrash* to fulfill themselves in the Zionist idea until he eventually came to Eretz Israel himself.

I worked then as a member of the Jewish community committee and I could see up close how important it was that the Zionist movement, in all of its streams, should capture the minds of the communities. Reb Menachem Meir's influence over the Jewish residents of the Zychlin was huge. He was originally a follower of the Ger Hasidim, but their opposition to Zionism forced him to break away. He founded and led the Zychlin branch of the religious party Mizrahi and disseminated the Zionist idea among all the layers of the Jewish community. It was not an easy task because Zychlin was a stronghold of the Ger Hasidim and the town's rabbi Avraham Mordechai Alter was close to them. Their power was great, not so much in their numbers, but in their firmness and their brashness to declare that all scholars or God-fearing Jews with any type of connection to Zionism were criminals who harmed the People of Israel. Not everyone was able to stand up to such pressures and accusations in order to be counted as a "Zionist".

Reb Menachem Meir, a Jewish scholar, was a pillar of light for all those who dared to break the barrier and connect to the Zionist movement. Being part of the rabbinical institutions, he could not be elected to the governing committee of the community, but he supported the election of most of the members from the Zionist parties. This factor helped overcome the objections of the Ger Hasidim and the town's rabbi, facilitating the dissemination of Zionist ideas in the synagogue and the *beit hamidrash* when Zionist lecturers or envoys from Eretz Israel visited Zychlin.

Reb Menachem Meir Rozenbaum

by Yosef Rozengarten

Translated by David Goren

[Original book: pages 100-101 Hebrew section, 276-277 Yiddish section]

IMenachem Meir Rozenbaum was known as a God-fearing scholar and a passionate Zionist. He worked as a butcher in several communities, encouraged youths to study the profession before emigrating to Palestine, and was one of the founders of the Union of Ritual Slaughterers in Poland. He became *shoychet* in Zychlin in 1900 to the great dissatisfaction of the Ger Hasidim, who opposed his Zionism and called him names like "*apikores*", "rebel", amd "scavenger." More than once they tried to disqualify the *kashrut* of his slaughter. He was a member of Mizrahi, the party of the religious Zionists, but his home was open to people of all the Zionist organizations. We, the members of the secular youth movements Hechalutz and Tzeirei Zion, often sought his advice. When we distributed shares of Bank HaPoalim he gave us lots of helpful advice to ensure the success of our endeavor. He always tried to make peace among the various Zionist factions.

He came to Eretz Israel in 1934. Very soon he had disputes with the religious establishment and spoke against its leaders. For that he was punished: he was de-certified as *shoychet* and his name was widely smeared.

Despite the difficulties, he was able to see the fulfillment of his vision. He raised children, grandchildren and great grandchildren, and all in Israel.

When he was 85, he invited me over and said with a smile: "God bless that my health is good, my mind is clear, and I was never forced to compromise my views. Every day I learn a chapter of *Sha's* alone and another chapter in a group. These days I am finishing the entire *Sha's* and, God willing, I will start it again.

When I wished him a long life to 120, he gave me a playful look and said "Yoselah, why are you limiting my life? Why shouldn't I be like Methuselah, who lived 969 years?"

Menachem Meir Rozenbaum died at the age of 88. He will always be remembered for good by all those who knew him.

[Published in the newspaper Davar, September 26, 1954].

Aharon Kanarek (Zamir)

by Yosef Rozengarten

Translated by David Goren

[Original book: pages 107-108 Hebrew section, 281-281 Yiddish section]

Aharon Kanarek (Zamir)

Aharon Kanarek was one of twelve siblings. In his youth he studied in the *beit hamidrash* and the *yeshiva*. He was considered one of the brightest youngsters in Zychlin, a man of HaTzfirah (the Hebrew newspaper published in Warsaw). He was an avid reader of Hebrew books and active in the Bnei Zion Association. In 1923, when the Zionist movement in Poland split into the Al HaMishmar and Et Livnot factions, he joined Al HaMishmar and his relationships with me and other members of the group Eretz Yisrael HaOvedet (Workers of the Land of Israel) were very warm.

After his arrival in Palestine in 1925, he worked for some years with the Nesher publishing company, but he was forced to leave his work due to severe illness. He was bed-ridden for fifteen years during which his wife had to support the family on her own (may she live a long life).

He was sixty years old when he died, leaving a son and a daughter. May his memory be blessed.

[Published in the newspaper Davar, March 9, 1956].

Menachem Olsztyn

by Yosef Rozengarten

Translated by David Goren

[Original book: pages 108 Hebrew section, 282 Yiddish section]

Menachem Olsztyn

Menachem Olsztyn worked in Israel for forty years, first with his son Leibish at the University in Jerusalem and, after his son died, at Moshav Tel Adashim until he became blind. He was a devoted labor man in Israel as he had been in Zychlin, where he had worked from early morning until late at night. More than a worker, he was an artist in his profession. I once passed by the Zychlin synagogue to find him doing reparations on the roof. My blood froze in fear of a disaster, but he was doing it with great pleasure.

All the members of Moshav Tel Adashim liked him. He worked tirelessly, but on the eve of Shabbat or a holiday he would take off his work clothes, dress up in his best attire, and go to the synagogue. When the services finished he would leave glowing. His children sang special Shabbat songs until the late hours of the night for everyone's pleasure.

He died at the good old age of ninety-five leaving five daughters and a son, thirteen grandchildren and twenty-three great-grandchildren.

[Published in the newspaper Davar, February 21, 1966].

Leibush (Aryeh) Olsztyn

by Yosef Rozengarten

Translated by David Goren

[Original book: pages 109 Hebrew section, 282-283 Yiddish section]

Leibush (Aryeh) Olsztyn

Leibush (Aryeh) Olsztyn was a worker's worker. From a young age he toiled in metalwork, a profession that he had learned from his father, who had started working at age eight and continued working all of his life. After the First World War, when Poland's public, political and cultural life was flourishing, Leibush joined the Zionist labor movement. Because he was artistically inclined, he was assigned cultural tasks such as organizing a choir, a string orchestra, and a drama circle.

In 1924, he was among those who came to Palestine as part of the fourth *aliyah* wave. He quickly arranged for all his family (eight people) to join him. Leibush was the only Zychliner who did not stop until his entire family was reunited in Eretz Israel.

He worked hard his entire life. Despite having cancer, he did not quit his professional work until the very last minute. He was involved in the metalwork of all the public buildings of Jerusalem including Binyanei HaUmah (the Jerusalem Convention Center). In the last days of his life, lying in the hospital, he was still making plans for that important project and thinking of ways to implement them on time.

Leibush (Aryeh) Olsztyn was taken from us when he was only fifty-three. He was a good friend and a good man. He was modest and maintained his connection with the Israeli labor movement until his passing.

[Published in the newspaper Davar, October 1, 1950].

Avraham Getzel (Ben-Yaakov)

by Yosef Rozengarten

Translated by Leon Zamosc

[Original book: pages 280-281 Yiddish section]

Avraham Getzel (Ben-Yaakov)

The news of the death of Avraham Getzel have shocked all of us. I was privileged to work with him in the Tzeirei Zion and Hechalutz organizations in Zychlin, a few years before coming to Eretz Israel.

In 1917, upon returning to my hometown Zychlin from Lodz, I met again with the young people with whom I had studied in the *heder* and the *yeshiva*. We were all very close. The oldest was Avraham Getzel, who had just returned from Warsaw, where he had been working as an employee. He led our group as we took the first steps to participate in public life. With the independence of Poland, socio-cultural and political organizations could now legally operate in the open.

In addition to founding the Zychlin branch of Tzeirei Zion, Avraham Getzel was one of the main speakers at the organization's first regional cross-conference in Plock. The delegates established the district chapter of the Zionist Socialist party (which was Tzeirei Zion's political arm), electing Abraham as regional secretary.

In late 1918, the Socialist Jedrzej Moraczewski was appointed as prime minister of Poland. At the time, Workers' Councils were being formed all over the country, often with the participation of Jewish socialist movements. Abraham Getzel was elected to the Zychlin Workers' Council and became one of its leading members, fighting for the interests of the working class and the poor, who saw him as a true representative.

He came to Palestine with the third *aliyah*, changing his name to Avraham Ben-Yaakov. He working in the construction of the Haifa-Jeda highway and in the stone quarry in Jerusalem. When he became seriously ill, doctors ordered him to travel abroad to recover and Berl Katzenelson, the editor of Davar, helped make the trip a success. Coming back from abroad, he was unable to return to physical labor, but he worked as head of the insurance department of the Histadrut's Solel Boneh construction company,

Unfortunately, his beloved son was killed during the war in 1948. The tragedy had a fatal effect on Avraham. He avoided his friends and acquaintances. Once, I met him in Tel Aviv and invited him to walk by the sea - he refused. After that, I never saw him again.

He died suddenly in the United States while on a trip related to his insurance work.

Those who were close to Abraham will always remember him.

My friend, Avraham Getzel (Ben-Yaakov)

by Yaacov Lemberg

Translated by David Goren

[Original book: pages 118-120 Hebrew section, 293-294 Yiddish section]

Avraham Getzel had left Zychlin before the First World War. Feeling confined in our small town, he had moved to Warsaw, where he worked as a salesman in a garment store. But he decided to return to Zychlin when the Germans captured Warsaw during the war. He entered public service and was elected as a member of the first committee of the sports organization Turen Farein in Zychlin. In 1918 he was among the founders of the Bnai Zion Association, which attracted youngsters who had not found their place in the other Zionist parties. He was always in a good mood. His soulful balance, congeniality and good temper always illuminated his environment. He captured all our hearts.

Celebrating the departure of Abraham Getzel (Ben Yaakov) to Palestine. Standing from right: Michael Lajzerowicz, Zechariah Targovnik, Avraham Hodes, Yehoshua Wojdeslawski. Seating: Tzvi Lemberg, Zlotogorski, Avraham Getzel, Aryeh Opatowski, Yosef Rozengarten. Below: Yaakov Zhukhovski, Yaakov Lemberg.

Avraham was sent to represent Zychlin at the 1918 regional meeting of Tzeirei Zion in Plock, where he was elected as the organization's secretary for the region.

With the restoration of Poland's independence, elections were held in Zychlin for a Workers' Council. We decided to participate in the elections, despite the fact that our organization's center in Warsaw had not yet issued a positive opinion regarding participation in the council.

Poalei Zion and the Bund, which were also operating in Zychlin, took advantage of the unclear position of our Warsaw centrer to disqualify our participation in the Workers' Council, saying that we were just "children" and not "kosher" proletarians. We sent Avraham Getzel and Avraham Wrontzberg to Warsaw to convey our decision and convince the center to approve our position. After heated discussions, the center decided to allow the decision to be made locally. After receiving this approval, we participated in the stormy election and succeeded in placing two members on the Workers' Council – Avraham Getzel and myself. In the first May Day public demonstration there was great participation of factory workers and farmers of the area. Avraham gave a speech on the importance of the holiday and blessed the meeting in the name of all the Jewish workers of Zychlin. His speech made a deep impression and he was elected as secretary of the Workers' Council.

Deeply shocked by the terrible news of the pogroms in Pinsk and Lviv, Avraham embraced the cause of emigration to Palestine. He came in 1919 with the third *aliyah*, and his first job was working on the highway between Haifa and Jeda (today Ramat Yishai). When the road was complete, he settled in Haifa and learned masonry.

He entered public service in Eretz Israel with great enthusiasm. He was active in labor politics, in the Histadrut, and in the Haganah. In 1921 he was sent to defend Hulda during the Arab riots. In 1925, on his way back home after receiving medical care in Vienna, he paid a short visit to Zychlin. His mood was uplifting. He taught Israeli songs and dances to the youth.

I came to Palestine in 1926, arriving in Haifa in the midst of the great financial crisis. Despite his difficult economic circumstances, my friend Avraham hosted me for several days. He was in his usual great mood – one of the Trask Troupe.[5]

---

[5] The Trask Troupe (Hevra Trask) was a group founded in Tel Aviv in 1917. Its purpose was to bring joy to Tel Aviv at a time when there were not enough places of entertainment in the city. The group, which was active until the late 1920s, was famous for its big parties, its Purim costume parades, and the pranks of its members (such as locking Meir Dizengoff, the mayor of Tel Aviv, in his office).

Avraham Getzel eventually established a family and had two children - a son and a daughter. But life did not pamper him. He fell ill with a serious disease and became handicapped on both legs. He took a senior job at the construction company Solel Boneh in Haifa and, for a hobby, he installed in his home a large aquarium. Through this hobby, he was in contact with people from around the world, which gave him comfort.

The death of his son during the War of Independence devastated him. He walked around like a lunatic. He ruined his aquarium and could not find comfort. In addition, the passing of a dear and loyal friend influenced him a lot. Melancholy took over him. He died while visiting his brother during a trip to the United States.

Michael Lajzerowicz

by Yosef Rozengarten

Translated by David Goren

[Original book: pages 106-107 Hebrew section, 283-284 Yiddish section]

Michael Lajzerowicz

Michael Lajzerowicz was a baker, a hard worker from his youth. He was an active member of our Polish Zionist youth movement Tzeirei Zion. In his spare time he was an avid reader and was very respected by the Zionist youth of Zychlin. He was called the "dreamer poet" because he gave more to society than it was willing to receive from him. He liked to discuss literary topics and was always keen on convincing others about his opinions.

Michael came to Eretz Israel in 1922. His first stop was Jerusalem, where he worked in various jobs. In 1924 he moved to Tel Aviv and was active in the bakers' union. Then he moved to Haifa, where he was an independent worker. His entire livelihood came from his manual labor and he worked tirelessly. He was a fighter in the Haganah, sustaining injuries on two occasions during his service. He had a secret place in his Kriyat Eliyahu home where he kept a stash of Haganah weapons. The British raided his home and bakery several times, arresting him on two occasions. To his great fortune, the weapons were never discovered.

He educated his children in that spirit. His two sons were singers and entertainers who went on a tour to perform in the United States. To please their parents they invited them to accompany them. During the trip Michael developed cancer. After a couple of months he passed away at age 65, leaving a wife, two sons, a daughter and three grandchildren.

[Published in the newspaper Davar, May 16, 1966].

Eliyahu Goldfarb

by Yeshayahu Meiri

Translated by David Goren

[Original book: pages 124-125 Hebrew section, 297 Yiddish section]

Eliyahu Goldfarb

Eliyahu Goldfarb was born in Zychlin during the First World War. He grew up absorbing the influences of traditional and modern Jewish Poland, learning to live as a quiet, modest Jew who was proud of his origins. Maintaining these characteristics throughout his entire life, he was able to overcome difficulties, fight during the Shoah, arrive in Israel in 1949, and start a new life participating in the construction of the country.

Eliyahu had a difficult beginning in Israel. He struggled a lot until he began working for the Israeli Electric Company in 1952. He reached a good level there but he was not at peace. He worked shifts, morning, evening and night, Shabbat and holidays, always motivated by his desire to advance and carry the burden of responsibility. He had a wide circle of friends and acquaintances who valued his qualities and knew that he had a warm Jewish heart. He was always willing to help the less fortunate as much as he could, if not beyond that.

Always aware of everything that was happening in Israel, he liked to engage in discussions and arguments, always in a gentle, calm, modest and responsible way. His friends of the Electric Company's workers union do not recall Eliyahu making claims or demands. They remember him as someone who made professional and social requests politely and with integrity. This inspired others to treat him in the same manner. There was a desire to listen to his way of defining problems and finding solutions.

Eliyahu liked to act according to the notion that "the words of the sages should be heard in peace". What he did came from his heart, and he always found ways to be heard.

He raised a family in Israel, with two daughters of whom he was very proud. He saw them build their own homes and contribute to Israel's progress. When he died, he was still working and he had great hopes for the future.

May his memory be blessed.

Moshe Kelmer - From Zychlin to the Knesset

by Yosef Rozengarten

Translated by David Goren

[Original book: pages 110-111 Hebrew section, 284-285 Yiddish section]

Moshe Kelmer

Deviating from the "straight path", a group of Zychlin yeshiva boys began to associate with Reb Menachem Meir Rozenbaum - a committed Zionist and one of the most honest men in the town. Reb Menachem Meir was a member of the Zionist religious party Mizrahi. When he set out to organize a youth branch of the party, Moshe Kelmer was the first of his adherents. Moshe was the fifth of seven siblings – six sisters and one brother. As they grew up, they all joined Zionist labor parties and were devoted activists.

The youngsters gathered frequently at Reb Menachem Meir's home, where he would quiz them on their *yeshiva* and *beit hamidrash* studies and their knowledge of the Talmud. After these exams, he would tell them stories to nurture love for the Zionist idea in their hearts. Reb Menachem Meir was blessed with many daughters. One of them was Tova, with whom Moshe Kelmer was in love and he would eventually marry.

In 1920, Reb Menachem Meir asked Rabbi Nisenbaum, a leader of the Mizrachi party in Poland, to allocate a visa certificate to his future son-in-law. After receiving the visa, Moshe came to Eretz Israel in 1921, immediately starting his public activity within the framework of the Hapoel Mizrachi party.

Between 1922 and 1924 he worked in Jerusalem as a construction worker while completing his studies in the teaching certification program of Mizrachi. He then moved to Haifa where he continued his activism with Hapoel Mizrachi while administering two buildings for the contractor Nirenshtein. After that, he entered the political scene of Tel Aviv, where he served as secretary of the city branch of the Hapoel Mizrachi party.

With the merging of the HaBoneh and Mashkantaot construction companies in 1935, he was appointed manager of Mashhav, the new combined company. He worked there until his death.

Moshe Kelmer was a central figure in the Zionist congresses, a board member of the Keren Kayemet, and a founder of the bank Adanim. He established Hapoel Mizrachi's work center and was a member of the party's national leadership, becoming a member of parliament during the first, second and fifth Knessets. He was dispatched on six occasions as emissary to the United States and Canada. He also participated in a special Knesset delegation to Ireland. In 1965, he was formally certified as a lawyer.

Regardless of their political views, the Zychliners living in Israel were proud of Moshe Kelmer's career to the pinnacle of public service. His illness and sudden death were a source of sadness for all Zychliners in Israel and around the world.

Yosef Rozengarten

by Yeshayahu Meiri

Translated by Janie Respitz
Edited by Leon Zamosc

[Original book: pages 125-126 Hebrew section, 300 Yiddish section]

Yosef Rozengarten

His heart was filled with love for his people, his homeland, and the workers' movement. Yosef Rozengarten of blessed memory absorbed all of that in his old home, his birthplace Zychlin. The historical context of his youthful years and his strong will formed a Jewish man who relentlessly fought for high ideals.

I met him when he worked in the Tel Aviv workers' council, first in the "Red House" and later in Beit Brenner. I saw his devotion and loyalty to his work as a community activist. His sincerity was renowned and all his friends learned to respect "Yosef's truth".

We learned a lot from him about how to promote a honest way of life in the community. How to value and respect the rights of others while at the same time not abandoning your commitment to the social issues dear to our party.

In a conversation with him, you knew that Yosef was listening attentively and that his advice was always honest and friendly.

Until the last day of his life he was active in providing for the needs of the people. On the day of his death he attended a meeting which took place in Tel Aviv's city hall. Upon returning home he died at the threshold of his house.

We all honour his memory.

Michael Schwartzberg

by A. Z.

Translated by Janie Respitz
Edited by Leon Zamosc

[Original book: pages 306-307 Yiddish section]

Michael Schwartzberg

The news of the untimely death of Michael Schwartzberg hit the Yiddish-speaking community of Melbourne like a thunderbolt. He was a dedicated Jew from old Polish stock. In Melbourne, he was active in the Kadimah Cultural Centre, the Zionist council, the Labour Zionists and other Jewish institutions. He firmly believed that in the far reaches of Australia he could keep alive the golden chain of the millennium of Jewish life that had been destroyed in Poland. He held this belief until the moment of his sudden death on June 6, 1971.

Michael Schwartzberg was born in Zychlin in 1907. His father, an old timer who belonged to the Hovevei Zion, instilled in the young Michael a deep feeling of love and responsibility for the Jewish people, which would take him to all sorts of Zionist undertakings. In his youth, Michael was a member of Tzeirei Zion, representing his party in various Zychlin delegations to conferences and negotiations.

When the Second World War broke out, Michael Schwartzberg and many others fled to the area of Poland that had been occupied by Russia, knowing that they would have a better chance to survive than under the Germans. Unlike other refugees, however, Michael took the enormous risk of returning to Poland in order to rescue his wife and smuggle her, along with many friends, back across the Russian border. While in Russia he devoted himself to social work in faraway regions of the country.

When he returned to Poland after the war, Schwartzberg went to Zychlin and found out that the Jewish community had been completely destroyed. He temporarily settled in a different town of the western region of Poland, where he helped establish the first Jewish school and youth organization.

After immigrating into Australia Michael Schwartzberg remained true to his lifetime goal to live out his final years in Israel, a goal that had been frustrated twice at the last minute. The first time was when he was in a Zionist training camp in Grochow and his immigration certificate to Palestine was given to someone else. Then, after the war, he had been set on finding a way to go to Eretz Israel, but the plan was called off when his wife's cousin, who was a close friend, asked them to come to Melbourne with him, so they could be together.

One week before he passed away, Michael sold his house and began to pack his bags for the third time in preparation to go the Jewish state. He already had a departure date for November 1971. However, once again he was unable to realize his dream. Death took him from us quickly and unjustly.

Hundreds of people came to his funeral in Melbourne. Friends from Kadimah, the Zionist Council and his party Poalei Zion delivered eulogies by his grave.

Honor his memory!

[Published in the newspaper Australian Jewish News, June 1971].

Nicknames from our town

by Yosef Propen

Translated by Janie Respitz
Edited by Leon Zamosc

[Original book: pages 307-308 Yiddish section]

Various characters from Zychlin stand before my eyes, some of whom were treated with derision by the younger generation.

In the town everyone had a family name that appeared in official records and passports, but many had nicknames that were used in everyday life, when people rarely called each other by their official names. The nicknames described the character of the person according to occupation, individual peculiarities, family traditions, or other special circumstances. The following are some examples.

The Old Goat
David the Old Goat's son
Reb Chaim the Teacher with a Goose Feather
The Gombin teacher
Tuviya the female teacher (he was a man)
Chaimke Dumpling
Yankl the Nobleman's Teacher
Zelig Tzivye's
The Budzavaner
The Aforementioned
The Little Rabbi Skygazer
Simpleton
Auntie Yoyne
Khaim Khume's
Yakov Khume's
Zechariah Khume's
Itche Aron Tuviya's
The Red Head Watchmaker
Yehoshua Feyvl of the Community Committee
Shloyme Khaya House
Avrom Yitzkhak the Watchmaker
Henekh the Watchmaker
Berish the Goldsmith

Yoyne the Hat Maker
Yukele the Shoemaker
Mates the Hat Maker
Yehoshua the Cork
Mendl Blachazh
The Red Head Blachazh
Chil Tziviye's
The Little German
Nute the Butcher
Nute's Zalmen
Nute's Eliezer
The Red Head Sholem
Mordkhai the Butcher
Shmuel the Non-kosher Butcher
Leibish the Butcher
Gilye the Butcher
Raytze the Borscht Lady
Raytze's Chave
Shprintze Neche
Moishe Aron the Cake Baker
Chanuke the Baker
The Dirt Road
The Goat
Fraitche the Dirt Road
Golda Yerl the Herring Lady

The Deaf Brukyazh
Reb Mendl Meir the Ritual Slaughterer
Reb Feyvish the Ritual Slaughterer
Avrom Moishe the Boot Stitcher
Efraim the Tailor
The Glazer
The Mechanic
The Miller
Yosele with a Growth
The Sugar Maker
The Frantic One
Itche the Brat
Moishe Cham
Khaim Yuvin
Ayzik Meir with the Cold Feet
Kasriel the Hat Maker
Columbus Kola the Impulsive
Sholem Bomb
Aron the Groper
Mendl Zumbul
The Red Head Manufacturer
Simcha the Silent
Esther Khaya the Silent
Yakov Tumek
Moshe Aron Yakov Tumek's
Berl with the Goiter
Hershl Brayne Gitl's
Moishe Bogder
Avreymele the Priest
Yisroele with Ringworm
Leibele Niemolovaniye
Itele Yisruel's
Khaml the Water Carrier
Matis the Hunchback
Shimen the Hunchback
The Great Sabbath with a Short Friday
Aronke the Cigarette Seller
Mordkhai Vaynacher
Dovid Blacksmith
The Rabbi's Assistant
The Stork
Anshl the Rag Dealer
Aronke the Governor
Avreyml the Governor

Golda Feyge
The Crazy Mckhliekhe
Royze's Dobrish
Royze's Rashi
Chane Shtrontze
Mashke's Esther
Chanele the Rabbi's Wife
Mrs. Balbuna
Itzik the Baker
Yukele the Baker
Yakov Wolf the Baker
Moishe the Stallion
The Four Sisters
Zalmen's Chayele
Tzemach's Ronye
Yakov's Moishe
Shloymke the Baker
Noiech his Son
Avreymele the Ladies' Tailor
Leibishl the Tailor
Zelig Moishe the Tailor
Skurke the Patchlayer
Hershl the Tailor
Bobsel the Shoemaker
Bovele the Shoemaker
Dovid Chudiel
Wolf the Shoemaker
Yitzhak Aron the Shoemaker with a
Bastard
Wolf's Berish Yaakov
Wolf's Moishe Yaakov
Aroniche Fisher from Zychlin
Hershele from Ostropol
Itzik's Leah
Lipesh the Beadle
Itche the Beadle's Son in Law
Zalmene the Beadle
Cantor Pomerantz (Orange)
Avereymele the Shulklapper
The Gombin Medic
Chaim Leyb the Enema Maker
Gershon the Medic
Shaul the Pigeon Catcher

and many others...

The Destruction

In the Zychlin ghetto

Translated by Leon Zamosc

[Original book: pages 129-132 Hebrew section, 311-315 Yiddish section]

This chapter is based on the testimonies of Eli and Anna
Goldfarb, Zandberg, Sasha Kowent and Zechariah Rozenkopf.

In September 1939, the Germans occupied Zychlin almost without a fight.
Only a small group of Polish soldiers offered some resistance. The next day,
senior managers from the Dobrzelin sugar factory appeared in the town dressed
in SS uniforms. They were Volksdeutsche (ethnic Germans). Taking advantage
of the fact that he was married to the daughter of Walter (a Pole of German
descent who owned a pub on Pasieka street), the head of the Polish Socialist
Party in the town, Markowka, suddenly became a Volksdeutsche. It should be
noted, though, that the Volksdeutsche of Zychlin did not participate in the
persecution of the Jewish population. In many cases, they helped the families of
the Jewish tailors and shoemakers who had worked for them. The Volksdeutsche
who harassed the Jews were not local. The Germans brought them to Zychlin
from other places.

During the first days of the occupation, the Jews hid in their homes, afraid
to take to the streets. The Polish soldiers and some civilians who had been
wounded were taken to the church, where they received treatment from Polish
and Jewish young women.

A few days later, the Germans pounded drums in the streets and issued a
proclamation ordering all the Jews to gather in the market square. While they
were there, the soldiers searched their homes, ostensibly looking for weapons,
but in fact taking everything they wanted. Many Jews were seized for compulsory
work, such as sweeping the streets and cleaning the living quarters and offices
of the Germans.

In November, the Jews were ordered to wear a yellow ribbon on their sleeves
and paint the word "Jude" on the doors of their homes. Shortly afterwards, the
yellow ribbon was replaced by a yellow Star of David that the Jews had to wear
on their chests. A curfew was also set from 6 pm to 6 am. Jews were not allowed
to be seen on the street during those hours.

The Germans established a Jewish council - the Judenrat. The chairman was Alter Rozenberg, who had been chairman of the community committee. The other members were Yosef Chelmski, Yitzhak Kelmer, Yehoshua Zyger, Yitzhak Zeifert, Noyech Kelmer, Mordechai Zyger and Dr. Winogron. A Jewish police force was also established, headed by Yosef Oberman. The policemen received a salary and many of them wore police hats. They served as policemen in the ghetto and provided food to the residents. Initially, the ghetto was established on Narutowicz street, from Shalom Zyger's house to Buszkower street. The Jews whose homes faced Narutowicz street were ordered to block their windows and doors with planks, so that it would not be possible for them to look out onto the street. This was the large ghetto, in which about 1,800 people were concentrated.

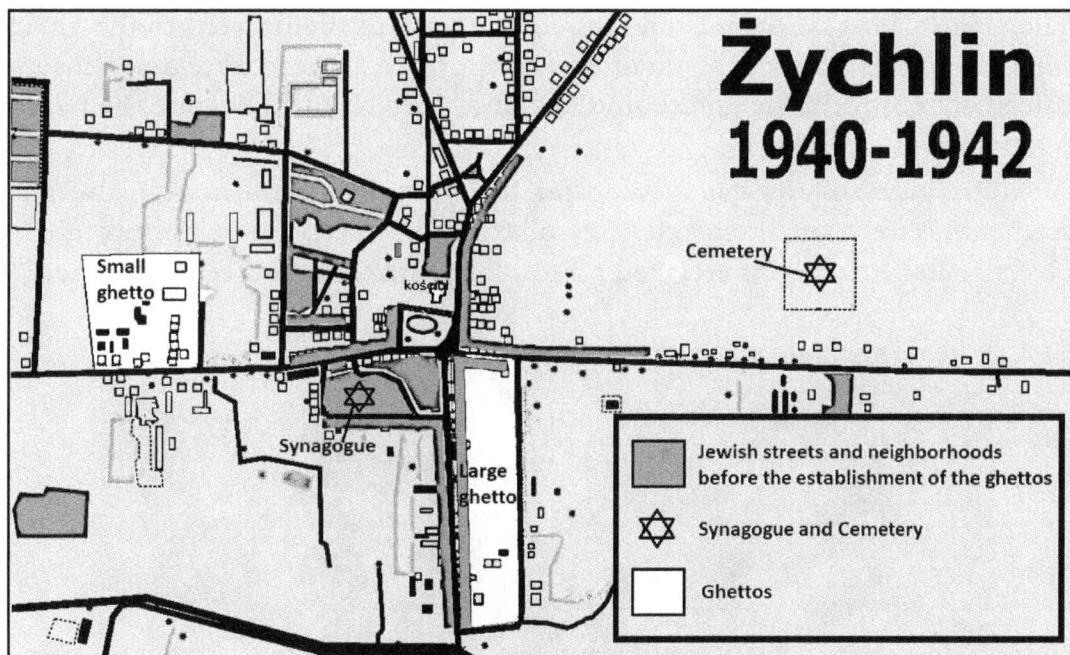

Zychlin map showing the two ghettos.
[Not in the original book. Image source: Żychlin Historia]

A second ghetto was established near Pabianów. There were 300 people in that ghetto, where the housing situation was horrendous. Three families, up to 20 people, had to share a two-room apartment. Everyone had brought with them their miserable possessions, which caused continuous strife. The members of the Judenrat and the policemen had to come and calm things down every day. The Judenrat's office was located in Shalom Zyger's house.

The German commander in Zychlin was less brutal than the commanders in some neighboring towns, which prompted Jewish families from Sanniki, Kutno and Wloclawek to secretly move into Zychlin ghetto as refugees.

To prevent the savage hunting of Jews for compulsory work, a labor office was established, headed by Yehoshua Zyger. He sent people to work in orderly shifts. Those who could not work would pay others to replace them. The economic situation of the craftsmen was still tolerable. The farmers in the area still came to place orders for clothes, shoes, etc. They paid in kind with food and other agricultural products. The barter trade was conducted in the yard of Shalom Zyger's house. The Germans did not obstruct it, but they posted a German guard in front of the house to make sure that the Jews did not go out onto Narutowicz street.

There were Jews who sneaked out of the ghetto at night, went to the villages, brought foodstuffs and sold them at exorbitant prices. There were also those who produced schnapps in the ghetto and sold it to the Gentiles, despite the fact that it endangered their lives.

A public kitchen was established for the former merchants and the ghetto residents who were unemployed. They distributed free soup in the two ghettos. The baker Alter Rozenberg received a license to supply bread to the ghettos.

Zychlin ghetto. [Not in the original book. Image source: Żychlin Historia]

The terrible overcrowding and the severe sanitary conditions caused various diseases as well as a typhus epidemic. A Red Cross dispensary was established, headed by Eli Goldfarb and Monique Morgentaler. Dr. Winogron, along with a group of girls, provided medical help to the needy.

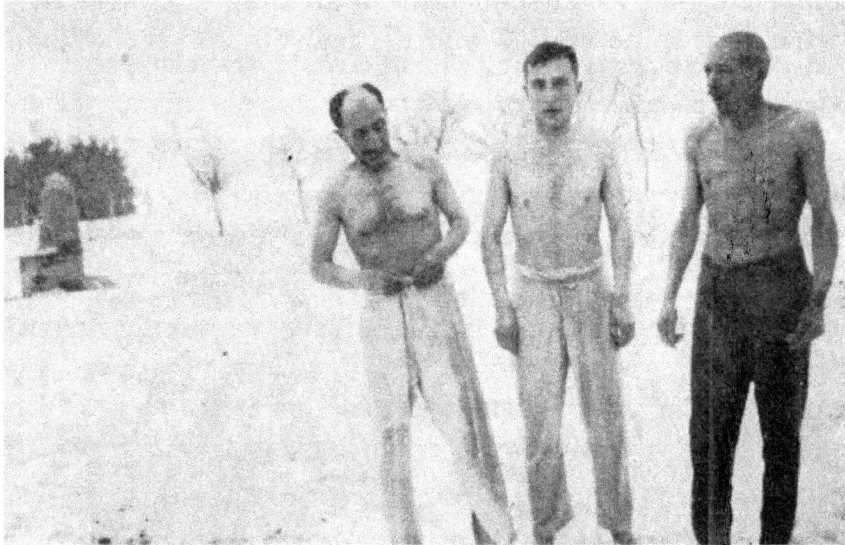

Forced Jewish workers in Zychlin, naked in the show.

In August 1941, young people began to be sent to forced labor camps in remote places. The first group, 400 men, was sent to the camps in the Poznan area. None of them returned. A group of 60 people, mostly women, was sent to a village for agricultural work. They worked for a landlord that protected them and provided good food. By the end of 1941, four groups had been sent to work.

Two Zychliners were hanged in the Potulice concentration camp in Naklo. They were caught while sneaking out to fetch some potatoes from the field near the camp. In Zychlin, some youngsters escaped from the ghetto and wandered around seeking refuge. Only a few of them managed to reach Russia.

Until the end of 1941, it was possible to bury the deceased in the town's Jewish cemetery. The Germans did not interfere with the funerals. The cemetery guard was not forced into the ghetto. He was allowed to live in his house next to the cemetery.

Yitzhak Kelmer took care of public and cultural life within the ghetto, as well as Zionist work. From time to time gatherings were held, in some cases to collect funds for social assistance.

In 1942, after the German invasion of Russia, the Nazis began to hasten the execution of their plan to exterminate the Jews. The Nazi commander from Kutno, who excelled in his cruel treatment of Jews, came to Zychlin. Old and sick people were murdered on the spot. The Judenrat's chairman Alter Rosenberg and the police chief Yosef Oberman were also murdered. Yehoshua Zyger, who dared to resist, was immediately shot. It has been said that when the Germans demanded him to surrender the remaining money in the Judenrat's cashbox, he took out some marks from his pockets and threw them into their faces.

Yaakov Meir Rozendorf, his wife Rachel Blime, Mordechai Koren, and Neche Lifshitz (Bajzer) about to be sent on their final journey to Chelmno death camp.

In March 1942, when the Zychlin Jews were deported to the Chelmno death camp, only a few managed to escape.

This marked the end of a vibrant Jewish community that had been distinguished by its cultural, political and Zionist activism. The cemetery and its gravestones were also completely razed. There is nothing left of Jewish Zychlin.

"Magnified and sanctified is the great name..." (first words of Kaddish prayer).

The liquidation of Zychlin ghetto

by Helena Bodek (Tzinamon)

Translated by Leon Zamosc

[Original book: pages 133-137 Hebrew section, 315-321 Yiddish section]

It was a great shock when people were first hunted to be sent to faraway forced labor camps. It took time, but things calmed down to some extent. Everyone wanted to take comfort in the thought that it would not happen again. In their innocence they did not know that it had been nothing but a sign of what was to come, which would be far worse in its scope and cruelty. There were moments in which one hunting was immediately followed by another. We were persecuted like wild animals and there was no refuge from the murderers. The Germans were assisted by the Jewish police, who knew every nook and cranny in the Zychlin ghetto.

While the first hunt may have been randomly done, the hunts that followed were made by precise selection. Everybody knew that it was Yosef Oberman, the chief of the Jewish police, that prepared the lists of people to fill the quotas set by the Germans. He was the lord of life and death. Awe-inspiring horror. I tried to avoid him, so that his eyes would not focus on me and he would not put me on his blacklist. His influence was so great that he was able to remove from the Judenrat the members that he did not like. Because of him, one of the most honest members of the committee was detained and deported. Bribery and protectionism flourished. The first victims were those who did not have the means to save themselves.

As the deportations to the camps intensified, the population in the ghetto dwindled. There was no family that did not experience the loss of one of its sons. Young girls were also sent in the shipments, among them my friend Melah Rubin. Her brother was a policeman, but his intervention was to no avail. I prepared myself for the worst. But maybe because of my unfortunate father, who had done so much for the town, or simply because it was a matter of fate, some human spark remaining in their hearts prevented them from sending away the only daughter of a mother in despair after losing her husband.

Deportation of Zychlin ghetto Jews to forced labor camps.

The wave of deportation of Jews to the camps subsided. The relative calm lasted a long time. There were rumors of the defeat of the German army on the Eastern Front. Will our situation improve? Unfortunately, we would soon realize that it would be the opposite. In the meantime, I continued to give lessons to the children in the ghetto, where life was now supposedly "normal." The number of students was considerably small. One day, Chelmski's niece little Mira did not come to class. When I asked her why she had been absent, she told me a fantastic story about the killing of Jews by gassing. I did not take that "nonsense" seriously, but Mira insisted that the story was true. On Saturday I went to the Chelmski apartment to visit her mother. I found there a very depressed man, a refugee from Krosniewice.

Scared all over, he recounted his horrific experiences. Together with all the Jews of his town he had been taken to the forests at Chelmno. They had been told that they were being going to labor camps. In Chelmno, however, groups of men, women and children were loaded to hermetically sealed trucks. When the engines were turned on, the toxic gases were fed into the trucks. When the corpses arrived at the destination they were burned. He, along with other men, was forced to work unloading the victims. Only miraculously he was able to escape from that place of death.

Shocked, I returned home. That night I could not close my eyes. Zychlin was very close to Krosniewice. It was clear that we were facing the same fate.

At lightning speed, the terrible news spread throughout the ghetto. It was also confirmed by other refugees. Horror, panic and despair gripped the ghetto residents. What to do? There was talk of escaping to Warsaw. People believed that such a large center of Jews could not be destroyed by gas. It was just not technically possible. However, a lot of money was needed to get to Warsaw and there was also the danger of being caught by Germans on the way. Despite the dangers, the wealthier people prepared to escape secretly. For us, that possibility did not exist, first of all because of lack of means. One hundred marks – that was our capital. We had sold everything that could be sold. Komwa, a Volksdeutsche woman who lived near the ghetto, had bought carpets, curtains and other things from us.

The only place we could escape to was the town of Strzegowo. My brother-in-law lived there with his family. We sent them a postcard saying that there was a fire in our house and asking if they could accommodate us in some corner of their house. For fear of censorship we signed with a false name, Nadarski. From their answer, which we got without delay, we realized that they had no clue of what was happening to us. They told us that they would send us a food package.

In the meantime, life went on "normally", but everybody was frantically looking for a way to escape. That evil was coming to us was no longer in doubt. The question was: when? Behind the apparent calmness, there was intense tension in the ghetto.

I tried not to think about what awaited us. I worked, ate, talked to people and also laughed sometimes, but in my mind the question was constantly poking: how could we escape? Since, as they said, I had "good looks", maybe I would be able to escape. But what about my mother? If we had to die, we would die together. Saying goodbye was out of the question. We were in a hopeless situation. And it was precisely then that the Andrzej's telegram arrived, delivered by Dr. Winogron. Just a few words: "My dear, if this telegram reaches you, I ask you for an immediate answer". I was confused. After so many years, that sign of life from Andrzej came at the most critical hour for us. It was the finger of God. I was sure he would do anything to save us, and I was not mistaken. After receiving my reply, he immediately came to us to make arrangements for our escape. Due to the lack of direct contact between Wloclawek and Zychlin he walked from Kutno on foot, despite the frost and the snowstorms.

Meanwhile, life in the ghetto had become unbearably difficult. The German police appeared every day. They conducted sudden searches, beating people to death or shooting them with the most trivial excuses. One woman was murdered just because she got too close to the barbed wire that surrounded the ghetto.

Because of the fear, people did not venture outside. Life was slowly dying. The anxiety reached its peak with the arrest of Oberman and Alter Rozenberg, the head of the Judenrat. Those who had connections with the Germans panicked. The Jewish policemen were fleeing. The giant policeman Toroncyk was caught at the border with his son, a 3 or 4 year old boy. They were brought back to the ghetto and murdered near the buildings of the Jewish community in front of the Poles. One of the Poles who was there before the execution was shocked at the sight of the unfortunate father hugging the child in his arms.

Huda came to us annoyed and frightened. He asked us to hide him in the basement offering five kilos of onions as a trade. The German police were after him. In his innocence, he did not imagine that the day would come in which the Germans would erase the traces of their contacts with Jews. Therefore, Huda, whose contacts took place in his home, had to die. His beautiful young daughter had to die too. For that same reason Oberman and Alter Rosenberg had been hanged at the prison. Unaware of her husband's tragic death, Oberman's wife showed up at Rotpel's place early in the morning asking for help. Rotpel could not do anything. He had been fired from his job and denied the right to leave the ghetto.

Panic struck us all. The ground was burning under our feet. People walked around terrified, the fear of death literally in their eyes. Everything pointed to the imminent liquidation of the ghetto. Disconnection from the outside world was a warning signal to us. We had to flee, immediately. Then or never. It was Saturday. The meal was being cooked on the stove. In winter the days were short. It would soon be night. We could not waste a single moment – the following day would be too late. Any moment the Germans would surround the ghetto. We got dressed. Garment on top of garment, no patch on our coats. We said goodbye to the Rotpel family and left.

From a nearby hut we heard the screams of the policemen. There was a search going on. On our windowsill was our cat, howling bitterly. At that moment I envied her. She stayed at home while we had to run away like hunted animals. From the ghetto we crossed the courtyard of a German house on Buszkower street, where we once had lived. We went right, in the direction of the road leading to Gombin. There was a strong blizzard. The passers-by hastened their steps. Nobody noticed us. I stopped a passing cart. The carter said that he was going to Gombin and agreed to take us there for a small fee. There was a lot of snow and the horse was barely able to pull the cart. But we were able to reach Gombin.

In the Gombin ghetto there was silence. I stayed at the home of Holtzman, a member of the Judenrat. My mother was received at another family's home. The news we brought shocked the Jews of Gombin. We were the first refugees from Zychlin. We were followed by more refugees. The appearance of Zychliners on the streets of Gombin was a danger. A young woman from Zychlin was caught by the local police and shot dead. On the third day of our escape, a group of young men arrived. Somehow they had managed to escape deportation. In exchange for valuable gifts, a Polish policeman in Zychlin called Pick had allowed them to hide in his house. When the Gestapo surrounded the ghetto, he feared that the Germans would find out. So he ordered the young Jews to go away.

Deportation of the Zychlin Jews: taken on horsecarts
to the train station.

In Zychlin, the Germans gathered all the Jewish policemen, lined them up, and killed them one by one. Yehoshua Zyger gave his life shouting "Long live the people of Israel". Oberman's wife was taken out of her house and promised that she would meet her husband. After taking a few steps, she was shot in the back and fell to the ground. The fate of Oberman's elderly parents was the same. Of the entire family, only a small child remained. When a neighbor tried to help him, she was shot by the Germans. The child stood in the frost and cried. People were afraid to approach him. Alter Rozenberg's brother was also shot. The German police took groups of Jews to the cemetery and murdered them. The blood of the Jews flowed in the street gutters outside the ghetto. Dr. Winogron's wife was killed for trying to hide a diamond in violation of the Germans' order to surrender all the jewelry.

There were desperate acts of madness. Rozia Gelman, a young woman in her ninth month of pregnancy, tried to escape jumping into the river in front of the Gestapo. The German bullets got her. Chelmski's mother, an old woman, was hiding in a coffin for fear of the Germans. She died of suffocation.

In the morning, the Germans brought the carts they had confiscated from the farmers of the surrounding area. The Jews were loaded standing up. They had to cling to each other to avoid falling. The children cried and the women howled as the caravan moved towards the train station. There, they were locked in train wagons intended for animals and taken on their final journey...

Zychlin had become a Judenfrei town (free of Jews). The ghetto no longer existed.

All this happened on the holiday of Purim. It was precisely on the children's holiday, a day of rejoicing, that the Jews of Zychlin were led to their deaths.

Grave for the martyrs of Zichlin, containing ashes
brought from Chelmno.

The last days of the Jewish community

by Moshe Kelmer

Translated by Leon Zamosc

[Original book: pages 138-141 Hebrew section, 322-326 Yiddish section]

In 1938, before the outbreak of the war, Zychlin was a town of 8,000 inhabitants, of whom about 3,500 were Jewish. The Jews lived around the market square and on three main streets: Budzyner (later renamed Narutowicz), Pasieka, and Buszkower. Most of them were tailors, shoemakers, carpenters, butchers, watchmakers, and artisans of all kinds. The rest of the Jews made a living from petty trade. Many made the rounds of the surrounding villages, purchasing cattle that they then sold to butchers in the town. There were also poultry and egg traders. Sometimes these businesses were conducted on a bartering basis: the Jew would take textiles and other goods to the villages and come back with the farmers' eggs, poultry and sometimes even veal. There were also some small general stores, grocery stores, taverns and restaurants, liquor stores, a pharmacy, a bank, and the Jewish community offices. There was a Jewish elementary school of 4-5 grades. After graduating, few Jewish students were unable to continue their studies, since that required attending the Christian school, where they did not accept more than 5-10 Jews at a time.

The Jewish youth of Zychlin had a lively social life. Various organizations and political movements had branches in town, including Poalei Zion Right, Poalei Zion Left, Hashomer Hatzair, Hechalutz, General Zionists and more. There were also local branches of sports associations, such as Hapoel, Gwiazda-Shtern and Maccabi. The youngsters had access to a cultural library and opportunities to attend Hebrew classes. In the evenings, they would walk from the end of Pasieka street to the end of Narutowicz street, chatting and discussing world news and other topics. Their arguments often continued until midnight, but nobody tried to prevent them from doing what they wanted. There were occasional fights between Jewish and Christian youngsters, but there was no fear in the hearts of the young Jews.

This continued until the mid-1930s. In 1935 and 1936, however, things changed. The peace and quiet gave way to anxiety, and social life was significantly affected. Night walks in the outskirts of town became dangerous and

193

economic life was shaken. The Poles were influenced by the example of German anti-Semitism and began boycotting the Jewish businesses. The outbreak of the war and the German occupation of Zychlin in 1939 put an end to the activities of the organizations and parties. The town's Jews were left to fend for themselves.

I was drafted into the Polish army, captured by the Germans, and later released. I returned home to Zychlin to find our beautiful town in fear and danger. After 5 pm the Jews were not allowed to be on the streets. Those who were caught outside were shot on the spot. Of course, social visits ceased altogether, and public life was completely quashed. In their homes, the Jews lived in fear. Whenever they heard footsteps, they panicked thinking that it was the gendarmes. And when the gendarmes did enter a Jewish house, it could end in brutal beatings and sometimes even death.

During the day, the Jews were rounded up for hard labor, always under the vigilance of Germans, Poles or gendarmes. They were harshly punished for the slightest motives. Eventually, an office was established to organize the supply of workers. It was located in Yaakov Kelmer's restaurant and was run by Yehoshua Zyger, who had to meet the Germans' demands for labor on a daily basis. Of course, he could not send the elderly and the sick to hard labor. To comply with the Germans' orders, he sometimes had to go out himself to catch friends and send them to work. This caused a lot of resentment. Moreover, some Jews who would get someone else to replace them in the fulfillment of the obligation to work, of course for a fee. This too was a source of bitterness.

In the summer of 1940, all the Jews were ordered, without exception, to leave their apartments, businesses and jobs and move to the ghetto, which bordered on one side on Buszkower street and on the other on Narutowicz street. In the ghetto, two or three families were crammed in one apartment. All the windows facing Narutowicz street were sealed with planks. Life became much harder. There was only one doctor in the ghetto, there were no pillows, it was forbidden to go to the pharmacy, and the diseases multiplied by the day. There was very little food. As far as supplies were concerned, we depended completely on the Judenrat, which was headed by Alter Rozenberg and Yosef Oberman. They received the food from the Germans. Of course, the quantities were not enough for everyone's needs. There were also injustices in the distribution.

The Germans organized a Jewish police force, which had to maintain order within the ghetto. Every day they demanded 100-200 Jews for work outside the ghetto. The work was gruelling and it was always accompanied by beatings. Yehoshua Zyger continued to manage the supply of workers. But then the things changed. Now, the Germans wanted to send people to faraway forced labor camps. Nobody wanted to leave their families behind without knowing where they were going. Every shipment of workers caused a terrible panic and harrowing scenes. The transports were usually made at night, and the tragedy was repeated again and again. Almost all the young people were sent to the camps.

Israel Zolna, Yoel Lifshitz and Gombinski (ghetto policemen)
with a picture of David Gersht.

In that new situation, the Germans began to kill the Jews, starting with those with whom they had been in closest contact, such as the suppliers of food and those who were responsible for distributing it. Alter Rozenberg was the first to be murdered with his entire family, followed by Yosef Oberman and his wife, Yidel Gelman and others. Then the Germans appointed a commandant of the ghetto, Yaakov the son of Reuven Gombinski. He was forced to collect from the Jews five marks per person, which was like a fine for the killing expenses. Threatening to shoot anyone who refused, the Jewish police collected everybody's furs and jewelry in one place and delivered the whole hoard to the Germans.

Yaakov Gombinski held office for a very short time, because the order came to deport all the Jews from the ghetto. We understood the meaning of this development. Two men had reached Zychlin from a neighboring town. They told us what had happened to the Jews who had been deported. Some of us believed what we heard, but there were others who did not want to believe. Families and friends gathered in one place to be together at that critical time.

On the way to annihilation. On the cart, from right, Leah Tatarka,
Rachel Gleider, Sara Ketman, Yidel (her daughter), Ita Royza Cohen,
Chaya Leah Zyger.

On a cold night of Purim 1942, the gendarmes raided every house in the ghetto. They concentrated all the Jews in an open square, loaded them on horse-drawn carts, and drove them in the direction of Krosniewice. Our family and the Morgentaler, Borowiak and Bawa families, were together in one of them. There were gendarmes guarding the carts. I knew very well where I was going and what the end would be. I made a decision in my heart and, without saying a word to anyone, jumped out of the cart while the gendarme was not watching. Salk Zlotek and Michael Orenbach did the same and we ran into the woods. They shot at us, but luckily, we were not hit. All night we wandered in the woods until we reached Gombin. We were there two days and in the end they took us to a forced labor camp. Of the three of us, I was the only survivor.

Appeal to the American Joint Committee

Jews of Dabrowice in Zychlin

Translated by Leon Zamosc

[Original book: pages 143-143 Hebrew section, 329-332 Yiddish section]

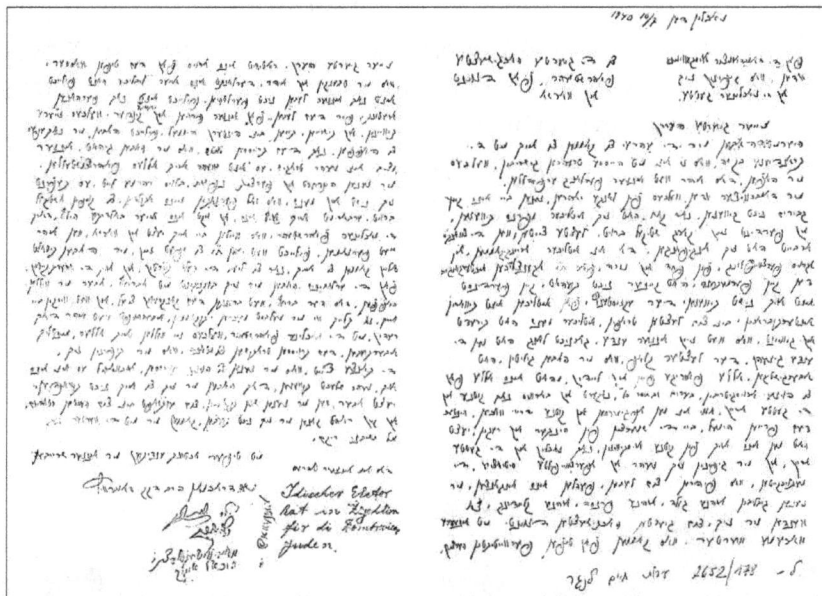

Letter from the Dabrowice Jewish refugees in the Zychlin ghetto.

July 10, 1940

To: Representatives of the American Joint in Warsaw

From: Jews deported from Dabrowice, currently in Zychlin ghetto

Respected Gentlemen!

We are approaching you with an urgent request written in tears, and we hope you will respond to our petition.

We, the Jews of Dabrowice, have not had a wealthy person among us for many years. Each one of us has barely made a living, just earning for our daily bread. In recent days, following the introduction of forced labor, we are suffering terrible despair and fear of extinction. None of us has property and our existence is completely broken. We cry and wonder what will be our end. Our anguish and torture surpasses all our previous sufferings. We were expelled from our homes, naked and destitute, and taken to the Kutno ghetto, where we lived under the open sky for three weeks and suffered from hunger and the rain falling on us.

We have now been deported from Kutno to the Zychlin ghetto and we are in a state of despair. We have no way of getting bread. We were left without money, without a livelihood and without appropriate clothing.

We turn to the esteemed officers of the Joint with words from a sore heart: Dear Sirs, save us from the deep water in which we are drowning. Reach out to us for help! Maybe we are not completely lost yet. We hope our weeping reaches to heaven. Maybe there is hope to save us. Our situation is very tragic and it is difficult for us to describe everything.

We are one hundred and forty people, all very poor. There is no one among us with money in his pocket to buy a slice of bread.

Have mercy on us and send us immediate help through the Zychlin delegates who are now with you in Warsaw. Do not delay, lest it be too late, God forbid.

The Jewish families from Dabrowice, expelled to Kutno ghetto and later to the ghetto in Zychlin.
[Not in the original book. Image source: Kutno and surroundings Yizkor book]

We intended to go with the delegates to visit you but, due to the costs and the difficulties in obtaining a travel permit, we can only send you this letter, and we hope that you will respond as if we were there in person. The Zychlin representatives will inform you about our tragic situation. When we were in our own homes we did not request your help despite the fact that we were already facing difficulties. But now, when we have reached a state of despair and hopelessness, we appeal to you with these words: Please, do not ignore our petition.

With deep appreciation, we end our request.

Committee members: Rabbi Moshe Drachman of Dabrowice, Meir Vigodski, Michael Isaac (last name unreadable)

From the ghetto and the camps to freedom in Israel

by Tzipora Maroz

Translated by Leon Zamosc

[Original book: pages 141-142 Hebrew section, 326-328 Yiddish section]

My grandmother Esther had the good fortune of passing away right before the outbreak of the Second World War, which spared her the sufferings that Hitler inflicted upon the Jews. My grandfather, Reb Yehoshua Rozengarten, was left alone in his old age, along with my sick aunt Ytele. At the time, my parents and the four of us were living in Kutno, and when the Nazis occupied the town we were interned in the Kutno ghetto. We decided to do everything we could to be with our old grandfather and aunt. We managed to bribe the Germans with money and jewelry, and they allowed us to move to Zychlin, where we joined my aunt and grandfather in the town's ghetto.

In the Zychlin ghetto. From right: P. Wolkowicz, L. Pytel,
L. Glewinski and Chaim Leib Wasertreger

The Zychlin ghetto was located on Budzyner street, where grandpa lived. The apartment had two rooms and we all lived together, eight people in total. Later the *shamash* Yitche also came to live in our apartment with seven more relatives. So we were 15 people in two rooms, without any sanitary facilities.

By order of the Germans, a Judenrat and a Jewish police force were established. They were responsible for maintaining order in the ghetto. In the fields bordering Buszkower street, the Jews traded with the Gentiles of the surrounding area. Those who had money and jewelry could buy groceries. The Judenrat cared for the poor, providing them a hot meal once a day.

To comply with the Germans' demands, the Judenrat prepared lists of the Jewish population, especially of the young people, to supply workers for the forced labor camps. The Jewish police hunted them down, snatching them from bed in the middle of the night. I was sixteen when I was cut off from my loved ones and sent to work in the camps with dozens of other girls of my age.

I later learned that my grandfather died in the ghetto. He was privileged too, because in those days it was really a blessing to pass away of natural causes. In 1943, when I was already in Auschwitz, we received a letter from a Christian neighbor informing us that all the Jews of Zychlin had been deported to the death camp in Chelmno, where they had been exterminated.

As the Russians approached Poland, I was taken out of Auschwitz in the infamous death march to Ravensbrück camp and from there to the concentration camp in Neustrelitz. We were freed on May 5, 1945. After liberation, I wandered across countries and cities until I reached Kutno, where I hoped to find someone from my family. But none of them remained. They all perished in the hands of the murderers. In Kutno, I met with a classmate who was destined to be my husband, and we decided that the only way open to us was going to Palestine.

In Poland, we met with other members of Hashomer Hatzair. We organized into a group and contacted the leaders of the movement. We arrived in Germany with fake identification papers. There we joined a Aliyah Bet group named after Tosia Altman. We were taken to Italy and from there we sailed to Eretz Israel. We arrived at the port of Haifa on April 1, 1946, but the British Mandatory authorities did not allow us to disembark and deported us to Cyprus. We spent more than a year in a camp, where our first son was born. The Jewish Agency had requested the British government to at least release the families with small children and allow them to enter Palestine. Thus, thanks to our baby, we arrived there even before the independence declaration of the State of Israel.

We first lived in an immigrants' camp in Raanana, then in Kibbutz Hazorea, and in 1947 we were among the first settlers of Kibbutz Gazit. Our path was full of suffering and anguish, but we were finally able to begin a new life of freedom in Israel.

Act of heroism

by Yaakov B.

Translated by Janie Respitz
Edited by Leon Zamosc

[Original book: pages 144 Hebrew section, 334-335 Yiddish section]

In one of the Nazi forced labor camps, a Jewish boy that worked in the camp's kitchen was caught burying a few potatoes. The Nazis decided to carry out a public execution of the unlucky child in order to instill fear in all the Jewish prisoners.

In the evening they ordered a roll call. All the camp's inmates had to line up on one side, across from the SS murderers. They brought the child who had dared stealing the potatoes to calm his bitter hunger.

Without saying a word, one of the officers, smiling like the devil, approached the boy, pulled out his pistol and emptied the entire bullet cartridge into his small body. The child fell to the ground covered in blood. The murderer looked around with sadistic enjoyment and holstered his gun.

There were Jews from Zychlin in the camp, among them Moshe Kelmer, the son of Hirsch Mordechai Kelmer. When he saw the child's shooting, Moshe's eyes darkened. He felt a deep, immense hatred toward the murderers. He jumped out of line, grabbed an iron bar that was lying on the ground and threw it at the SS officer hitting him on the head.

The Germans immediately opened fire on this heroic young man, killing him on the spot. He fell near the boy whose spilled blood he had acted to avenge. With his martyr's death, that young Jewish man from Zychlin sanctified the heroism of those who resisted Hitler's murderers.

In Auschwitz and Buchenwald

by Leibish Tadelis

Translated by Janie Respitz
Edited by Leon Zamosc

[Original book: pages 333-334 Yiddish section]

I, the son of Binyamin and Esther Tadelis, born and raised in Zychlin, lived in the Zychlin ghetto under Hitler's occupation during the years of the Second World War. When the Germans rounded up 110 Jews and sent them to the forced labor camps, I was one of them.

After a few months in the camp, the children of Yoruchem Levin came and crying bitterly told us that their father had died. Since Yoruchem was a Cohen (from the priestly class), we thought that it was a bad sign, a sign of an epidemic in the camp. And that was what actually happened. Right after him 10 more Jews died. The eleventh was another Levy, Mordechai the Watchmaker's son, Levkovitz.

I met other people form Zychlin in the camp. Among them was Aron Sanitzki. He told us that the Germans had executed Boruch Rubin, Yitzhak Sochaczewski, and Berl Sarna. They were hanged because they had asked for a piece of bread.

In 1942 I was sent to Auschwitz. There I met Faleh Zlatkin who helped me a lot. I also found my brother Yaakov but I was only able to stay with him for three days.

After three years in Auschwitz I was sent to Buchenwald, where I spent two weeks before they took us, 2,000 Jews, on a death march to Dachau. Anyone who was unable to walk briskly was shot on the spot. On the road I met Hanoch Bielawski, Yakel Diner's son in law. From then on we were together. We had practically nothing to eat or drink for three months. We were exhausted. One night, as we dragged ourselves like corpses, Hanoch told me he was going to escape. When he jumped into the bushes I did the same.

This was on April 23, 1945. The Americans liberated the region a few days later.

After liberation I was in Germany. We communicated with Sam Berman of the relief committee of the Zychliners' society in America and received addresses of our families in America. I also found my brother in Feldafing. We remained together until we immigrated to America.

203

Memories of the war

by Moshe Zyslender

Translated by Janie Respitz
Edited by Leon Zamosc

[Original book: pages 335-336 Yiddish section]

September 1, 1939. The war broke out. Hitler's Germany attacked Poland.

Men were mobilized, Jews and Christians. They were accompanied to the gathering points by their parents, wives and children, with tears in their eyes.

After the bombing of cities and towns a regular stream of refugees began. Many of them wandered through Zychlin.

My mother Fraydl of blessed memory took the initiative to organize a kitchen in our store and cooked soup and tea for the refugees. She only took a bit of money to cover expenses. She arranged for two families from Turek to sleep in our shop at no cost.

On September 12, the Germans entered Zychlin. Bread was rationed and the Poles were pushing the Jews out of the bread lines.

The Germans began to press-gang Jews for various jobs. I was in Lodz and heard that many Jews were escaping to the Soviet-occupied part of Poland to save themselves from the Nazis. My mother agreed that I should run away. Israel Lenchinski and his cousin Moshe Lenchinski escaped with me.

After great effort and exertion we arrived in Bialystok on our way towards the Urals. I worked hard to receive a bit of soup in the factory's kitchen. We had to stand in line for hours to buy a loaf of bread. To calm my hunger I had to sell my last possessions. The climate was also difficult. I was not used to the freezing cold and contracted typhus. It was a miracle that I recovered without any treatment. But the illness made me very weak and I was assigned to easier work with a locksmith.

From there I went to Lviv where I met people from Zychlin. Since I did not have a Soviet passport I was arrested and sent to Yaroslavl to work in the forest at starvation wages. Every day a few would die from hunger. The Russian guards teased us, saying that we would all meet the same end.

I returned to Lodz when the war ended in 1945. I visited Zychlin but there were no Jews in the town. I walked through all the streets and could not find anyone.

My family's roots in Zychlin went back for generations. But nobody remained, even the cemetery's graves had disappeared. There were no Jews living or dead.

The Poles walked through the streets. Some were murderers who had helped the Germans annihilate our people.

My great grandfather, Israel Eisenstadt, had a brewery in Pasieka. In 1860, during the uprising of the peasants, the local nobility escaped to Paris and my grandfather took over the management of the estates, providing arms and supplies to the rebels. My grandmother, who was then a young girl, smuggled the weapons and food to the peasant fighters in the forests.

Today, there is no trace of anyone, not even tombstones in the Jewish cemetery...

The bitter end

by Michael Schwartzberg

Translated by Leon Zamosc

[Original book: pages 144-145 Hebrew section, 337-340 Yiddish section]

The war came to Zychlin on Friday, September 1, 1939, at 6 am with ululating sirens, the terrifying sound of aircraft, and shell explosions. There were fires and cries of fear. There was blood. Throughout the day the city was bombed and there were many casualties. Zychlin, which was an important transit station for the Polish army, suffered more bombing than other cities and towns.

The outbreak of war had caused an immediate shortage of food. Together with other activists, Yitzhak Kelmer set up a committee to help the refugees who came to Zychlin from other towns. The committee operated while the fighting between the Polish and German armies continued. At that time, we removed from the library the whole archive, hiding some documents and burning the rest, to avoid endangering our main public activists.

On September 17, the Germans occupied the town. As soon as they entered, they expelled the Jews from their homes around the market square. We stood there for a few hours, surrounded by guards who fired over our heads to scare us and finally made us run back to our homes. In the following days, Jews began to be rounded up on the streets or taken out of their homes for various jobs. The Jews were told that they were no longer allowed to trade in foodstuffs. The Jewish grocery stores, butchers and bakeries were closed. The bakers were put in prison to extort ransom. The decree was then revoked and the bakers were released.

Very soon the Germans issued new decrees. Jews were not allowed to be on the streets after 5 pm. Anyone who violated the order would be shot. In any case, the Jews were already refraining from leaving their homes for fear of being caught for work. They were also afraid of other abuses, since the Germans enjoyed tearing the men's beards together with the facial skin, or taking off their shoes and sending them home barefoot through the mud and snow. On top of being left without a livelihood, the Jews had to do compulsory work for the Germans. An employment office was set up to provide Jewish workers to the Germans.

In November, the Jews were ordered to wear yellow badges on the left side of their outer garments, both on the front and the back. They were not allowed to use the sidewalks. Instead, they had to walk in the street "with the horses" (as written in the ordinance). The Jews had to take off their hats when they saw a German in the street – otherwise they would be severely punished. The Polish neighbors were indifferent to the persecution of the Jews. In many cases they actually assisted the criminal acts of the Germans. Part of the Jewish youth fled east, to the territories that had been occupied by the Russians. They thought that redemption would come from there ...

Forced labor in Zychlin.

In June 1940, two ghettos were established in Zychlin. Hundreds of mothers with their children walked the streets in the direction of the ghetto, dragging their belongings with them. But that was immediately stopped when the Germans forbade the Jews to remove their property from the homes they were leaving. Inside the ghetto, three or four families had to share a small room. This caused a great deal of distress, quarrels and fights among the families.

I went to Warsaw and contacted the Kibbutz Borochov training farm, which had been moved to Lodz at the beginning of the war. I assisted in the transfer of the pioneers that had been preparing for *aliyah*, from Warsaw to Bialystok. From there they tried to get to Palestine in one way or another. But only a few were able to reach their goal. Many died on the roads, and some took part in the Bialystok ghetto uprising.

I drank the cup of poison to the fullest. Many times I saw death before my eyes. I stayed alive because I was lucky, not because I was smarter. When I returned to Zychlin after the war I did not find anyone. It all went up in the smoke of the cremation pits at the Chelmno death camp. That was the end of a Jewish community that had existed for generations.

Remembrance ceremony at the martyrs' grave in the Zichlin Jewish cemetery, which contains ashes brought from Chelmno.

Zychlin survivors at a memorial meeting after liberation.

Yizkor – Memorial

List of Martyrs

A memorial to the martyrs of Zychlin who perished in Kiddush Hashem, murdered by the German Nazis and their helpers during the years of the Shoah (1939-1945).

The list was compiled by the book editors with the names provided by landseit from our town, but we are aware that there are many omissions. These are their names.

FAMILY NAME, Given name (MAIDEN N.	Sex	Status	Father	Mother	Spouse
Alef					
ORBACH, Feiwel	M				
OLSZTYN, Joel	M	Married			Necha
OLSZTYN, Necha	F	Married			Joel
OLSZTYN	F		Joel	Necha	
ELSNER					
ALTER, Rabbi Avraham Mordechai	M				
OPOLEN, Feiwel	M	Married			Gitla
OPOLEN, Gitla	F	Married			Feiwel
OPOLEN, Mozes Aharon	M				
OPOLEN, Sara Rywka	F				
OPOLEN, Ruchla	F				
ADLER, Yitzchak Lejbisz	M				
ADLER, Yechiel	M				
JATKIEWICZ, Brajna	F				
Bet					
BICZ, Yechiel	M				
BUTLER					
BORNSZTAJN, Laja Rajzla	F				
BORNSZTAJN, Chaja Tzipora	F				
BONDER, Mozes	M	Married			Sara
BONDER, Sara	F	Married			Mozes
BIDERMAN, Mozes	M	Married			Pessa
BIDERMAN, Pessa	F	Married			Mozes
BIDERMAN, Szmuel	M				
BIDERMAN, Dwora	F				
BIDERMAN, Yehoshua	M				

FAMILY NAME, Given name (MAIDEN N.	Sex	Status	Father	Mother	Spouse
BERMAN KAC, Yehuda Arje	M	Married			Frajda Bracha
BERMAN KAC, Frajda Bracha	F	Married			Yehuda Arje
BERMAN BORNSZTAJN, Laja Rajzla	F				
BERMAN BORNSZTAJN, Chawa	F				
BERMAN BORNSZTAJN, Tzipora	F				
BOL, Neomi	F				
BOL, Rywka	F				
BOL, Mozes Josef	M	Married			
BOL	F	Married			Mozes Josef
BOL, Jakow	M				
Gimel					
GORKI, Mozes	M				
GLAJDER, Mordechai	M	Married			Chana
GLAJDER, Chana	F	Married			Mordechai
GOLDFARB, Eliezer	M	Married			Rywka
GOLDFARB, Rywka	F	Married			Eliezer
GOLDFARB, Mozes	M				
GOLDFARB, Zev	M				
GOLDFARB, Avraham	M				
GOLDFARB, Yechiel	M				
GOLDFARB, Yechiel	M				
GOLDFARB, Itka, (ORBACH)	F				
GELBART, Chajm	M				
GELBART, Jossel	M				
GETZEL, Pinchas	M	Married			Chawa
GETZEL, Chawa	F	Married			Pinchas
GOSTYNSKI, Aharon	M	Married			
GOSTYNSKI	F	Married			Aharon
GOSTYNSKI, Betzalel	M	Married			
GOSTYNSKI	F	Married			Betzalel
GOSTYNSKI, Moshe Yosef	M				
GELBART, Szamai	M				
GALINSKI					
GOTHELF, Yitzchak	M				
GOTHELF, Fajga	F				
GOSTYINSKI, Elijahu	M	Married			Gitl
GOSTYINSKI, Gitl	F	Married			Elijahu
GOSTYINSKI, Pinchas	M				

FAMILY NAME, Given name (MAIDEN N.	Sex	Status	Father	Mother	Spouse
GOSTYINSKI, Brajna	F				
GOSTYINSKI, Henja	F				
GOSTYINSKI, Josef	M				
GOTHELF, Elijahu	M				
GOTHELF, Eliezer	M				
GOTHELF, Szmayahu	M				
GOTHELF, Lemel	M				
GOTHELF, Rajzel	F				
GIERSZ, Szyfra	F				
GOTHELF, Hershl	M				
Dalet					
DAVIDOVICZ, Lejbisz	M	Married			Sara
DAVIDOVICZ, Sara	F	Married			Lejbisz
DAVIDOVICZ, Pinchas	M				
DAVIDOVICZ, Heshel	M				
DAVIDOVICZ, Szajna	F				
DAVIDOVICZ, Roza	F				
DAVIDOVICZ, Hynda	F				
DAVIDOVICZ, Sara	F				
DAVIDOVICZ, Chana	F				
DAVIDOVICZ, Josef	M				
DANCZYKER, Yechiel	M	Married			Hela
DANCZYKER, Hela	F	Married			Yechiel
DUMBINSKI, Chajm	M				
Hey					
HELMER, Yehoshua	M	Married			Esther
HELMER, Esther	F	Married			Yehoshua
HELMER, Chaja Ruchla	F				
HELMER, Arje	M	Married			Drizel
HELMER, Drizel	F	Married			Arje
HELMER	M		Arje	Drizel	
HELMER, Mordechai	M				
HELMER, Chana	F				
HELMER, Micha'el	M	Married			Bracha
HELMER, Bracha	F	Married			Micha'el
HAMBURG, Jakow	M	Married			Bajla
HAMBURG, Bajla	F	Married			Jakow
HODU, Hentshe	F				

FAMILY NAME, Given name (MAIDEN N.	Sex	Status	Father	Mother	Spouse
HELMER, Chaja (TORONCHIK)	F				
HODU, Mozes	M				
Vav					
WOJDYSLAWSKI, Gerszon	M	Married			Sara
WOJDYSLAWSKI, Sara	F	Married			Gerszon
WOJDYSLAWSKI, Jakow Dawid	M	Married			Gitl
WOJDYSLAWSKI, Gitl	F	Married			Jakow Dawid
WOJDYSLAWSKI, Avraham	M	Married			Avraham
WOJDYSLAWSKI, Henja	F	Married			Henja
WOJDYSLAWSKI	F		Avraham	Henja	
WOJDYSLAWSKI WAJNSZTOK, Josef	M	Married			Marjem
WOJDYSLAWSKI WAJNSZTOK, Marjem	F	Married			Josef
WOJDYSLAWSKI WAJNSZTOK	M		Josef	Marjem	
WOJDYSLAWSKI, Mozes Majer	M				
WOJDYSLAWSKI, Avraham	M				
WOJDYSLAWSKI, Abba Josef	M				
WOJDYSLAWSKI, Ruchla Laja	F				
WOJDYSLAWSKI, Bajla Chaja	F				
WOJDYSLAWSKI, Gerzhon	M				
WOJDYSLAWSKI, Brajna	F				
WAJNSZTAJN, Josef	M	Married			Balche
WAJNSZTAJN, Balche	F	Married			Josef
WROBEL, Gerszon	M	Married			Laja
WROBEL, Laja	F	Married			Gerszon
WESELOWSKI, Yitzchak	M	Married			Brajna
WESELOWSKI, Brajna	F	Married			Yitzchak
WAJNKRANC					
Zayin					
ZYGIER, Yisrael Szulim	M	Married			Dwora Necha
ZYGIER, Dwora Necha	F	Married			Yisrael Szulim
ZYGIER, Jakow Yehoshua	M				
ZYGIER, Sara	F				
ZYGIER, Sara Laja (SHATAN)	F				
ZYGIER, Malka (SHWARCBERG)	F				
ZYGIER, Beryl	M				
ZYGIER, Henech	M				
ZYGIER, Yehoshua	M				
ZYGIER, Mordechai	M	Married			Rywka

213

FAMILY NAME, Given name (MAIDEN N.	Sex	Status	Father	Mother	Spouse
ZYGIER, Rywka	F	Married			Mordechai
ZYGIER, Jakow	M				
ZYGIER, Chaja	F				
ZYGIER, Yechiel	M				
ZYGIER, Szlomo	M	Married			Marjem
ZYGIER, Marjem	F	Married			Szlomo
ZYGER, Jochewed	F				
ZYGER, Lewi	M				
ZYGER, Gita	F				
ZYGER, Yechiel	M				
ZYGIER, Yechiel	M				
ZLOTNIK, Roza	F				
ZLOTNIK, Szimon	M				
ZLOTNIK, Szmuel	M				
ZLOTNIK, Chaja	F				
ZYGIELMAN, Josef	M				
DZIEROWSKI, Avravam	M	Married			Malka
DZIEROWSKI, Malka	F	Married			Avravam
ZAJDE, Bluma	F				
ZANDBERG, Chajm Wulf	M	Married			Luba
ZANDBERG, Luba	F	Married			Chajm Wulf
ZANDBERG, Pesach	M				
ZANDBERG, Rywka Rojza	F				
ZANDBERG, Wiktor	M				
ZANDBERG, Hynda	F				
ZANDBERG, Hersh	M				
ZANDBERG, Yitzchak	M				
ZANDBERG, Esther	F				
ZAJFERT, Itche	M	Married			Rachl
ZAJFERT, Rachl	F	Married			Itche
ZYGIELMAN, Yechezkel	M	Married			Tzila
ZYGIELMAN, Tzila	F	Married			Yechezkel
ZYGIELMAN, Tzwi	M				
ZYGIELMAN, Mozes	M				
ZYGIELMAN, Dawid	M				
ZYGIELMAN, Sara Bajla	F				
ZYGIELMAN, Hershel	M	Married			Jente
ZYGIELMAN, Jente	F	Married			Hershel

FAMILY NAME, Given name (MAIDEN N.	Sex	Status	Father	Mother	Spouse
ZYGIELMAN, Szimon	M				
ZYGIELMAN, Jakow	M				
ZYGIELMAN, Hynda	F				
ZYGIELMAN, Sara	F				
DZIEROWSKI, Avraham	M				
DZIEROWSKI, Yitzchak	M	Married			Jente
DZIEROWSKI, Jente	F	Married			Yitzchak
DZIEROWSKI	M		Yitzchak	Jente	
ZYK, Yisrael	M	Married			Bronche
ZYK, Bronche	F	Married			Yisrael
ZYK, Rywka	F				
ZYK, Aharon Dawid	M				
ZYK, Tzirale	F				
ZYK, Ruchla	F				
ZYK, Majta	F				
ZYCHLINSKI, Rabbi Menachem Yedidja	M	Married			Rajzala
ZYCHLINSKI, Rajzala	F	Married			Menachem Yedidja
ZYCHLINSKI, Rabbi Szmuel Avraham	M	Married			Rodkele
ZYCHLINSKI, Rodkele	F	Married			Szmuel Avraham
ZYCHLINSKI, Perela	F				
ZYCHLINSKI, Malka	F				
ZYCHLINSKI, Mordechai	M				
ZYCHLINSKI, Efrojm	M				
ZYCHLINSKI, Avigdor Baruch	M				
ZYCHLINSKI, Yitzchak Jakow	M	Married			Fruma
ZYCHLINSKI, Fruma	F	Married			Yitzchak Jakow
ZYCHLINSKI, Micha'el	M				
ZYCHLINSKI, Szulim	M				
ZYCHLINSKI, Frajdla	F				
ZYCHLINSKI, Szyfra	F				
ZAFRAN, Mozes	M	Married			Jochewed
ZAFRAN, Jochewed	F	Married			Mozes
ZAFRAN, Hela	F		Mozes	Jochewed	
ZAFRAN, Yisrael	M	Married			Chawa
ZAFRAN, Chawa	F	Married			Yisrael
ZAFRAN, Mundyk	M				
ZAFRAN, Ruchla	F				
ZAFRAN, Hilel	M				

FAMILY NAME, Given name (MAIDEN N.	Sex	Status	Father	Mother	Spouse
ZYCHLINSKI, Betzalel	M	Married			Ester Fajga
ZYCHLINSKI, Ester Fajga	F	Married			Betzalel
ZYCHLINSKI, Rywka	F				
ZYCHLINSKI, Lajzer	M				
ZYCHLINSKI, Szamai	M				
ROZENTAL, Jakow Yehuda	M	Married			Chaja
ZYCHLINSKI ROZENTAL, Chaja	F	Married			Jakow Yehuda
ZYCHLINSKI, Ruchla	F				
ZYCHLINSKI, Dwora	F				
ZYCHLINSKI, Tzila	F				
ZYCHLINSKI, Rachum	M				
ZYCHLINSKI, Plata					
ZYCHLINSKI, Rywka	F				
ZYCHLINSKI, Lejzer Naftali	M				
ZLOTAK, Majer Henech	M	Married			Sara
ZLOTAK, Sara	F	Married			Majer Henech
ZLOTAK, Fajga Ruchla	F				
ZLOTAK, Esther Gitla	F				
ZLOTAK, Pessa	F				
ZLOTOK, Szulim	M				
ZLOTOK, Szmuel Dawid	M				
ZLOTOK, Yakow Mozes	M				
ZYSLENDER, Josef	M	Married			
ZYSLENDER	F	Married			Josef
ZYSLENDER, Avraham	M				
ZANDBERG, Esther Frajdla	F				
ZYGIER, Jakow	M	Married			Laja
ZYGIER, Laja	F	Married			Jakow
ZYGIER, Mordechai	M				
ZYGIER, Naftali	M				
ZYSLENDER, Frajdla	F				
ZYSLENDER, Pessa	F				
Chet					
CHODA, Hersh Wulf	M	Married			Chana
CHODA, Chana	F	Married			Hersh Wulf
CHALEMSKI, Josef	M				
CHALEMSKI, Rywka	F				
HERSZ, Bajla	F				

FAMILY NAME, Given name (MAIDEN N.	Sex	Status	Father	Mother	Spouse
CHYBERT, Szulim	M				
CHODA, Feiwel	M				
CHODA, Chana	F				
CHODA, Alter	M				
Tet					
TATARKA, Szimszon	M	Married			Laja
TATARKA, Laja	F	Married			Szimszon
TATARKA, Jossel	M				
TATARKA, Esther	F				
TATARKA, Tova Roza	F				
TATARKA, Tzwi	M			Tova Roza	
TATARKA, Jossel	M			Tova Roza	
TATARKA, Chana	F				
TATARKA, Sara	F				
TATARKA, Bajla	F				
TATARKA, Szulim	M				
TORONCZYK, Ruchla	F				
TORONCZYK, Chaja (HELMER)	F				
TORONCZYK, Rywka (BLUMENFELD)	F				
TORONCZYK, Chajm	M				
TORONCZYK, Dawid	M				
TUSZYNSKI, Betzalel	M	Married			Laja
TUSZYNSKI, Laja	F	Married			Betzalel
TUSZYNSKI, Szlomo	M	Married			Rywka Laja
TUSZYNSKI, Rywka Laja	F	Married			Szlomo
Yod					
JATKOWSKI, Mozes	M	Married			
JATKOWSKI	F	Married			Mozes
JATKOWSKI, Yitzchak	M	Married			Tzirale
JATKOWSKI, Tzirale	F	Married			Yitzchak
JATKOWSKI, Chana	F				
JATKOWSKI, Hynda	F				
JATKOWSKI, Mozes	M				
JATKOWSKI, Laja	F				
JATKOWSKI, Chana	F				
JATKOWSKI, Mozes	M	Married			Hynda
JATKOWSKI, Hynda	F	Married			Mozes
JAKUBOWICZ, Yitzchak	M	Married			Masha

FAMILY NAME, Given name (MAIDEN N.	Sex	Status	Father	Mother	Spouse
JAKUBOWICZ, Masha	F	Married			Yitzchak
JAKUBOWICZ, Necha	F				
JAKUBOWICZ, Marjem	F				
JAKUBOWICZ, Fryda	F				
JAKUBOWICZ, Lejzer Lipa	M				
JAKUBOWICZ, Yehuda	M				
Kaf					
KAC, Avraham	M				
KOHEN, Yissakar	M				
KOHEN, Ezra	M				
KOHEN, Golda	F				
KOHEN, Sara	F				
KOHEN, Yitzchak Majer	M	Married			Chana Myndla
KOHEN, Chana Myndla	F	Married			Yitzchak Majer
KOHEN, Tojbe	F				
KOHEN, Eliezer	M				
KOHEN, Simcha Bunim	M				
KOHEN, Hynda	F				
KOHEN, Josef Chajm	M	Married			Marjem
KOHEN, Marjem	F	Married			Josef Chajm
KOHEN, Avraham	M				
KOHEN, Frajda	F				
KOHEN, Ruchla	F				
KOHEN, Eliezer	M				
KOHEN, Chaja Sara	F				
Lamed					
LENCZYCKI, Hersh Feiwel	M				
LEMBERG, Binem	M				
LEMBERG, Avraham Arje	M				
LEMBERG, Hersh Henech	M	Married			
LEMBERG	F	Married			Hersh Henech
LEMBERG, Yehuda	M	Married			
LEMBERG	F	Married			Yehuda
LEMBERG, Aharon	M	Married			
LEMBERG	F	Married			Aharon
LEMBERG, Avraham Majer	M	Married			
LEMBERG	F	Married			Avraham Majer
LEMBERG, Jiska	M				

FAMILY NAME, Given name (MAIDEN N.	Sex	Status	Father	Mother	Spouse
LEMBERG, Necha	F				
LEMBERG, Masha	F				
LEMBERG, Sara	F				
LEMBERG, Chana	F				
LEMBERG, Lyfshe	F				
LEMBERG, Hendla	F				
LENCZYCKI, Pinchas	M	Married			Laja
LENCZYCKI, Laja	F	Married			Pinchas
LEWKOWICZ, Jakow	M	Married			Sara
LEWKOWICZ, Sara	F	Married			Jakow
LEWKOWICZ, Chanoch	M				
LEWKOWICZ, Lyba	F				
LEWKOWICZ, Mozes	M				
LEJZEROWICZ, Efrojm	M	Married			Towa
LEJZEROWICZ, Towa	F	Married			Efrojm
LEJZEROWICZ, Yitzchak	M				
LEJZEROWICZ, Gedalja	M				
LEJZEROWICZ, Roza	F				
LEJZEROWICZ, Bela	F				
LASMAN, Szmuel	M	Married			
LASMAN	F	Married			Szmuel
LASMAN, Abba	M				
LEJZEROWICZ, Szimon	M	Married			
LEJZEROWICZ	F	Married			Szimon
LEJZEROWICZ, Yehuda	M				
LEJZEROWICZ, Jermiyahu	M				
LENCZYCKI, Chajm Dawid	M	Married			Sara
LENCZYCKI, Sara	F	Married			Chajm Dawid
LENCZYCKI, Hela	F				
LENCZYCKI, Jakow	M				
LENCZYCKI, Reuwen	M				
LENCZYCKI, Marjem	F				
LEWKOWICZ, Mordechai	M	Married			Rywka
LEWKOWICZ, Rywka	F	Married			Mordechai
LEWKOWICZ, Yitzchak Josef	M				
LEWKOWICZ, Esther Chana	F				
LEWKOWICZ, Laja	F				
LEWKOWICZ, Yehuda	M				

FAMILY NAME, Given name (MAIDEN N.	Sex	Status	Father	Mother	Spouse
LENCZYCKI, Jakow	M	Married			Golda
LENCZYCKI, Golda	F	Married			Jakow
LENCZYCKI, Feiwisz	M				
LENCZYCKI, Esther	F				
LENCZYCKI, Avraham Majer	M				
LENCZYCKI, Zyssa	F				
LENCZYCKI, Bajla	F				
LENCZYCKI, Pinchas	M				
LENCZYCKI, Laja	F				
LENCZYCKI, Mozes	M				
LENCZYCKI, Hersh Feiwisz	M	Married			Chaja
LENCZYCKI, Chaja	F	Married			Hersh Feiwisz
LIBFRAJND, Mendel	M	Married			Chaja Sara
LIBFRAJND, Chaja Sara	F	Married			Mendel
LIBFRAJND, Irena	F				
LIBFRAJND, Sara	F				
LANDSZNAJDER, Avraham	M	Married			Chawa
LANDSZNAJDER, Chawa	F	Married			Avraham
LANDSZNAJDER, Laja	F				
LANDSZNAJDER, Sara	F				
LANDSZNAJDER, Chana	F				
LANDSZNAJDER, Shoshana	F				
LANDSZNAJDER, Jakow	M				
LEMBERG, Wulf	M				
LIBFRAJND, Lejbisz	M	Married			
LIBFRAJND	F	Married			Lejbisz
LIBFRAJND, Simcha	M				
Mem					
MORGIENTALER, Avraham	M	Married			Tzipa
MORGIENTALER, Tzipa	F	Married			Avraham
MORGIENTALER, Josef	M	Married			Sara
MORGIENTALER, Sara	F	Married			Josef
MAJDET, Zelig	M				
MAKOWER, Szmaryahu	M				
MIEDZINSKI, Fyszel	M				
MIEDZINSKI, Elimelech	M				
MICHALEWICZ, Godl	M				
MICHALEWICZ, Yitzchak	M				

FAMILY NAME, Given name (MAIDEN N.	Sex	Status	Father	Mother	Spouse
MAKOWER, Ruchla	F				
Nun					
NISYNBOJM, Mendel	M	Married			Laja
NISYNBOJM, Laja	F	Married			Mendel
NAJFELD, Nachum	M	Married			Chawa
NAJFELD, Chawa	F	Married			Nachum
NAJFELD, Chana	F				
NAJFELD, Aharon Lejb	M				
NASILOWICZ, Mordechai	M	Married			Hynda
NASILOWICZ, Hynda	F	Married			Mordechai
NASILOWICZ, Majer	M				
NASILOWICZ, Lewi	M				
NASILOWICZ, Chana	F				
NAJMAN, Dawid	M				
Samech					
SADOWSKI					
SANNICKI?, Josef	M	Married			Pessa
SANNICKI?, Pessa	F	Married			Josef
SANNICKI?, Manja	F				
SLOMA, Majer	M				
SLOMA, Golda	F				
SLOMA, Szulim	M				
SLOMA, Mozes	M				
Peh					
PYTEL, Chaja	F				
PYTEL, Lejzer	M				
PYTEL, Hershel	M	Married			Laja
PYTEL, Laja	F	Married			Hershel
PYTEL, Mendel	M				
PANCER					
FAJERSZTAJN					
FAJERSZTAJN, Feiwel	M	Married			
FAJERSZTAJN	F	Married			Feiwel
FRAJMAN, Mordechai	M				
FRAJDES, Yitzchak Aharon	M	Married			
FRAJDES	F	Married			Yitzchak Aharon
FRAJDES, Menashe	M	Married			
FRAJDES	F	Married			Menashe

FAMILY NAME, Given name (MAIDEN N.	Sex	Status	Father	Mother	Spouse
FRAJDES, Jossel	M	Married			
FRAJDES	F	Married			Jossel
FIRST, Micha'el	M				
FENIGSZTAJN, Esther Bluma	F				
FENIGSZTAJN, Szajna	F				
FENIGSZTAJN, Jakow	M				
FUKS, Chana	F				
FUKS, Szlomo	M				
FUKS, Ruth	F				
FRANKIENSZTAJN, Chajm	M				
FRANKIENSZTAJN, Alter	M				
FRANKIENSZTAJN, Chawa	F				
PLONSKI, Benjamin	M	Married			Chawa Laja
PLONSKI, Chawa Laja	F	Married			Benjamin
CIEPLINSKI, Avraham	M				
CHANEMAN	M				
Tzadik					
TZENTNER?, Jossel	M				
TZENTNER?, Jakow	M	Married			Joshka
TZENTNER?, Joshka	F	Married			Jakow
TZENTNER?, Malka	F				
TZENTNER?, Tzirel	F				
TZENTNER?, Szajna	F				
TZENTNER?, Roza	F				
TZENTNER?, Gitla	F				
TZENTNER?, Hersh Mozes	M				
ZUK, Szulim	M				
Kof					
KOWENT, Elijahu	M				
KOWENT, Jakow	M				
KOWENT, Josef	M	Married			Bajla
KOWENT, Bajla	F	Married			Josef
KOWENT, Lybe	F				
KOWENT, Jakow	M				
KOWENT, Nachum	M				
KOWENT, Szmayahu	M	Married			Jochewed
KOWENT, Jochewed	F	Married			Szmayahu
KOWENT, Szmuel	M				

FAMILY NAME, Given name (MAIDEN N.	Sex	Status	Father	Mother	Spouse
KOWENT, Gerszon	M				
KOWENT, Zlata	F				
KOWENT, Yisrael	M	Married			Laja
KOWENT, Laja	F	Married			Yisrael
KOWENT, Avraham	M				
KOWENT, Szmuel	M				
KOWENT, Yitzchak Mozes	M	Married			Bajla
KOWENT, Bajla	F	Married			Yitzchak Mozes
KOWENT, Elijahu	M	Married			Gitl
KOWENT, Gitl	F	Married			Elijahu
KOWENT, Rajzla	F				
KOWENT, Bela	F				
KOWENT, Mozes	M				
KOWENT, Mordechai	M	Married			Dwora Lybe
KOWENT, Dwora Lybe	F	Married			Mordechai
KOWENT, Josef	M	Married			Gutshe
KOWENT, Gutshe	F	Married			Josef
KOWENT, Szmayahu	M	Married			Tzwija
KOWENT, Tzwija	F	Married			Szmayahu
KOWENT, Nisan	M				
KOWENT, Chanche	F				
KORN, Towa	F				
KORN, Esther	F				
KORN, Micha'el	M				
KORN, Hershel	M	Married			Frajda
KORN, Frajda	F	Married			Hershel
KORN, Golda	F				
KORN, Rywka	F				
KORN, Chaja Sara	F				
KORN, Lybe	F				
KORN, Jakow	M				
KORN, Mendel	M				
KANARIK, Mordechai	M				
KIELMER, Ayzyk	M				
KLECZEWSKI, Szmuel	M	Married			Sara
KLECZEWSKI, Sara	F	Married			Szmuel
KLECZEWSKI, Yitzchak	M	Married			
KLECZEWSKI	F	Married			Yitzchak

FAMILY NAME, Given name (MAIDEN N.	Sex	Status	Father	Mother	Spouse
KLECZEWSKI, Tuwja	M				
KLECZEWSKI, Rywka	F				
KLECZEWSKI, Syma	F				
KLECZEWSKI, Malka	F				
KRAJZER, Golda	F				
KRAJZER, Ruchla	F				
KIELMER, Jakow	M	Married			Roza
KIELMER, Roza	F	Married			Jakow
KIELMER, Hersh	M	Married			Chana Laja
KIELMER, Chana Laja	F	Married			Hersh
KIELMER, Jochewed	F				Yehoshua Feiwisz
KIRSZSZTAJN, Balche	F				
KIRSZSZTAJN, Fyszel	M				
KIRSZSZTAJN, Brajna	F				
KIRSZSZTAJN, Abba	M				
KIRSZSZTAJN, Feiwel	M				
KIRSZSZTAJN, Laja	F				
KIRSZSZTAJN, Ruchla	F				
KUTNOWSKI, Jona	M				
KARMEL, Nachum	M	Married			Jochewed
KARMEL, Jochewed (ZYGIER|	F	Married			Nachum
KANARIK, Esther Malka	F				
KANARIK, Zalman	M				
KANARIK, Noach	M				
KANARIK, Mendel	M				
KANARIK, Zelde	F				
KANARIK, Bajla	F				
KLINGIER, Rafael	M	Married			Ruchl
KLINGIER, Ruchl	F	Married			Rafael
KLINGIER, Avraham Jakow	M	Married			Chana
KLINGIER, Chana	F	Married			Avraham Jakow
KACZYSOWICZ	M	Married			Maryla
KACZYSOWICZ, Maryla	F	Married			
KIRSZSZTAJN, Jakow	M	Married			Elka
KIRSZSZTAJN, Elka	F	Married			Jakow
KIRSZSZTAJN, Chawa	F				
KIRSZSZTAJN, Henech	M	Married			Chawa
KIRSZSZTAJN, Chawa	F	Married			Henech

224

FAMILY NAME, Given name (MAIDEN N.	Sex	Status	Father	Mother	Spouse
KIRSZSZTAJN, Perela	F				
KIRSZSZTAJN, Yitzchak	M				
KIRSZSZTAJN, Avraham	M				
KIRSZSZTAJN, Yitzchak	M				
KIRSZSZTAJN, Zyssel	M				
KIRSZSZTAJN, Laja	F				
KIRSZSZTAJN, Dwora	F				
KIRSZSZTAJN, Towa	F				
KIRSZSZTAJN, Lybe	F				
KIRSZSZTAJN, Tzwrja	F				
KLINKOWSZTAJN, Bajla	F				
KLINKOWSZTAJN, Rywka	F				
Resh					
RAPKOW, Jakow	M	Married			Laja
RAPKOW, Laja	F	Married			Jakow
ROZENBERG, Szlomo	M	Married			Golda Marjem
ROZENBERG, Golda Marjem	F	Married			Szlomo
ROZENBERG, Mozes	M	Married			Chana
ROZENBERG, Chana	F	Married			Mozes
ROZENBERG, Marjem	F				
ROZENBERG, Majer	M				
RYSTER, Eli	M	Married			Menucha
RYSTER, Menucha	F	Married			Eli
ROZENBOJM, Shoshana	F				
RUBIN, Shoshana	F				
RUBIN, Nechama	F				
RUBIN, Syma	F				
RUBIN, Sara	F				
RUBIN, Marjem	F				
RUBIN, Towa	F				
RUBIN, Frymet	F				
RUBIN, Gitla	F				
RUBIN, Szlomo	M				
RUBIN, Baruch	M				
RUBIN, Lapidot?	M				
RUBIN, Yitzchak	M				
RUBIN, Mozes	M				
ROZENKRANC, Abba	M				

FAMILY NAME, Given name (MAIDEN N.	Sex	Status	Father	Mother	Spouse
ROZENKRANC, Mozes	M				
ROZENKRANC, Yitzchak	M				
ROZENBERG, Szmuel Dawid	M				
RUBIN, Yisrael	M	Married			Chana
RUBIN, Chana	F	Married			Yisrael
RUBIN, Mozes	M				
RUBIN, Bunim	M				
RUBIN, Mala	F				
RUBIN, Gedalja	M				
RUBIN, Yitzchak	M				
ROZENBLUM, Berish	M	Married			Rywka Lybe
ROZENBLUM, Rywka Lybe	F	Married			Berish
ROZENBERG, Jakow	M	Married			Esther
ROZENBERG, Esther	F	Married			Jakow
RUBIN, Aharon Dawid	M	Married			Rywka
RUBIN, Rywka	F	Married			Aharon Dawid
ROZENKRANC, Mozes	M				
Shin					
SZERETSKI, Yitzchak	M				
SZERETSKI, Feiwisz	M	Married			Rywka
SZERETSKI, Rywka	F	Married			Feiwisz
SZERETSKI, Zelig	M				
SZERETSKI, Dwora	F				
SZERETSKI, Chaja	F				
SZERETSKI, Hela	F				
SZERETSKI, Yakow	M				
SZWARCZBERG, Mozes	M	Married			Pessa
SZWARCZBERG, Pessa	F	Married			Mozes
SZWARCZBERG, Jakow	M				
SZATAN, Majer	M	Married			Jitta
SZATAN, Jitta	F	Married			Majer
SZATAN, Avraham	M	Married			Sara Laja
SZATAN, Sara Laja	F	Married			Avraham
SZATAN, Yechiel	M				
SZATAN, Yitzchak	M				
SZATAN, Jakow	M				
SZATAN, Roza	F				
SZATAN, Szmuel	M				

ZYCHLIN MEMORIAL BOOK

FAMILY NAME, Given name (MAIDEN N.	Sex	Status	Father	Mother	Spouse
SZLACHTUS					
SZWARCBERG, Wulf	M				
SZWARCBERG, Yitzchak	M	Married			Dwora
SZWARCBERG, Dwora	F	Married			Yitzchak
SZWARCBERG, Chawa	F				
SZWARCBERG, Rojza	F				
SZWARCBERG, Szajna	F				
SZWARCBERG, Jochewed	F				
SZWARCBERG, Yechezkel	M				
SZWARCBERG, Dawid	M				
SZWARCBERG, Jasza	M				
SZWARCBERG, Avraham	M	Married			
SZWARCBERG	F	Married			Avraham
SZWARC, Rywka	F				
SZTAJNBERG, Lewi	M				
SZTAJNBERG, Esther	F				
SZTAJNBERG, Jakow	M				
SZTAJNBERG, Beta ?	F				
SZTAJNBERG, Szmuel	M				
SZMULOWICZ					
SZTOLZAFT, Szlomo	M	Married			Szprintza
SZTOLZAFT, Szprintza	F	Married			Szlomo
SZTESIGIEL, Genja	F				

Additional Materials

Zychlin

Pinkas Hakehilot

Translated by Leon Zamosc

[Not included in the original book]

This is a translation of the entry corresponding to Zychlin in *Pinkas Hakehilot: Encyclopedia of Jewish Communities, Poland, Volume I, Lodz and its region,* pages 116-119, published by Yad Vashem, Jerusalem, 1976.

Zychlin (Kutno District)

Year	Total Population	Jews
1764/65	(?)	311
1808	801	457
1827	1,277	782
1857	1,611	1,062
1897	4,840	2,268
1921	7,098	2,701
Sept. 1, 1939	(?)	2,600-2,800

Jewish settlement until 1918

Zychlin was first mentioned in a document from 1332. It gained city status in 1450 as a private aristocratic city. Despite the fact that there were clear signs of urban development in terms of population, it lost its city status in 1867 as punishment of the Russian government for the residents' support to the Polish rebels in 1863. In 1924, Zychlin recovered its city status.

While no legal or administrative restrictions to Jewish residence in the town are known, there are no records about the presence of Jews in Zychlin until the 18th century. Those first records indicate that they worked in petty trade and the crafts, mainly as tailors and shoemakers who sold their products on market days. Some also traded in horses and cattle during the fairs. In the middle of the 19th century, the food industry in the town developed to a certain extent, with a considerable number of Jewish factory owners participating in it. In 1894, Jews owned most of the town's industrial plants, including a steam mill, a leather factory, a soap factory, and two oil factories. However, the most important sources of livelihood for the Jews continued to be the small commerce and the crafts: of the 184 shops in this period only 7 were not owned by Jews, and among the 16 bakers there were only 4 non-Jews.

At first, the community of Zychlin was subordinate to the communities of Kutno or Gostynin. In 1766 the Jewish community of Zychlin was already independent and, during its first decades of existence was run by notable "homeowners". By the end of the 19th century, the Gur Hasidim became the majority group, took over the reins of the community, and continued to rule it until the end of the First World War. Zychlin's original synagogue, a wooden building, was erected in 1780. One hundred years later it was replaced by a stone building. There was also a *beit hamidrash* and some *shtiebels* of Hasidim. In 1912, the opponents of the Gur Hasidim established a *shtiebel* of their own under the name Linat Zedek. Later on, this *shtiebel* served as a base for the local branch of the Mizrachi party in Zychlin.

By the second half of the 18th century the community had grown. One of the first rabbis in Zychlin was Shlomo ben Avraham, formerly a *maggid* in Dobra and Kalish. His essay *Benin Shlomo* was published in Shklov in 1789. In the 1840s, other Hasidic rebbes settled in the town, founding what would become the Zychliner dynasty. In 1824, after the death of Rabbi Efraim Fishel of Strykov, some of his followers had crowned Rabbi Shmuel Abba (who at the time was living in Buduanov) as Rabbi Fishel's successor. In 1844, Rabbi Shmuel Abba moved to Zychlin, engaged in practical Kabbalah, and became known as a miracle worker. The common people flocked to him. In his area of control and influence, especially the "enlightened" cities and towns of the Prussian occupation, Rabbi Shmuel Abba fought the harbingers of progress, the people of education and reform. After his death, the leader of the Hasidim was his son, Rabbi Moshe Netanel Zychlinsky (who died in 1912), and then his grandson Rabbi Menachem Yedidah, who died in the Zychlin ghetto in 1940. Rabbi Shmuel Avraham, the son of Rabbi Menachem Yedidah, continued as head of the Hasidim until Purim 1942, when the Germans killed him by firing squad on the day before the liquidation of the ghetto and the deportation of all the Zychlin Jews to their death.

The first Jewish political organizations were established In Zychlin at the beginning of the 20th century, including the Bund in 1903, the Zionist-Socialists in 1905, and Poalei Zion in those same years. With the news about disturbances against the Jews in 1905, the local "revolutionaries" (apparently, members of the organizations mentioned above) organized self-defense groups to face possible troubles. During the reactionary period after the revolution of 1905-1906, these groups disintegrated due to the persecution of the authorities. Political activism resumed when the German armies occupied the town during the First World War. That period saw the foundation of the organizations Bnei Zion, Tzeirei Zion and the Jewish Scouts. In 1914 there was an attempt to establish a non-partisan professional union, Tsukunft (Future), but the occupation authorities soon abolished the union. After the end of the war, the Poalei Zion party founded in 1918 the Arbeter Heim club, and next to it the Union of Needle Workers and the Leather Workers' Union. With the news of the harassment of Jews by units of General Haller's army in 1918, a local self-defense group was organized in Zychlin by the youngsters of the sports organization Turen Farein. In the years 1916-1918, there was a public school with 4 class levels for Jewish children, supported by the municipality.

Between the two world wars

During the interwar period, there was no change in the occupational structure of the Jewish community in Zychlin. Most Jewish residents were among the poor, making a living as small merchants and craftsmen. There were only a few affluent Jews leasing forest plots for logging and operating as tenants of dairy farms that belonged to landowners. No Jews were hired in the large non-Jewish industrial plants found in the area, which included two sugar factories, a beer factory, and a brick factory. Only two Jews worked in the flour mill, which was owned by Jews. A new industry, which employed less than twenty craftsmen, was the knitting of socks by order of contractors from other cities. In this situation, many Jewish families (especially youngsters) migrated to larger cities.

The Zionist organizations played a crucial role in the political life of Zychlin. Local branches of the General Zionists, Mizrachi, Hapoel-Mizrachi, Poalei Zion-Left, Poalei Zion-Right, and the youth movements Hashomer Hatzair and Hanoar Hatzioni were active in the town. In the 1930s, the Hechalutz branch was founded, which brought together the pioneering youth of all the organizations. In 1932, Poalei Zion established in Zychlin a training agricultural school for future life in the kibbutz. At the initiative of Poalei Zion-Left, a local trade union council that grouped Jews and non-Jews was founded in the town in 1924. Under the union's leadership, there was a successful bakers' strike on that year. The results of the elections to the Zionist Congresses indicate the influence of the various parties. In the elections to the 20th and 21st Congresses, there were about 270 *shekel* buyers who voted as follows: General Zionists 101 votes in 1937 and 79 in 1939, and the Workers' League for the Land of Israel 120 votes in 1937 and 142 in 1939 (in alliance with Poalei Zion-Left). The other Zionist parties won 10-20 votes each. The Bundists and Folkists were few in numbers. Agudat Israel was active in the community and in education. After World War I, the Zionists defeated the Gur Hasidim of Agudat Israel and took over the community's administration. In the 1931 community elections, the Zionist parties won 5 seats, Agudat Israel 2, and the artisans' list 1.

The influence of the Jewish parties in the municipality was demonstrated by the fact that, in line with the results of the 1927 election, a Jew was supposed to occupy the position of deputy major. In the end, the position was lost because the representatives of the Jewish parties did not reach agreement on the candidate (rather than voting for the Jewish candidate, a representative of Poalei Zion-Left voted for the candidate of the Polish Socialist Party). In 1927, under the influence of the Jewish councilmen, the municipality allocated a thousand zlotys to the Jewish Craftsmen and Traders Bank, which was founded on that year.

Prominent among the Jewish institutions in Zychlin during this period was the Gemilat Hesed fund, which in 1936/37 alone provided 450 loans to the needy. Linat Zedek and Bikur Cholim, which had existed in the town for years, continued to provide health relief. The Jewish Craftsmen's Association took care of obtaining craft licenses for its members and assisted them with low-interest loans. The Jewish Merchants' Association also had a lending fund.

The high status of the Zychliner Hasidic dynasty cast a shadow over the local rabbinic authorities. After the First World War, the rabbi of Zychlin was Yechiel Yitzchak Rappaport, activist of the Mizrachi party. His Agudat Israel opponents spared no effort to undermine him, denouncing him to the Polish authorities in 1920 as a "Bolshevik". As a result, rabbi Rappaport spent some time in prison. The last rabbi of Zychlin was Avraham Mordechai Alter, born in 1872. He was a Ger Hasid and was considered a great scholar. He did not transcribe his many innovations out of humility "so as not to flaunt the crown of the Torah." He perished during the Nazi occupation.

Despite the small size of the community, there were many Jewish educational institutions in Zychlin. The community ran a Talmud Torah for the poor. Immediately after the First World War, Agudat Israel established a *yeshiva* and a school for girls, Bnot Yaakov. The Zionists opened the Tarbut school, offering evening classes for Hebrew, the Bible and the history of Israel. Due to lack of resources, the Tarbut school was closed in 1928. The already mentioned 4-grade municipal school for Jewish children was transformed in 1922 into a 7-grade school that was attended by most children of the town. The principal and the teachers (except for one) were Jews, which was not typical of such public schools in other towns of Poland.

During the interwar period there were three Jewish public libraries in Zychlin. The two larger ones were run by Poalei Zion-Left and Poalei Zion-Right. In addition to the already mentioned sports organization Turen Farein, the football club Hapoel was also established in 1927 by Zionist youngsters and Poalei Zion.

In the years leading up to the Second World War, the Jews of Zychlin were subjected to harassment. In March 1939, a gang of the Polish right-wing party Endecja forced a local Jewish peddler to remove his stand. The despairing peddler responded with a shout, and for this he was tried and punished "for insulting the Polish people."

The Holocaust

Zychlin was occupied by the German army on September 17, 1939. The next day the Germans abducted a group of young Jews, took them to a remote village 20 kilometers away, locked them up for three days in a church, and then allowed them to return to Zychlin. A few days later, the Germans concentrated the Jews in the market square. Many of them were drafted for manual labor, such as sweeping the streets and cleaning the apartments and offices of the Germans. The press-ganging of Jews for forced labor became a daily routine in the town. After a while, the authorities imposed a ban on Jewish bakeries, arresting and imprisoning the Jewish bakers who continued to bake and sell. After vigorous lobbying and high penalties paid by the bakers, the ban on baking was lifted. Two additional penalty taxes were imposed on the Jews of Zychlin, including one as "punishment" for allegedly burning the synagogue after the Germans torched it themselves. In November 1939, the Jews were ordered to wear a yellow ribbon on their sleeves, and after a while the ribbon was replaced with yellow stars that had to be worn on the chest and on the back. The Jews were required to affix the sign "Jude" on the doors of their houses and observe a curfew from 5 pm to 6 am. In April 1940, the local authorities imprisoned the Polish and Jewish *intelligentsia* in Zychlin, especially the teachers. The prisoners, including many Jewish teachers, were sent to concentration camps in Germany.

The Zychlin ghetto was established in the summer or fall of 1940. It had two sections. The "large ghetto" was set on the right side of Narutowicz Street and was crammed with approximately 1,800 people. The "small ghetto" was located on the outskirts of the town, in a suburb called Pabianów. Both sections were overcrowded, with several families in each apartment and more than ten people occupying the same room. The Jews were ordered to seal their windows facing Narutowicz Street in order to insulate them from the "Aryan" side. The living conditions in Pabianów were extremely harsh. It was a wet and swampy area, with dispersed primitive houses that had no sewage and no well water to drink. The Jews had to dig their own well. It appears that no part of the ghetto was fenced off. Apparently, only one German policeman guarded the ghetto, near the building where the Judenrat was located. Officially, Jews were allowed to leave the ghetto only in exceptional cases, and only with a special license from the authorities (for example, to visit a doctor) and accompanied by a Jewish policeman. The Jewish policemen and members of the Judenrat were free to move throughout the town. The Jews who left the ghetto without permission were beaten, robbed and imprisoned. Contact with the non-Jewish populations of the city and the countryside was easy. The "Aryans" - the Poles and the Volksdeutsches (ethnic Germans) - often entered the ghetto, ordered clothes and shoes from Jewish tailors and shoemakers, and bought ready-made items. They paid with money or food. In an empty lot next to the Judenrat building, and in a field near Buszkower Street, an illegal trade flourished: the Jews sold their products or the rest of their property, the Christians sold food. Many Jews secretly slipped out to buy food in the surrounding villages, and the Jewish workers who were daily escorted by policemen to work outside the ghetto would also bring food on their return. Illegal trade and smuggling of foodstuffs were made possible by regular bribes to German policemen and Volksdeutsche auxiliaries.

While the living conditions of the Jewish residents were not too difficult, most of those who came to Zychlin as displaced refugees from other towns suffered starvation. On January 1, 1940, there were about 600 refugees in Zychlin among the 3,000 Jews. Their numbers increased, and so did the overcrowding in the ghetto, which on the eve of its liquidation had 3,200 Jews (March 1942). Most of the refugees came from Kutno, Dabrowice, Sanniki and Wloclawek. The housing difficulties of the refugees were enormous. For example, a large group of Dabrowice Jews were housed in a half-ruined brick factory. Many refugees, however, were forced to live outdoors. Most of them were penniless, could not buy food, and had to survive on the meager German food rations (the daily ration of bread in the ghetto was 120 grams per person) and leftovers that they rarely received. In the "large ghetto", the Judenrat opened a public kitchen, which distributed soup to the poor from both ghettos, once a day. In Pabianów it was not possible to open a kitchen because there was no suitable building. The Judenrat received only one grant from the Joint Distribution Committee's office in Warsaw.

The chairman of the Judenrat was the head of the community administration before the war, Alter Rozenberg. Its members were: Max Rozenberg, Yosef Chelmski, Yitzhak Kelmer, Yehoshua and Mordechai Zyger, Yitzhak Zeifert, Dr. Winogron. The chief of the Jewish police force was Yosef Oberman. Every day, they selected the workers according to a list and hired replacements for those who were able to pay to avoid being drafted for work.

With this organization of the labor supply, the press-ganging of workers ceased in Zychlin. But this did not prevent the deportation of young Jews to the labor camps. These drafts were a nightmare for the ghetto residents. From August 1941 until the end of the year, several hundred men were sent to the forced labor camps in the Poznan area. The living conditions in those camps were terrible, and none of them returned to the ghetto. Two Jews from Zychlin were hanged in the Naklo camp for trying to steal some potatoes from a nearby field. About 60 women from Zychlin were also sent to do field work on one of the estates. Luckily, the farm manager treated them decently. The Judenrat, or the chief of the Jewish police, had to prepare the list of men selected for deportation, which were collected during the night by the Jewish police. Understandably, people in the ghetto detested the Jewish police and especially its commander.

Under the appalling sanitary conditions, typhus cases appeared in the ghetto. The only doctor in the ghetto, Dr. Winogron, organized a small primitive hospital without proper equipment and medications, trying to eradicate the plague with the help of two assistants.

Signs of the imminent liquidation of the Zychlin ghetto came with the news that arrived in early 1942 about the liquidation of the ghettos in the Kolo district, especially Klodawa. It is believed that some Jews who managed to escape from Chelmno, the site of the mass extermination, reached Zychlin. There was also a hardening in the attitude of the local authorities. For example, the postal connection between the Zychlin Jews and the Jews in other places was severed and the Jews captured outside the ghetto began to be killed. Smuggling, which had been largely ignored by the German police, was now severely repressed. Regular searches began in the ghetto, accompanied by robbery. Many Jews considered fleeing to Warsaw on the assumption that the Germans would not eliminate its large Jewish ghetto. But the trip involved large expenses, and only a few rich people were able to leave Zychlin. One of such groups was caught on the road and the Jews were shot on the spot. Only a handful of Jews had the opportunity of hiding outside the ghetto with Polish acquaintances.

By the end of February 1942, the German police arrested the chairman of the Judenrat and the chief of the Jewish police. They were hanged in prison. In the following days, the ghetto was liquidated. The police broke into the houses, looted property, and killed Jews in apartments and streets. The members of the Judenrat and all the Jewish policemen and their families were publicly executed in the market square. The family of the chairman of the Judenrat and the wife of the Jewish police chief were apparently murdered even earlier, immediately after they were hanged in prison. A member of the Judenrat, Yehoshua Zyger, tried to resist the German policemen before he was killed. With the ghetto strictly surrounded by police guards, about 200 people perished in this "aktion". On March 3 1942, the entire population of the ghetto, 3,200 Jews, were taken to the market square and loaded on carts confiscated from the local farmers. The operation was rife with beatings and shootings. Failing and slow people were shot on the spot. The deportees were taken to the train station in Krosniewice, loaded onto wagons and transported to the extermination camp in Chelmno. The policemen who conducted the "action" and escorted the carts told the Jews openly that they were being transported to death. Only a very small number of young Jews managed to escape from the wagons.

Of the Jews who lived in Zychlin at the outbreak of the war, only 68 survived: 41 in the Nazi camps, 14 who escaped to the Soviet-occupied area of Poland, and 13 who were given refuge by Poles or managed to obtain false "Aryan" identity papers.

History and construction of the Zychlin synagogue

by Michal Ryter

Translated by Leon Zamosc

[Not included in the original book]

Zychlin was granted town privileges before 1385. For most of its history, it was a private city, playing the role of the center of a large complex of land estates, often changing owners. At the end of the reign of King August III, the city became the property of Kazimierz Pruszak and remained in the hands of this family for the next three generations.

Probably the first Jewish settlers appeared in Zychlin only at the beginning of the 18th century. Traces of this settlement can be found in the tax documents of 1734-1735, where the Jewish community in Zychlin was mentioned for the first time, as a *kehila* of the Kutno commune that paid 140 zlotys in tax. According to data from 1765, 311 Jews from the town and surrounding villages belonged to the *kehila*. Around 1780, it gained the status of an independent community, as evidenced by the poll tax register, probably from 1781.

In 1789-90 there were 66 houses in Zychlin. According to the tariffs of the chimney tax from that period, 29 houses belonged to Catholics, 23 to Jews, and 14 were owned by the church. With the creation of the independent *kehila* in Zychlin, the Jews began their efforts to build a new synagogue beffiting their their status as a community. The new building was to replace the old prayer house that had been erected around the third decade of the 18th century. After the project was endorsed by the town's owner, Tomasz Pruszak, an approval request was submitted to the archbishop of Gniezno, Antoni Ostrowski. With a document issued in Skierniewice on August 18, 1780, he complied with the request of the *kehila*, ordering that, "to avoid scandal or agitation during the proclamation of the word of God, it should be erected in a place distant from the parish church, not as a bricked building, but made of wood." The document mentioned the old synagogue: "The Jews of this town have had their synagogue here from ancient times. Since the old synagogue is in poor condition, destroyed with the passage of time and now dilapidated, they have humbly asked our approval of their plan to rebuild, or to complete a new construction in the place". For the permission to build a synagogue, Jews were required to pay two

Hungarian ducats to the local parish priest each year and to give one tallow stone for the candles.

The new synagogue was built as a wooden structure on a rectangular plan resembling a square. According to the municipal cadastral records from 1818, it was 27.5 x 25.5 Warsaw cubits (15.5 x 14.6 m). We know absolutely nothing about its architectural form, as no source materials have survived. However, this synagogue was thoroughly rebuilt around 1850. The condition after the reconstruction is documented by a preserved photograph, most probably taken at the beginning of the 20th century, which shows that the common body covered all the main rooms. The rooms for women, located above the vestibule, were reached by a staircase located in the front. In the ground floor, from south and north, there were rectangular doors leading to the vestibule. The walls of the building in the side elevations were regularly pierced by two pairs of windows, smaller ones in the women's section and much larger ones illuminating the prayer room. The whole building is covered with a multi-storey mansard roof protected with shingle.

Wooden synagogue rebuilt around 1850.
Image source: Żychlin Historia

In the 1840s, along with the increase in the number of Jewish inhabitants of Zychlin, an ambitious plan of communal construction investments was launched under the patronage of the then *kehila* elders Abram Zandberg, Abram Debinski and Man Kilbert. A completely new complex of synagogue buildings was to be erected in place of the existing wooden and old synagogue buildings, which were in poor condition. It was supposed to include a brick synagogue and, to be built again in wooden materials, a house for a rabbi with a *beit hamidrash* and a *mikveh* building with a hospital. The work on the design documentation was commissioned under the ordinary administrative procedure to the builder of the Gostynin district, Sylwester Baldi, whose duties included architectural design of public buildings with their estimated cost.

In mid-August 1844, the builder completed the design work and the investment documentation package containing a cost estimate, two drawings of architectural designs, a building site plan covering an adjacent part of the city, and a consultation protocol for further official approval. On June 8, 1844, the synagogue supervisory authorities requested the approval of the Masovian Gubernia authorities to carry out the construction by the community itself under the so-called "administrative system" (rather than the "bidding system"). The "administrative system" consisted in the submission of a written declaration by the interested parties providing their own valuation of the works, which allowed the investment of amounts that were lower than the calculation based on the plans and cost estimates. The main reason for this was not just the rationalization of investment costs, but also the fear that the lack of financial resources would delay the commencement of construction works and thus adversely affect the date of their completion. Considering the existing bureaucratic procedures, such a danger was by all means justified, considering that in Kutno, for example, a much more modest investment in the construction of a new choir in the old synagogue had lasted nearly seven years.

Despite the fact that the "administrative system" was most often used when the sources of financing came from a single investor, the initiative was supported by the head of the Kutno Poviat. He considered that doing the works under the "administrative system" would be more economical for the community and that, in the longer term, would contribute to the collection of larger voluntary donations for the construction. He also considered that the representatives of the synagogue district would donate from their own funds to "rush the construction without asking for interest."

The request included the approval of the administrative committee, selected from among the most prominent representatives of the city's Jewish community. The committee members were Josek Krajer, Wolek Rozenbaum, Pawel Lasman, Zelik Klinger, Michal Helmer, Josek Zajderman and Abram Hersz Lasman. The supervisory staff and the rabbi were also supposed to watch over the proper implementation of the investment. In addition, the supervision requested that, before drawing up and approving the distribution of the community fees, the provincial authorities inform the members of the committee about their disposition to start the construction "at the right time" under the oversight of the county builder.

Meanwhile, the lengthy bureaucratic machine was launched, beginning with the inspection of the cost estimates by Stefan Balinski, construction assessor of the Masovian Gubernia. The revision resulted in a reduction in the cost estimates of all the designed synagogue buildings. The cost of building a brick synagogue, taking into account the declaration of the city owner, Aleksander Pruszak, who offered to donate 111,000 burnt bricks and 19,000 carp tiles for the construction of the synagogue, was calculated at 2,450 rubles. The construction of the rabbi's house and the prayer room was estimated at 853 rubles, while the construction of the hospital and the apartment for the *mikveh* manager was estimated at 515. Total overhead costs for the entire complex of synagogue buildings were to amount to 3,818 rubles.

On November 14, 1844, the provincial government presented the synagogue buildings in Zychlin for approval of the Government's Office for Internal and Religious Affairs in Warsaw. The documentation was sent to the Department of Industry and Craftsmanship, which revised the cost estimates again and checked with the Construction Council the calculation of the list of costs of all synagogue buildings using old materials. In the end, the cost estimate of the brick synagogue, after being checked by the government builder Damazy Borzecki, decreased to the amount of 2,032 rubles. At the same time, the government builder made minor changes to the architectural plan of the synagogue in relation to the original design by Sylwester Baldi. Anyway, nothing is known about them, because the architectural drawings of the synagogue have not survived, contrary to the accompanying cost estimates. According to them, the synagogue was to be erected on a rectangular plan, 38.5 x 23 cubits (i.e. 22 x 15 m), on the top of a cornice made of lime-burned brick, with a roof covered with plain tiles in a lace manner. In the case of the rabbi's house and the hospital, the Department of Industry and Craftsmanship decided that these buildings should also be made of brick, as it was forbidden to build wooden houses in cities. The Department of Denominations also commented on this matter, noting that according to the regulations of the Construction Police of September 26, 1820, it was only possible to erect wooden buildings in cities whose surrounding areas were completely devoid of bricklaying materials and that, in the case of Zychlin, there was no information on the topic. In this situation, the Denominations Department informed the provincial government on February 20 1845 that it would suspend issuing a final decision on the building of wooden houses for the rabbi and the hospital until the matter was resolved. In response, the provincial government sent to the Office for Internal and Religious Affairs in Warsaw a protocol that was jointly drawn up by the municipality and the synagogue supervision, explaining the reason for erecting wooden buildings in Zychlin. Based on these explanations, the Office for Internal and Religious Affairs approved on August 13 1845 the cost estimate of all the synagogue buildings along with their architectural plans for a total amount of 3,343 rubles. On that basis, the provincial government issued the final decision which allowed the construction works to begin.

First, the *kehila* committee started to build the rabbi's house with a house of study and the *mikveh* with a hospital, considering that they were more urgent and less costly and that, at that stage of the construction, the expenses were only covered with the private funds of the committee members. The plans were fully implemented, as shown by acceptance reports drawn up by the magistrate, the synagogue supervision and the district builder on November 17 1850 and August 28 1851. The house for the rabbi and the prayer room were built in a log structure on a foundation, with outer and middle walls made of 4-inch sawn logs connected with a lock and pillars. According to the records, it was built on a rectangular plan with dimensions of 30 x 20 cubits (17 x 11.5 m) and 6 cubits high from the foundation up to the beams. The roof with two gables was made of a timber frame filled with lime-fired brick, and the whole roof was shingled. The mikveh was 27 x 20 cubits and 4 cubits 18 inches high from the foundation up to the beams. It was a log structure on a stone and brick foundation above the ground, laid on lime, and in the ground on clay with circular walls made of 5-inch logs, and central 4-inch walls joined with a lock and poles.

According to the acceptance protocols, the synagogue administration spent 879 rubles for this purpose, and "asked" for them to be returned from the community treasury in order to complete further construction works. The Gubernia authorities complied with the committee's request, but they considered the return of the entire sum impossible due to the lack of sufficient funds in the synagogue fund, in which only 822 rubles were deposited. However, the payment did not take place because of the cholera epidemic raging in Zychlin in 1852. The members of the committee Wolek Rozenbaum and Josek Krajer, who were in charge of the construction works and were fully trusted by the commune, were victims of the epidemic. The foremen used for the construction also died. Most of the funds deposited in the cash register were spent on material aid for impoverished residents. In such a difficult situation, the construction of a brick synagogue was abandoned, the more so because a large part of the wealthier Jews left the city during the cholera epidemic.

The project of building a brick synagogue was resumed twenty years after those dramatic events. In 1875, an engineer from the Kutno Poviat sent a cost estimate for the construction of a brick synagogue in Zychlin for the amount of 10,501 rubles to the construction department of the Gubernia. The cost estimate was accompanied by architectural plans, a protocol from the meeting of members of the commune regarding the investment, and an excerpt from the Bank of Poland confirming that the funds needed for the construction were available in the supervision's account.

Brick synagogue built around 1880.
Image source: Żychlin Historia.

The architecture of the synagogue was designed by Jan Kowalski, an engineer of the Kutno Poviat, who most likely based it on the previous design by Sylwester Baldi. The synagogue project was then sent to the architect of the Warsaw Gubernia, Aleksander Woyde, but it is difficult to ascertain whether he made any fundamental changes to Kowalski's design.

The positive decision of the authorities regarding the construction of the synagogue in Zychlin was made on May 21 1876, and its final implementation took place in 1880 at the latest. It was erected near the old wooden synagogue, which had been rebuilt in the middle of the century. The brick synagogue was a 16 x 22 m rectangular building with a square prayer room on the east and a vestibule on the west. The walls of the building were regularly pierced by tall arched windows. The height of the windows, due to the fact that there were galleries in the main hall, allowed the illumination of the interior on all levels. Windows were the main compositional element of the building's exterior architecture, which was designed very modestly. The body of the building was covered with a gable roof with triangular gables. By the very end of the century, the wooden *mikvah* building was demolished and replaced by a brick building with a boiler room.

In the 1920s, construction work was carried out on the walls of the synagogue changing the composition of the side elevations. At that time, rectangular openings leading to the vestibule were carved on the north and south with rich architectural frames.

The Zychlin synagogue today.
Image source: Wirtualny Sztetl.

During the German occupation, the high windows were bricked up, leaving only their upper fragments to illuminate the interior. The synagogue has survived in this architectural shape to this day. Inside, a gallery has survived, running around the main hall on three sides, supported by cast-iron fluted Corinthian columns, with a high wooden balustrade filled with rows of panels with painted decorations. On the eastern wall, near the recess for the Aron Kodesh, the remains of wall paintings have survived.

History of the Zychlin Jewish Cemetery

by Marysia Galbraith and David Goren

[Not included in the original book]

The Jewish cemetery in Zychlin is located about 600 meters east of the town center, 90 meters north of Lukasinskiego Street. It is surrounded by farmland with a farmhouse to the east. The cemetery is enclosed by a chainlink fence, with an unlocked iron wrought gate facing the road. No signs on the road mark the location of the cemetery, though it is indicated on Google Maps. The size of the cemetery is variously listed as 1.25 or 1.46 hectares.

View of the Jewish cemetery in Zychlin.
Image source: Towarzystwo Przyjaciół Ziemi Kutnowskiej.

The cemetery was established during the first half of the 18th century, around the time the first Jewish settlers arrived in Zychlin. According to the 1928 list of real estate owned by the Jewish Religious Community in Zychlin, there were two cemetery plots: an old one, and a new one. Their combined value was about

8,000 zlotys, and they produced and income of about 600 zlotys annually. A caretaker building was located in the old cemetery. Since there are no further details about the location of the new cemetery plot, Polish historian Tomasz Kawski suggests that new land was probably purchased next to the old cemetery. On maps of the town from the 1920s and 1930s, as well as on contemporary Google Maps, the cemetery is shown as covering a square-shaped area.

Zychlin satellite map showing the location of the Jewish cemetery.
Image source: Google Maps.

Testimonies indicate that, during the Second World War, the Germans shot Jews from Zychlin at the cemetery and that numerous other victims were buried in the cemetery grounds. During the liquidation of the ghetto in March 1942, when over 3,000 Jews from Zychlin were deported to the Chełmno death camp, there were mass executions in the town. Postwar testimonies at the Polish Institute for National Memory include the names of 176 of the approximately 180-200 Jews who were murdered on the spot and buried in the cemetery, including sick and infirm people, and more than twenty children (the list is included in the "Additional Materials" section of this book). According to a survey of the European Jewish Cemeteries Initiative, about 200 forced laborers were also killed in the cemetery a few months later, in the Fall of 1942. Analzing LiDAR aerial imagery, Zychlin's local historian Henryk Olszewski has detected the possible location of two mass graves in the cemetery grounds (light detection and ranging LiDAR data are collected from aircraft that scan the reflections of a laser beam to build a high resolution model of ground features).

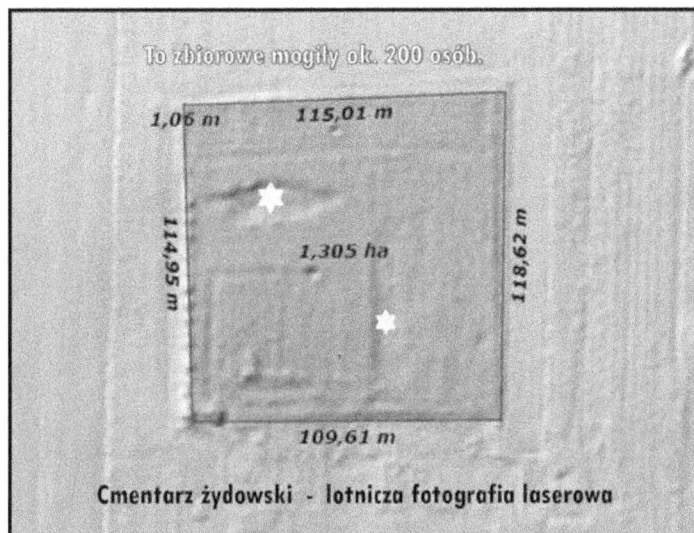

LiDAR image showing the possible location of two mass graves in Zychlin's Jewish cemetery. Image source: Henryk Olszewski.

Following the liquidation of the Zychlin ghetto, the Jewish cemetery was devastated by the German occupiers, who used the tombstones for construction work, including the building of a pigsty on a nearby property. There are also reports that some tombstones were used by local residents in housing construction after the war.

During the postwar years, the cemetery gradually deteriorated. On September 25, 1965, the Presidium of the Municipal National Council in Zychlin adopted a resolution to demarcate the cemetery with an area of 1.33 ha. In 1966, Szyja Hamburg, a former inhabitant of Żychlin, wrote in a letter to the Jewish Religious Union in Poland: "A neighbor of the cemetery set up a pasture for cattle there (...), he tried to cultivate a piece of the cemetery for planting potatoes, in the place where the murdered Jews rest". After the intervention of the Jewish Religious Union, the authorities of the Kutno district enjoined the Zychlin municipality to terminate the cemetery's lease agreement and install information boards prohibiting grazing animals and digging ditches.

In 1989, the Association of Zychliners in Israel and America launched an initiative to memorialize the Zychlin Jews and restore the Jewish cemetery of the town. The project was led by the president of the organization in Israel, Moshe

Zyslender, an architect and painter who lived in Haifa and was himself a Zychlin Holocaust survivor. Zyslender spent time in the Zychlin cemetery designing and building several concrete lapidary structures that incorporate about fifty recovered fragments of matzevot.

Main memorial monument commemorating the Jews of Zychlin. Image source: Marysia Galbraith.

One of the concrete lapidary structures with recovered fragments of matzevot. Image source: Leon Zamosc.

The main memorial monument features plaques in Hebrew and Polish with the following text: "In memory of our brothers buried in this cemetery for hundreds of years and those murdered by the Hitlerian criminals at Chełmno in 1942." The dedication ceremony, which took place on August 27, 1989, was described in the regional newspaper Tygodnik Płocki as follows:

> "The unveiling the monument was led by the Dean of the Catholic parish in Zychlin, Franciszek Sliwonik, the activist of the Association of Retired and Pensioners and author of a beautiful poem for the occasion, Irena Adaszewska, and Moshe Zyslender. The poem was read by Irena Dylik. The Rabbi of the Jewish community, who came from Warsaw, recited prayers in Hebrew.

Speeches were delivered by the city governor, the parish dean, the president of the Association of Refugees and party leader Ryszard Gawronski, social activist Ludwik Zalewski, and former Home Army soldier Henryk Popowski. Numerous delegations of institutions and businesses from Żychlin laid wreaths and flowers at the monument. The ceremony was filmed by a team of the TV Daily."

Unveiling the monument commemorating Zychlin's Jews in 1989.
From left: Moshe Zyslender, Franciszek Sliwonik, and Irena
Adaszewska. Image source: Tygodnik Płocki.

Five years later, in 1994, the Polish government recognized Moshe Zyslender with the Polish Knight's Order of Merit award.

More recently, Rabbi Israel Meir Gabbai's organization Agudat Ohalei Tzadikim, installed a monument to Rebbe Shmuel Abba (1809-1879), founder of the Hasidic Dynasty of Zychlin. The Hebrew plaque reads: "This matzeva is on the resting place of Rabbi Shmuel Abba of Zychlin, son of Rabbi Zelig, grandson of the holy Rabbi Fishel from Strykow. May his merits protect us. Taken to his grave on 1 January 1910".

Monument marking the grave of Rebbe Shmuel Abba of Zychlin.
Image source: Marysia Galbraith.

Today, the legal owner of the Jewish cemetery of Zychlin is the Foundation for the Preservation of Jewish Heritage in Poland (FODZ). The Association of Descendants of Jewish Central Poland (ADJCP), established in 2019 to recover and preserve the cultural heritage of the region's Jewish communities, works in cooperation with FODZ and local residents and organizations to clean, restore, maintain, and commemorate the Jewish cemetery in Zychlin.

Cleaning the Jewish cemetery as part of the program "In the Footsteps of Żychlin's Jews." Image source: Łowiczanin.info.

In 2022, Bożena Gajewska, director of the Society of Friends of the Kutno Region (Towarzystwo Przyjaciół Ziemi Kutnowskiej, TPZK), in collaboration with the School of Dialogue program, led a program for school children in Żychlin called "In the Footsteps of Żychlin's Jews." They learned about the Jewish history of the town, participated in the commemoration of the 80th anniversary of the liquidation of the Żychlin ghetto, and joined in clean-up activities at the Jewish cemetery. The Zychlin Group of the ADJCP plans to continue the maintenance and commemorative activities at the site in collaboration with the Matzevah Foundation and local partners.

Yeshiva Boys

by Hersz Bursztajn[6]

Recorded and edited by Fay Vogel Bussgang

[Not included in the original book]

Small Town Life

Most of the Jews in the small towns of Poland were small business people, working in grain, livestock, lumber, hardware, bakery, grocery stores, and the like. Most of the people were very poor, as there wasn't much money or much business in small towns. Usually the peasants came to town once a week, I think on Friday. The peasants brought their produce and sold it. They didn't have stores but just displayed their produce on benches. On the market day, the Jews did some business, but the other days, most of their time was free, so they usually had time to study. Although they had time to study, they barely made a living. Of course, it was desirable to be rich, and rich people were always honored, but few had that opportunity.

Zychlin was a typical Polish town with few Jewish people. There was no census in those days, but I suppose it had about 8,000 to 10,000 people. There was a Jewish tailor and a shoemaker who made shoes by hand, a baker, a grain merchant, a hardware dealer, a coal dealer, and a kerosene dealer, all Jews. A few Jews leased fruit orchards; they lived in town, but during the season for picking fruit, they took a small tent and went out to live in the orchards and then came back into town in the fall. But even these leaseholders were not usually very rich and simply sold their fruit on a small push cart. In towns all over Poland, the merchants were mostly Jewish.

Like other small towns, Zychlin had town officials who were responsible for road building. It had its own police as well. In Zychlin, there was a Christian grade school that was run by the town. Although it was run by the town, no Jews would teach in the school or attend as pupils.

---

[6] Editor's note: This account by Hersz Bursztajn (1890–1978), known in the U.S. as Joe Vogel, was given orally to his son, Ezra Vogel, in the late 1970s and recorded and edited by his daughter, Fay Vogel Bussgang.

The *Yeshiva*

When I reached thirteen, my father decided that I was far enough advanced in my studies to go to a *yeshiva*. I attended the *yeshiva* in Zychlin through arrangements that my mother made. Mother's cousin[7] was an ordained rabbi in Zychlin, but he did not practice. His wife operated a hardware store and provided a living for the family, so that her husband could spend his time in the synagogue for study and prayer. I studied under him. It was popular at that time in Poland that the wife provided for the family and the husband spent his time studying. He was goodness personified, and his wife was very proud of him. As her husband was very pious, she was sure the good Lord would compensate him and they would be together in Paradise, and all the good angels would be with them so that they would enjoy their reward for the good deeds they did while they were alive.

Mother's cousin was a great teacher, a conservative transmitting only the proven tradition. He was prominent among his contemporaries in town, and they all abided by his decisions as he expounded them, and they called him Rabbi with a capital R.

We were then living in Łódź, and I went with my mother in horse and buggy to Zychlin. She made all the arrangements for the *yeshiva* and stayed there a few days with me. I stayed with my mother's uncle, her mother's brother. He was a retired grain merchant.

There was no such thing as tuition in the *yeshiva*. It was supported by the community, and the community also bought the books that the boys used. The *yeshiva* was located in a special building belonging to the community, next to the synagogue. The men of the town usually gathered there to pray as anyone from the town was entitled to come there. A boy had to have some knowledge to come to the *yeshiva*, but it was democratic, and people usually studied several years and left when they chose. Usually to get in, a rabbi teaching there would give the boy a little exam to decide if he was ready.

Although there was no tuition, the real problem for the *yeshiva* boys who did not live in the town was room and board. There were no scholarships, but the Jewish people of the community, believing in education, supported the *yeshiva* students by offering them meals. It was arranged that a boy would eat one day each week at different houses. This was a kind of private charity, but it was very

---

[7] Editor's note: Later discovered to be Chaim Mendel Helmer.

painful for the boys receiving it. Most families were very poor, and it was a sacrifice to give up this food. Some boys didn't even get meals every day and had to do without for one or two days a week. Some people didn't treat the boys very nicely. I remember having to eat in the kitchen with the servant. It made me feel like a charity case, and I never forgave my mother for this. I didn't really want to go away to *yeshiva*, and I felt very disturbed when I arrived there. I felt humiliated, and so I became very depressed.

At the *yeshiva*, almost all our time was spent in study. Study, study, study. If a boy was bright, he would become a favorite of his teacher, and the teacher would take great interest in him. Although I did well, I looked around and saw all the poverty of life in the *yeshiva*, so I never felt there was any future in it.

I had a number of friends in the *yeshiva*, but I lost touch with them after coming to America. We boys spent the whole day in the *yeshiva*. I imagine that some of the boys managed to marry a rich girl, but most of them were wiped out by Hitler. When I returned home after a little over two years in the *yeshiva* to became a cutter, the boys of the *yeshiva* looked on me as an outcast. To be a working man instead of a scholar was very much against their way of thinking. I did get one letter, after I arrived in America, from a boy explaining his poor circumstances, and I think I sent him some clothes.

Before I left for the *yeshiva*, we prepared my clothes, and I got no new clothes that I remember during my two and a half years in the *yeshiva*. I never returned home during this period. Of course, my clothes became old and ragged and a little small for me during this time, but this was the usual way among boys in the *yeshiva*, so no one thought anything about it. Some students who didn't have a family to live with even stayed in school at night and slept on the benches. In the winter, there was some heat in the *yeshiva*, so this was not a serious problem. My parents sent me a little spending money while I was in the *yeshiva*. They didn't send more because they didn't have much, so about the only thing we could buy occasionally was sparkling water and some rolls to eat.

Although I slept at my relatives, all day from dawn till dark was spent in the *yeshiva*. There was no recreation. We simply stayed there and studied. Sometimes, someone had a new interpretation of a passage, and then we discussed the interpretation, arguing back and forth. Usually, it was one of the rabbis who had a new interpretation, but sometimes it was a student. Actually, the study was very democratic and free. A student could ask questions of the rabbi if he wished.

Although a boy did have to read certain parts of the Talmud, the same as the rabbi was reading, the rest of the time, he was free to read whatever parts of the

Talmud he wished. Sometimes, someone told stories about medieval times. There were lots of jokes and funny stories, and this was the main amusement we had. There were almost no magazines or newspapers, but there were a few books.

Most of the boys were very serious. Among the boys, the big shot was the one who knew the most. He would be respected by the rabbis and the other boys. There were also some "smart alecks." Some boys enjoyed telling ghost stories or else stories about angels. Even the "smart alecks" rarely talked about girls. There were not even dirty stories, and dates were unthinkable. The *yeshiva* boy rarely saw a girl before marriage. There was no physical exercise except for the shaking of the head during prayer, but as the whole body moved during prayer, this did constitute a kind of exercise.

The boys were mostly stiff around the rabbi, very serious. The joking was usually while the rabbi was out. But the boys were serious, too, as they wanted to learn.

The life of eating every day in a different place, seeing how all the poor Talmudists lived, deflated my spirit. They lived in the greatest poverty, and I became depressed and started to think about what I would do for a future. As there were no analysts to go to, I had to work out the problem by myself. I decided to quit studying, to leave the *yeshiva*. While I was thinking of being a drop-out, I went to talk it over with my *rebbe*, my mother's cousin, and he advised me to stay on a few months, until fall, after the Jewish holidays. I did so.

When I came home, I revealed my decision to become a tailor to my mother. When Mother heard this, she became very sad and started to cry, telling me I disappointed her in becoming a working man, a traitor to this way of life. Father didn't care so much, because he was born and raised in Brzeziny, but to Mother, it was a disgrace, since there were no working men in Mother's family. In my mother's family, there was a teacher, a hardware store operator, and a cantor, but no regular workers.

I knew a cutter in Brzeziny, but I first went home to Lodz after leaving the *yeshiva*, and then I went to Brzeziny and became a cutter.

New Winds of Culture

When I was studying in the *yeshiva*, Western culture began to penetrate the Jewish shtetls, and the youth became interested in other culture and literature. It was not so unusual to find some of us sitting with a secular volume in our hands underneath the table, with a copy of the Babylonian Talmud on top of our desk. Every day in the *yeshiva*, I saw around me the older Talmudists, what you would call graduate students today, all living in poverty.

I was among the youngest. Those who graduated and left lived a life of poverty except those who married a rich man's daughter. Just as a mother today wants her son to be a lawyer or a doctor, the mother of that time wanted her son to be a good Talmudist in order to marry a rich daughter. The reason was because all the rich Jews, who were not usually learned people, always wanted to mate their daughters with a scholar, so they could have a learned son-in-law.

While we were of school age, a great new Yiddish literature also appeared with more modern subjects. Ideas of socialism penetrated the modern Jewish mind. So, the Talmud began to lie around on our shelves and became less and less a book for devoted study.

To older Jews like my mother, it was a disgrace for people to work. There were many *luftmensch*, people with no work. So, when younger Jewish people actually went to the Land of Israel to work, there was a whole new movement. Even in my day, however, the majority still wanted the traditional education. Only a minority of the younger people wanted a secular education.

Surviving on the Aryan side

by Helena Bodek (Tzinamon)

Translated by Leon Zamosc

[Not included in the original book]

In June 1959, Helena Tzinamon-Bodek was interviewed by researchers of Yad Vashem in Holon, Israel. This is a translated version of her full testimony.

I was born in 1925 in Zychlin. My father Anshel Tzinamon was principal of a Jewish elementary school. After finishing elementary school I studied at the gymnasium in Plock, where I lived in a rented house. My family was not religious, but we kept the traditions. I was an only child. My father was killed soon after the German invasion. At the outbreak of the war I lived with my parents In Zychlin, a town in the Warsaw district. After the German invasion, the area of Zychlin was annexed to the Third Reich. The border (between the Reich and the so-called General Government of Poland) passed near the town. By the end of 1939, the Jews were ordered to wear a yellow badge on the back and chest are were not allowed to walk on the sidewalks. From the moment of the occupation, my father stopped working at the school. The building was confiscated and used as a jail for Polish prisoners.

Two or three months after the German occupation, relations in the city somehow normalized. There was no school for the Jewish children. My father started working as a teacher of Jewish children in our apartment on Narutowicza street. We suffered constant abuse from the Germans. The men of *Hilfspolizei* (auxiliary police), mostly *Volksdeustche* (local ethnic Germans) from neighboring areas, regularly raided the homes of the Jews and took away the most important things. In April 1940, mass arrests of the local Polish *intelligentsia* began - doctors, teachers, magistrates and civil servants. To round up the teachers they used the lists of the education bureau. My father was arrested on the night of April 14. He was one of the four Jews among the Polish detainees. They were taken to Kutno and, a few days later, further west. I know that, later on, some families received postcards from Dachau. But there were no signs of life from my father. Eventually, we heard that he had been killed at one of the travel stations. As far as I know, very few people returned from that transport. The few who came back had been assigned to places of work on the way. Those who reached Dachau were never seen again.

After my father was arrested, I stayed in our apartment with my mother Janina until May 1940. In May, the authorities ordered the Jewish population to concentrate in a ghetto. The order was given by the mayor - a German who had been brought from the Reich. The ghetto extended between Narutowicza (the main street) and Buszkowska street. Despite the fact that our apartment was inside the designated ghetto area, my mother and I decided to escape from Zychlin. A typhus epidemic had just broken out in the town and, by then, we already knew about what was happening in Lodz ghetto, where there was hunger, disease, and people were locked up. Zychlin was surrounded by guards and Jews and Poles were not allowed to leave, but we hid in the attic, packed our belongings in suitcases and fled through the fields bypassing the checkposts. We arrived in Plock, where we were received by the family of my mother's sister (her husband's family name was Kruk). Our belongings were brought to us by Polish acquaintances.

We stayed with the Kruk family for several months. They were poor and could not help with our livelihood. Meanwhile, we heard rumors that in the Zychlin ghetto that the situation of the Jews was tolerable, they had freedom of movement and they kept in touch with the Polish population. We began to consider the possibility of returning. I thought that the people who knew and appreciated my father would help us and I would be able to support both of us continuing his work as a teacher. So we returned to the Zychlin ghetto. Of course, our apartment was already occupied. But, thanks to the intervention of Chelmski, who was a member of the Judenrat, we got an apartment - first in a house bordering the ghetto and then in the ghetto area. I started working as a teacher and my mother ran the house.

The ghetto area was administered by the Judenrat, which included previous community leaders and especially new people who had been appointed through cunning or subservience to the *Schutzpolizei* (the German gendarmerie). The Jewish police also operated in the area (they wore armbands with an emblem of authority). The Jewish population survived mainly from the sale of belongings or valuables that they had managed to hide. The Jews could not leave the ghetto, but the Polish merchants were allowed to enter. The exchanges were facilitated by the Jewish police which, thanks to this "monopoly", gained increasing influence over life in the ghetto. Eventually, the people of the Judenrat lost control of the Jewish area. Taking advantage of the fact that he was in charge of the Jewish police, one of the Judenrat members, Yosef Oberman, ended up concentrating all the power in his hands. Assisted by the head of the Judenrat , a baker called Alter Rozenberg, he marginalized all the other members of the Judenrat and they became the masters of the ghetto. Oberman was a young man, originally from a good, rich family of Zychlin. He owed his power to his relationship with the *Hilfspolizei* and the *Schutzpolizei,* which had the authority over the Jewish police. This connection was not only administrative but also commercial. The members of the Judenrat and the Jewish police had freedom of movement outside the ghetto and the only way in which a Jew was allowed to leave the ghetto (for example, to the doctor, to an office) was in the company of a Jewish policeman. Later on, when people began to be sent to forced labor camps In Germany, the power of the Jewish police increased even more.

At first only men were taken to work, then women as well. The Jewish police were responsible for the quota of people. The execution was in the hands of the *Hilfspolizei* and the *Schutzpolizei,* who snatched the people from their homes in raids that usually took place at night. From the postcards that came from the camps, it was known that hard work and illness were crippling the workers. There were different people in the police, some of them decent, who just wanted to save themselves from being sent to camps, but there were also people of a different kind, such as Oberman and Rozenberg, who took advantage of their status for control, influence and enrichment. The rest were "little fish." It was rare for the Jews to try to leave the ghetto furtively. Some, especially the poor, would try to go out to nearby villages to get food. When they were caught they were abused, but most of the time the matter ended with the intervention of the Jewish police. There were frequent incidents, where the *Schutzpolizei* would enter the ghetto to steal under the pretense of confiscation of property. For the most part it was a matter of private initiatives that usually ended with the intervention of the Jewish police and the payment of a ransom. This was roughly the situation until the end of 1941.

At that time, rumors began to reach us about the extermination of the Jews in other towns. The first news was about the mass killing of the Jews of Klodawa. People who managed to escape from the place of annihilation reported that the Jews were brought to the forests of Chelmno and poisoned with gas in special trucks. Among the fugitives were eyewitnesses who had buried the corpses with their own hands. The atmosphere in the Zychlin ghetto changed to restlessness and panic.

At the beginning of 1942, relations within the ghetto deteriorated. There were several cases of Jews who were caught outside the ghetto and killed. In January or February 1942, Oberman and Rosenberg, the heads of the Judenrat, were arrested by the *Schutzpolizei*. A few days later there were rumors that they had been hanged. The *Schutzpolizei* began a hunt for one of Oberman's closest collaborators, who had fled or gone into hiding immediately after Oberman's arrest. They also arrested people who had previously had trade dealings with them. The corpse of a young Jewish girl was found in the Jewish cemetery. I do not remember her name, but it was known that she had connections with the *Schutzpolizei*. The few Jews who still worked in the German factories around the area were forbidden to go outside the ghetto.

There was panic among the Jewish population. There were many who thought about fleeing to the Warsaw ghetto. They knew that the Jews of the small towns were being killed, but they could not believe that the Germans would attempt to exterminate the entire Jewish population of such a big city. The youth also thought about the possibility of "resistance" in Warsaw. A group organized an escape to Warsaw, but they were caught and killed in Zychlin's cemetery.

The final sign that the liquidation of the ghetto was approaching was the suspension of mail delivery. This convinced us, my mother and me, that if we wanted to avoid deportation we had to flee. At the end of February we dressed in our best clothes, took off our "patches" and crossed into the Aryan side. The ghetto was not surrounded by a fence or barbed wire. Behind the last houses there were extensive fields, so that our escape was not difficult. There was only the fear that Poles or Germans would recognize us. We took the road leading to Gombin. On the way we stopped a farmer's cart and got a ride. In Gombin we stayed with an acquaintance, Holtzman, who was a member of the Judenrat. About a week after our arrival, a group of young men from Zychlin ghetto arrived in Gombin, bringing the news of the ghetto's liquidation. They escaped by chance because they were working outside the ghetto transporting things for the *Hilfspolizei*. From their stories, it became clear to me that the terror inside the ghetto had started a few days before the *aktion* of deportation. Every day Jews were killed on the street and blood flowed in the sewers. The Germans killed the entire Oberman family, all the members of the Judenrat, and the Jewish policemen. Under threat of death, people were ordered to hand over their furs and jewelry. The *aktion* took place on Purim. They brought peasant carts and loaded the Jews so densely that they had to stand holding on to each other. During loading, those who did not carry out the orders quickly enough were shot. Finally, the carts left town in an unknown direction.

We only stayed in Gombin for a few weeks, so I cannot provide details about the town's ghetto. As far as I know, the ghetto was not fenced. When the refugees arrived from Zychlin, the Jews of Gombin were surprised by the news they had brought. They had no idea that there was an ongoing operation to exterminate the Jews. One day, German police appeared on the Jewish streets of Gombin. The neighborhood was surrounded and closed. A few minutes later, the Jews were ordered to stay in their homes. The *Schutzpolizei* combed the houses and rounded up the men, leaving only the elders and the members of the Judenrat. That same night, all the men were driven in an unknown direction. There is no need to describe the mood on the next day.

Again without "patches" and without documents we set out through the fields with the idea of reaching Strzegow, where we had relatives with whom we had been corresponding. There were no Jews on the roads. We walked from Gombin to Plock. There, we stayed with Polish acquaintances who reluctantly agreed to host us for the night. From Plock we continued on foot to Plonsk, where we hired a cart that drove us to Strzegow. I describe our journey briefly, but it was very difficult. We were in constant danger of being caught because we did not have any papers. Evert time we tried to approach a Pole or a stranger, they would run away from us like a plague.

It was already the spring of 1942 when we arrived in Strzegow. The place, not far from Mlawa, was more a village than a town. How many Jews lived there I do not know, because I had never been there before the war. The Jews lived in a ghetto, surrounded by a wooden fence that was not difficult to cross. There was no German vigilance. The official entrance was through a gate guarded by Jewish policemen. We stayed with the family of my mother's brother Israel Rozen with whom, as I said, we had been in touch through letters. From them we learned that the Strzegow Jews knew nothing about the *aktionen* and killings in other Jewish towns. Our stories about Gombin and Zychlin caused panic among the Jews in the ghetto. Then came other refugees, who confirmed our stories.

I spent several months in Strzegow. If I remember right, there was a Jewish police in the ghetto and the leader of the Judenrat was someone called Bogen. Afraid of being arrested, he ran away and was replaced by his deputy Skowron. I did not spend enough time in Strzegow to learn much about the situation and the relations in the ghetto. Also, soon after our arrival I got sick with typhus and my mother and I spent most of the time at home.

Many Jews worked outside the ghetto. Almost all the young men went out every day accompanied by guards to work in the harvest on a nearby farm. In the fall, they started to take women out of the ghetto to work in peat mining in the area. This work was associated with a stay in a temporary camp. It was very hard work and I heard about many cases of women who died from the hardships and the awful sanitary conditions. The Jewish police was responsible for preparing the list of the workers and organizing their shipment. They came looking for me several times, but I hid in the attic. Due to the crowded living conditions (several families in one apartment), typhus transmitted by lice spread in the ghetto. Getting treatment was difficult because it was necessary to hide the outbreak of the plague from the Germans. The sick people were hidden in a hut and left alone. There was no Jewish doctor. The Polish doctor Wisniewski was a decent man who maintained secrecy and did not report anything to the German authorities. If the Germans showed up, the sick people would get out of bed to avoid the consequences of being discovered. The *Schutzpolizei* entered the ghetto frequently to hunt people down and make arrests on false pretenses (such as finding butter, etc.). It was said that they were members of the *Schutzpolizei* from Mlawa. They came in large numbers looking for prey.

I remember well the last manhunt I witnessed. The Germans burst into the ghetto at down, took out the entire population to the street and separated women and men. The men were organized in groups of ten and, as they said in the ghetto, were "locked up in the dungeon" for several weeks. The Jewish police guarded them. In the meantime, they brought back from Mlawa a number of Jews who had been caught in previous hunts. Among them was a relative of mine called Hersz Szurek. He had been held there for several days and now joined the group of detainees who were guessing what fate awaited them. My relative encouraged them to hold out and proudly bear their fate. On the day of the execution, a gallows was erected in the center of the ghetto. The entire population, including the children, was gathered there. Machine guns were placed behind the backs of the crowd. Between ten and twenty Jews were then hanged on that day.

My mother and I started thinking about escaping again. It was clear to us that we could not go to another ghetto. Only on the Aryan side there was a chance of survival. I had a friend in Wloclawek, a young Aryan guy with whom I maintained correspondence and on whose help we could rely. Wearing a peasant dress and carrying a hoe in my hand I left the ghetto. I knew that just being on the road posed a danger to me, regardless of my "Polish looks". Circulating on the roads was also dangerous for the Poles, because moving from one town to another required a transit permit. I made my way to Wloclawek partly on foot and partly on a truck. On the way, I spent the night with farmers. I told them that I had ran away from hunger and misery in the General Government, that I was looking for work as a housemaid or a nanny, and that I had to avoid the authorities because I did not have a work card. In those areas, every Pole had to carry an employment card that stated his place of work. Those who were caught away from their workplaces were sent to work in Germany. I had a card from one of my cousins, with a fingerprint, bearing the name Teresa Rozen. I had corrected the name to Rozenska.

To my dismay, when I arrived in Wloclawek I found out that my friend had been detained, so all my hopes were dashed. I stayed for several days with a teacher, whose address I had received from the farmers who had hosted me night before. When I told the teacher my story she was very moved and offered to keep me with her and enroll me in school. This was impossible because I did not have a registration certificate as a resident. In the end, I decided to go back to Strzegow. There, my mother kept insisting that we had to look for a shelter option outside the ghetto. I went to Slawecin, a pretty rich village in the same district, where I told the story that I was running away from the General Government and looking for some occupation. I managed to stay with the sister-in-law of Soltys (the head of the village), who offered me maintenance in exchange for work in the household and teaching her children. There were no schools and the Polish children had to study in secret. I was able to get a place for my mother as well, working as a housekeeper for the tailor Golebiowski. I brought her to the village after a few days. Thanks to my "Aryan looks" and my ability to speak good Polish, I did not arouse any suspicions. My mother, however, despite her excellent command of the language, was bound to be discovered. Her habits in the kitchen and household betrayed her. Growing up, I had spent a lot of time with Polish acquaintances and visiting their homes. But my mother, who had rarely left the Jewish environment, was easy to spot as a Jewess. After a few days, my mother was deported and showed up at my place. Our secret had been discovered and my landlady told us that we should both leave quickly. Since she liked me, she advised me to go to Raciaz and gave me some names and addresses.

One of the contacts in Raciaz was an old Polish woman named Gawronska, who lived alone in a dilapidated, dirty hut. She agreed to accept us for a modest fee. We had very little money and no belongings at all. The ground burned under our feet because we could not register as residents. My false certificate was of dubious value and my mother had no papers at all. Luckily, our landlady suggested we go to an acquaintance of hers, Halina Igielska, who also lived in Raciaz. She did not suspect for a moment that I was Jewish. She felt sympathy for me, believed that I was a refugee, and thought that her sacred duty as a Pole was to help me. One thing that I learned from my stays with the Poles was that the people of the Polish *intelligentsia*, who were also persecuted by the Germans, showed a great deal of solidarity and disposition for mutual assistance. Halina worked in some office and did some trading. She traveled frequently to the General Government and had connections with all sorts of notables in town. She had a friend, Alicja, who worked for the municipality and promised to arrange certificates for me and my mother. I do not know how she managed it, but the fact is that by Christmas we received certificates in the name of Helena and Janina Bodek. We gave Alicja a modest gift, but it was clear that it was Halina's mediation, and not the gift, that motivated her to help us. So by the end of 1942, I started working for a living teaching Polish children clandestinely. One of my students was Halina's younger brother. Most of my pupils were children of the *intelligentsia* and wealthy Polish families. They would pay me with food, which was the best payment at a time in which barter trade was all over the place. Thanks to my work, I made a lot of friendly connections with people, especially with the younger generation. Through these acquaintances, I was able to get a better apartment from the housing authority. I furnished it with the help of my students' parents. The fact that I was teaching clandestinely was risky, but I could feel a lot of sympathy, especially among the families of the *intelligentsia*. In any case, it was impossible to feel safe. I knew that there was gossip and that among my fans and acquaintances there were suspicions that we were Jewish. On one occasion, when I was visiting a neighbor, a woman said, "Did you hear the rumors about Jewesses living in our town?" "What are you blabbering about?" I replied, but a shiver went through my body. On another occasion, my mother was called "Jewess" on the street. But it was someone from the mob that did that. The people of the *intelligentsia* never bothered us. I would regularly attend church and we were invited to homes for family celebrations, Easter, and Christmas. My mother could not muster herself to go to church, so the opinion was formed that she was of Jewish descent and I was her daughter from a Polish father.

Another thing that worried me was the fact that my work was illegal and I was not registered with the labor bureau. What would happen to my mother if they caught me and took me to work in Germany? Poles who did not have regular jobs were forcibly drafted and sent to work in Germany. Near the end of the war, they started to massively deport people to work in excavation. It was very hard work and many Poles would mutilate themselves to avoid it. Miraculously, I was able to escape the round-ups several times, mostly thanks to my appearance. I looked more like a child than a young girl.

That was how my mother and I spent more than two years in Raciaz under the German occupation. We went from one dangerous situation to another until the arrival of the Russians in February 1945. My moment of greatest fear was when they issued new identity cards in 1943. To get the card it was necessary to present birth certificates, which of course we did not have. We were lucky that the brother of Halina Igielska helped us. He had been a student at a religious seminary in Plock and had connections with the clergy. I explained to him that I could not go back to the General Government to get the birth certificates. Fortunately, he was able to get valid certificates that we could use to get the identity cards.

Even after the Russians entered, we did not admit that we were Jewish. I continued my relationship with my former friends and, as it turned out, doing that may have saved our lives. By the end of the war, several Jewish young men and women who had managed to survive the camps returned to Raciaz. All the survivors lived in one apartment. One night an armed gang surrounded the apartment and killed them all, even pregnant women. After this incident we decided to leave Raciaz and went to Poznan. I found an apartment and started studying at the university in the Faculty of Agronomy. I registered as a Pole under the name Helena Bodek. In 1950 I passed the final exams and graduated. A few weeks later I came to Israel with my mother. Immediately after my arrival, I got a job at the Weizmann Institute in Rehovot, where I still work today.

* * * *

Translator's note: Helena Tzinamon-Bodek passed away in Israel in 2004. Her book of memoirs *Jak Tropione Zwierzęta (Like Hunted Animals)* was published in 1993 by Wydawnictwo Literackie in Krakow.

The boy in the closet

by Senek (Zelig) Rosenblum

Edited by Leon Zamosc

[Not included in the original book]

In May 1997, Senek (Zelig) Rosenblum was interviewed by researchers of the USC Shoah Foundation in Munich. This is an edited excerpt of his testimony, published with permission of the USC Shoah Foundation's Visual History Archive.

Senek with his father Henryk Rosenblum,
after liberation.

I was born on December 23, 1935 in Zychlin, a small town in Poland. My father was Henryk Rosenblum and my mother Fela Rosenblum, nee Czonskowski. My father was active in agriculture – he had a small mill and was a buyer of grain. We lived on the outskirts of town in a wooden house. Zychlin was a town of about 4,000 people. About half of them were Jews. It was a typical *shtetl*, very Jewish, and most of the business activities had to do with agricultural products.

My grandparents were very religious people, but my father already belonged to the liberal younger generation. I do not know about my mother's side of the family. I can only recall that my grandparents were both very religious and there were religious celebrations in the home.

My father was drafted into the Polish army when I was a small child, and he wasn't at home for a while. This was in 1939. From what he told me, I know that when the Germans occupied the country he fled to Romania to escape imprisonment. In the meantime, my grandparents, my mother, and I were alone.

My earliest memory is of the outbreak of war. I was three years old, but it was memorable because everyone was so agitated and there was intense bombing before the Germans arrived. I remember a group of German soldiers marching in a column. When one of them picked me up, the Polish children shouted to him, "Lord, Lord, don't carry him! He's a Jew!" So even at that early age I was aware that there were two classes in society - Poles and Jews.

I attended a religious school, a *cheder*, as a child. I have vague memories of it, and that we were allowed to stay in our house after the Germans arrived. Then, they took away our radio, horses, and other things. That was the first harbinger of disaster. There was terror in Zychlin after the German occupation. It wasn't like what came later, but Jewish children were removed from schools, and we were harassed in the streets by the Hitler Youth, the soldiers, and the administrators who came to the town.

After a time, my father returned and he hid with us. Life somehow became sort of normalized. We were not allowed to use the sidewalks and had to wear the yellow star. Then, we were evacuated from our home and had to go to the ghetto. The Polish and Jewish populations were separated. There were two ghettos in Zychlin. We were lucky to be in the little ghetto with the older people. Most of the town's Jews were cramped in the large ghetto, which was fenced off. The little ghetto had few houses and it wasn't fenced because the houses were in an open field, near other houses that were occupied by the German police and members of the SD (*Sicherheitsdienst*, the intelligence service of the SS). Escape attempts were unlikely because most of the Jews in the little ghetto were old people and the place was watched by the families of the German policemen. I lived in that small ghetto with my father and mother for two years, from the summer of 1940 to the winter of 1942. At times my maternal grandmother lived there too, and we had to share the house with other people whom I don't remember clearly.

I do remember that there was a hill in the small ghetto, with a little pond nearby. In winter, the frozen pond and the snowy hill were ideal for sledding and sliding down. The hill was a magnet for us children, but it was also a magnet for the children of the German policemen. They came into the ghetto to play with us - the lousy, seedy, half-starved Jewish boys. Looking back, it is almost unbelievable! The German children had all the equipment - sleighs, everything. For the first time in my life, I saw skis. They smelled good because their mothers smeared them with cream as protection against the frost. At first, they were reluctant to play with us, but they got used to us and we got used to them. And we played together as if it were the most natural thing in the world. Now and then, they brought us crisp bread and the *Wehrmacht* biscuits that were popular among the soldiers. Our parents never told us not to play with the German children. They would not have dared. We treated the German children like raw eggs - very carefully. We were very scared of their fathers. But, as I said, we got used to them, probably out of our youthful ignorance -- until the Germans started their *aktionen* against the Jews and everything was over.

In the ghetto, our freedom of movement was totally restricted. Some people, mostly youngsters, managed to get out of the ghetto to buy things, such as food and medicines. But this was forbidden and when they were caught, they were taken to the commandant's office where they were horribly beaten. As special punishment, their faces were painted with black tar. They were then sent back to the ghetto, which created quite a stir. Having so few resources in the ghetto, we were unable to clean the tar on their faces – it took weeks before the tar could be removed.

There were various German *aktionen*. I remember one in which young men aged twenty to twenty-five were picked up. In another operation, they rounded up men and boys as young as fourteen. The mothers put themselves between the SD and their children. Men ran the risk of being shot immediately if they protested, but they believed that as women they would be spared. So there were terrible scenes of teenagers being torn from their mothers. One of the most striking scenes was when the *Rebetzen* ran out into the market square and screamed in Yiddish calling her son, *"Gott'n nu schesi?" "Where are you?*

There was no synagogue in the small ghetto. I don't know if there were services in the town's main synagogue, but I do recall that religious celebrations at home continued to take place, even under the most adverse circumstances. I can remember that the little ghetto had a small *cheder*, but some children never showed up and others attended irregularly. At the time, there was already great hunger, and the children were plagued by disease. In autumn 1942, after the first German *aktionen*, no one was allowed to attend schools anymore and the members of the Council of Elders and the Judenrat were no longer allowed to leave the ghetto. If they were caught trying to leave the ghetto, people were no longer beaten or painted with tar at headquarters - at this point they were just put against the wall and shot.

Between 1940 and 1942, my father was involved with the Judenrat. He could speak some German, so he was kind of a liaison between the Judenrat and the German police. He had a brisk demeanor - he wasn't the typical frightened Jew. He had a way of calmly dealing with the German police, which was somehow recognized by the other side. And he also had, so to speak, a free ticket to get out of the ghetto. He made grain deliveries and purchased supplies for the ghetto. Of course, I didn't know the details, but I generally remember that he could get in and out of the ghetto and the German headquarters. He was committed to help improve ghetto life.

My father saved my life as a result of his interactions with the Germans, his knowledge of the area and his business with local famers. In his later years, he told me that he got a tip from a German police officer that there would be *aktionen* against the ghetto and the population would be destroyed. With that knowledge, he prepared for our escape.

When the military operation against the ghetto began in the winter of 1942, a farmer friend of my father's provided us a horse-drawn sleigh. The sleigh had been allowed into the ghetto to deliver grain and our family used it to escape. I remember that my grandmother dressed me in layers that I wouldn't normally wear. We also took clothes with us, everything that we could carry. I wanted to bring my rocking horse with me, it was my favorite toy. I had to be dragged away forcefully from that rocking horse. As a child, I probably didn't realize the situation we were in, but my parents did.

The day we left was very cold. My father carried me and the man driving the sleigh told us to hurry. He was uneasy because he would have been in deep trouble if caught smuggling Jews out of the ghetto. We were taken to a farm and then urged to move on late the next day. After that, we no longer had the sleigh and we started on a gruesome, arduous odyssey with my old grandmother and my mother, who already had severe kidney disease. We dragged ourselves to another farm.

My father planned to cross the border that the Germans had drawn between the Reich and Poland's General Government. Crossing the border was forbidden under pain of death. His goal was to get to Warsaw by train. He thought that the Warsaw ghetto, with its huge Jewish population – up to half a million – would be safe. It was a bold undertaking because we had to cross 140 kilometers in winter. My father hired someone who knew his way around, a local, to take us over the border. I can still remember that march, which started at night. The guide, dressed in white like a soldier on maneuvers, led our little group. At some point, he thought that the border guards had discovered us. He hid in a hollow and suddenly we were alone, unsure of where we were.

It was an extremely precarious situation. Exhausted, we managed to reach a farm where the farmer hid us in a barn. My mother said she just couldn't go any further, and that she wouldn't leave her mother either. She begged my father to continue with me, convinced that she wouldn't survive. It was a tragic night in that barn – my mother insisting that we should go on, and my father refusing to leave her. They argued for hours, until my father finally decided that we would continue without her. She and my grandmother allowed themselves to be captured. They ended up back in the ghetto and were wiped out along with the other women, children and old men. Years later, some Poles told me that she was last seen being deported to the gas vans with her mother. And that was it.

My father and I went on alone for weeks across the snowy, dreadful countryside, until we finally made it to Warsaw. We arrived in Warsaw in late December 1942. For me, it was a memorable day. Everything was new and different. In Zychlin, I had only seen horse-drawn carriages and carts. In Warsaw, there were brightly colored trams with bells. It was so impressive that I just forgot the danger we were in.

We stayed with relatives who were already living in Warsaw ghetto. The living conditions were terrible. We were all crammed together in a small apartment on Nalewki Street with other people. It was just horrible, not only because was there hardly any food and many were sick, but also because there were daily quarrels among those who shared the tiny rooms. Our daily life focused on those arguments and how to get food.

When you met people you knew on the street, they acted like it was the last time they were seeing you. People behaved like hunted animals because of the permanent German *aktionen*. Today, when I see pictures of the Warsaw ghetto, I see the same things that I witnessed back then. It is hard to describe now, but the images show exactly how it was – completely rundown characters walking down the streets, begging for something to eat.

Coming from a rural town, I had been used to fresh air. Suddenly, there was this bestial smell of so many people crammed together in the ghetto. There was simply no waste disposal or anything like that. They sprinkled something on the waste to prevent the spreading of diseases. The smell of those chemicals haunts my memory to this day.

I don't remember ever asking my father why I had to be there in the ghetto. But it was the result of the two-class society in which we were living in Poland – here are the Jews, and there are the Poles. I instinctively knew that I wasn't a Christian, that I was a Jew. And from the very first moment that the Poles attacked us, I also knew that I belonged to a minority, to the underdogs. This runs like a thread through my childhood.

At some point, my father understood that the Warsaw ghetto would also come to an end. He got in touch with someone in the Judenrat. They didn't want to believe that the Germans would dare to annihilate the mass of people in the Warsaw ghetto. But my father, knowing what had happened in Zychlin and in Kutno, was certain that there would be a systematic annihilation.

During this time, my father was in top form. He bribed the Ukrainian and Lithuanian guards and traded with the Poles over the ghetto wall, exchanging watches and rings for food, mostly fruit. And knowing what was going to happen in the ghetto, he made arrangements with a woman with whom he traded - when the time came, he would hand me over to her and she would hide me.

In the spring of 1943, the first of the big *aktionen* took place. There was terrible unrest among the ghetto residents. We didn't know: was this the final extermination operation or not? And more and more often, people were shot openly on the street. The streets were full of people, and I remember scenes of the crowds tried to escape in a panic. There were always rumors that there was a hole or passage where you could get out of the ghetto. I went to one of those places with my father, but the guards had already closed the path to escape. Like drowning people, we ran from one part of the ghetto to another. It was like being on a sinking ship.

While my father was preparing for my escape, he found out that there was a courthouse that had access from both the ghetto and from the so-called Aryan side. One day, he took me calmly past the Germans guarding this building. I remember that on the other side of the street there was shooting. The guards were distracted and my father took my hand and led me in. A Polish man was waiting for us inside. We exited the building on the Polish side. The man took me to an apartment where I stayed for weeks with other persecuted people. There were twenty people in the apartment. We barely moved during the day, crawling on our stomachs to avoid being seen through the window.

My father was only sporadically in the apartment. He went in and out of the ghetto and he got other people out. Based on what he testified after the war, he smuggled at least thirty more people who are still alive today. It was an enormous danger for him to go back into the ghetto again. But as I mentioned before, he did exceptional things during that period of his life. He seemed born for such a situation, with his finger on the pulse of what was happening.

Then one day, my father didn't go back to the ghetto. I think that it was when the Jewish uprising broke out. That sunny spring morning I left the apartment with my father. We went to a market, where a young woman approached us. He said, "This is your new aunt. You are going with her and I'll visit you." I already knew that things were a matter of life and death. I couldn't contradict him like a normal child saying, "I don't want to go with a stranger." The woman took me to the western part of the city, to a street named Groutschewska. I remember that very well.

This woman was the daughter of the lady with whom my father had traded over the ghetto wall. She was recently married. We went to her apartment, which was small but clean. Everything smelled completely different from the ghetto. She took off my clothes, washed me, and put me in a clean bed. During the day, she would hid me in a closet where I had to sit in a camouflaged section. That was my hiding place for the next eleven months. I sat there every day in utter silence. I had no toys, nothing at all. Only at night did she or her husband, a truck driver, let me out. The toilet for the apartment was communal, and nobody was supposed to know that someone was hidden there. She took me out at night to use the toilet. Over time, I became so weak that I couldn't stand alone, so she had to carry me.

This woman taught me to speak perfect Polish. Like most Jews of the small towns, my family spoke a mixture of Yiddish and accented Polish, which identified me as a Jew. The woman was very religious. I heard her singing Polish religious songs while I was hiding in the closet. She taught me Polish prayers and when she took me out of the closet at night she kept telling me that I had to kneel down in front of the bed and pray. She would say to me, "if you pray to the holy Mother of God every day, or better yet twice a day, you will survive the war." So I prayed.

The woman was very good to me despite the troubles I caused. Because of the loss of my mother, and seeing my father only sporadically, I started wetting the bed. Today, psychologists study the underlying causes of bed wetting, but at that time people didn't take circumstances into account. The woman was constantly changing the bed linens and there was no washing machine. Initially, she punished me for wetting the bed. But no punishment would solve it, and somehow she understood that.

I was often alone in the apartment during the day. It had been drilled into me again and again that I had to sit in the closet and make no noise, similar to Anne Frank's family in hiding. But I was alone - my only human contact was with the woman in the evening. Every few weeks my father would come to visit, and sometimes I made a scene trying to keep him from leaving.

My father passed as a Pole. He adopted the personality of a Polish officer who had fled from captivity. He wore good clothes and fashionable boots, and the Poles respected him. He spoke to the woman in the third person, which was common at the time when someone of a higher class spoke to others. He used that tactic to perfection and that helped him to survive. He brought his personality to bear in his dealings with the woman and he also paid her to compensate for hiding a Jewish child, which was forbidden under pain of death.

The worst part of my time in the apartment was when the Russians started bombing Warsaw. The apartment was on the third floor. When the bombs hit, everyone ran into the basement, leaving the windows open so that the air pressure of the explosions would not damage them. Nobody was supposed to know that a Jewish child was hidden there, so I had to stay upstairs during the raids. That was a terrible experience – everyone was in the basement and I was up there alone. Most of the bombing was at night, so the woman would open the closet and I sat in the apartment looking out of the window. The planes would first drop parachute flares that lit up the whole area with a pale, eerie light. Then came the bombers. It was incredibly scary the first couple of times, looking out at the whole inferno, fearing I would die. You have to imagine a little boy of six or seven sitting alone in a house with no one in sight. I had a harrowing feeling of loneliness, coupled with fear. The third or fourth time I just felt fear because many houses were destroyed. But there was also a dash of curiosity, which helped me overcome my fear.

Eventually, the neighbors found out that the woman, whose name was Irka Rudkowska, was hiding a Jewish child in her apartment. She couldn't conceal my trips to the communal toilet indefinitely. Someone discovered me and they told the young woman that they would denounce her to the Gestapo if I stayed there. She started to panic and her husband urged her to get me out of the apartment.

At that point, my father looked desperately for somewhere I could stay. He knew a farmer about 40 kilometers from Warsaw and he took me to his farm in early 1944. I was wise enough to know what was happening, and to do exactly as my father directed. I stayed on the farm for about two months.

It was a positive time. I felt relieved after my confinement in the closet and the horror of the night bombings. I will never forget the freedom I felt. I was suddenly out of my cage, on a farm with cows and horses (which I especially loved) where I could just frolic around freely, playing with the farmer's children. But it wasn't possible for me to stay with the farmer and his family. The farmer couldn't use me as a farmhand, he had enough children of his own.

Eventually my father found a place for me with another woman in the Praga district of Warsaw, on the eastern side of the Vistula. I went there in the early summer of 1944. The lady was a Polish widow with a four-year-old girl and made her living doing laundry for other people. She wasn't particularly good to me. She made me feel that when my father didn't come on time to deliver her payment. At that time, the Polish uprising broke out in Warsaw and my father stopped coming altogether. The woman treated me very badly. She drove me out a number of times, so I had to stay overnight with other families. As the front was getting closer, the Germans drove all the farmers out of the area and reassembled them as groups of refugees. The woman wanted me to move in with those people.

I continued to pretend that I was a Polish boy who had lost his father and mother and was taken in by the woman. With the Polish uprising, the whole food supply collapsed. A terrible famine broke out. The woman made me go to the villages and beg the farmers for food. For a few months, I was the only source of food for the woman, at the age of eight. Nonetheless, she cursed me because my father didn't come to pay her. She became more and more rabid and wanted to cast me out. She partially did that.

I was always longing for my father. But in the chaos that prevailed at the time, I was just one of thousands of orphaned children. Then came the bad days when the district was conquered by the Red Army. There was constant artillery fire and the building's residents were sitting in the basement during the siege. I was the only one without a parent. Someone had to go fetch water, and I had no protector. Collecting water was not just dangerous - it was a likely death sentence because whoever went up there had a fifty percent chance of not making it. I was always the one who was forced out of the cellar to get water. But I had a guardian angel - I always came back with water.

I saw my liberator, a Russian soldier, on one of those trips to get water. He was among the advance personnel who laid the telephone cables for the front line and he scolded me for tripping over some wires. I knew he wore a different uniform, not the gray of the Germans. I was no longer afraid. When he scolded me, it felt like freedom. I became friends with the Russians when they took up their quarters. I was a kind of mascot for them.

During one siege, I was especially lucky. The woman was away and I was alone in the basement with the other residents. They sent me to fetch the water again. When I came back, the house was no longer standing and everyone in the cellar was dead. Seeing the ruins of the house, I went to the woman's sister, who lived a few doors away. I kept hanging around in the hope that when my father came back he would find me there.

At this point, there was nothing to eat. The Russian soldiers themselves were starving. We began to go out to the countryside looking for food. There were three or four of us children in the group. There were minefields to left and right, but there were potatoes in those minefields. The adults didn't dare go into the fields, but they told us children that it was harmless to go dig for potatoes. We went in to gather the potatoes and one of us was just torn apart. In the end, I was the only one who survived. The other child starved to death.

We kept going further and further looking for food. One day I was dragging myself along alone, completely exhausted. I was so weak that I couldn't make it back. I sat down on a railway embankment to die. I was already in a state of delirium, between this world and the hereafter. Then a woman came up to me from afar. She was dressed peasant style, wrapped up in a cloth and she stopped in front of me. I asked in Polish, "*Niech bedzie pochwalony Jezus Chrystus* (Praise to Jesus Christ), would you have a piece of bread for me? " And the unbelievable occurs – she takes out a loaf of bread, breaks off a piece and gives it to me. Who had a loaf of bread at that point? Nobody, nobody. But it happened. I ate the bread and after a few hours was able to drag myself back. Somehow the days went by as the Red Cross offered soup and other foods. About half a year passed.

The front was right there -- the Russians on the edge of the Vistula, waiting for the Germans to crush the Polish uprising. I fraternized with the Russian soldiers, feeling the joy of not being afraid. The fear of death, the fear of being pursued by someone who is trying to kill you, can't be compared to anything else. When that's gone, you feel like you've got your life back somehow.

One day the front started moving. The Russians crossed the Vistula and liberated Warsaw. In less than a week, my father arrived. Amazingly, he was well dressed, well fed. However, little things could upset him. Maybe the passage of time made him weary. Outwardly, he was the same man, but probably he was broken in some ways too. When he arrived, he had money. And the woman's whole attitude toward me suddenly changed. He got us a room and arranged for me to sleep in a bed. He even got a doctor. Later, he told me that when he found me, I looked like an old man. If he hadn't arrived, it was only a matter of time, maybe weeks, and it would have been over for me. There was something wrong with my lungs. The doctor arranged hot baths for me. He also treated me for my bedwetting. And soon my suffering was gone. My father went away and came back after two or three days. He brought me clothes to replace the rotten ones I had been wearing. Then he took me with him. I remember that we drove through a tattered Warsaw. There were corpses everywhere, mostly fallen Germans. The dead Russian and Polish soldiers and civilians were taken away and buried. But not the Germans. You could see they were Germans by their uniforms. They had no shoes, socks, or hats, just their uniforms. Nobody wanted to touch a German uniform. They were the Poles' mortal enemy.

My father and I followed the front for weeks. We wanted to go back to our town. Then my father found his brother-in-law, who had also lost his whole family. He was our only surviving family member in Poland, this uncle, who passed away in the 1980s. He had been living in Radom, passing as a Pole. We stayed with him in Radom for a few weeks and then we again followed the front with my uncle, a horse, and a covered wagon loaded with boxes until we reached Kutno, a city near Zychlin where my father got an apartment as inheritance from an uncle who had been living in America for decades. In Zychlin, there was nothing left, so we stayed in Kutno, where we had that apartment, food, clothing, and school. I attended a Polish school there for the first time in my life.

I clearly remember the day the Germans surrendered. We still were fearful that the Germans would come back. That day, May 8 or 9, 1945 was one of the highlights of my life. I can remember it exactly. The whole populace was on its feet, soldiers shot their guns in the air. Everything was tremendously joyful and exuberant. We were in Kutno at the time. It was an event that all of Europe, and perhaps all of humanity, had been waiting for.

* * * *

Editor's note: In Kutno, Senek's father Henryk Rosenblum married a woman from Zychlin who had also survived the war. After crossing the border as refugees , the family settled in Germany. As a young man, Senek spent some time in the United States. He returned to Germany in the mid-1960s. Since then, he has been living in Munich, where he built a family and established a small business. His book of memoirs *Der Junge im Schrank: eine Kindheit im Krieg (The Boy in the Closet: a Childhood at War)* was published in 2009 by Verlag Btb Taschenbuch in Munich.

Images of the deportation of the Zychlin Jews, March 3 1942

[Not included in the original book]

Image source: Wikimedia Commons.

Image source: Wikimedia Commons.

Image source: Wikimedia Commons.

Image source: Wikimedia Commons.

Image source: Wikimedia Commons.

Image source: Wikimedia Commons.

Image source: Wikimedia Commons.

Image source: Wikimedia Commons.

Image source: Ghetto Fighters House.

Image source: USHMM.

Image source: Ghetto Fighters House.

Image source: USHMM.

Property of the Zychlin Jews, piled up in an open field after
their deportation. Image source: USHMM.

Burning the clothes left behind by the deported Jews.
Image source: USHMM.

List of Jews murdered on the day before deportation

[Not included in the original book]

Editors' note: The following list includes the names of 176 of the approximately 180-200 Jews who were murdered in Zychlin on the day before the liquidation of the ghetto and the deportation of its more than 3,000 remaining immates to Chełmno extermination camp. The list, which is part of a set of Zychlin documents and testimonies in the archives of the Polish Institute of National Memory (sygn. IPN BU 2448/634), was first published in the book *Zarys Historii Żydów Ziemi Kutnowskiej (Outline of the History of Jews in the Kutno Lands)*, edited by Karol Koszada, Elżbieta Świątkowska, and Bożena Gajewska, Kutno: TPZK, 2016, pp. 609-618. It is reproduced here by courtesy of the Society of Friends of the Kutno Region (Towarzystwo Przyjaciół Ziemi Kutnowskiej, TPZK).

A descriptive paragraph on top of the list reads: "On March 2, 1942 on the day before the liquidation of the Zychlin ghetto in Kutno district, the Schutzpolizei, with commander Albert Raschke at their head and policemen Herman König, Walter Modes, Wilhelm Bonicke and others shot 181 people of Jewish nationality. The bodies of the murdered were buried in the Jewish cemetery in Zychlin."

Last Name	First Name	Age	Occupation
Bander	Moszek	28	handlowiec (trader)
Bander	Hersz	32	handlowiec (trader)
Bander	Szlama	28	handlowiec (trader)
Bialek	Lajb	38	handlarz (tradesman)
Bialek	Ryfka	34	
Biederman	Moszek	38	handlarz (tradesman)
Biederman	Frejda	36	
Birnbaum	Josef	44	krawiec (tailor)
Birnbaum	Estera	42	
Blusztejn	Bluma	40	
Blusztejn	Szyja	43	kupiec (merchant)
Borensztajn	Abram	48	handlarz (tradesman)
Borensztajn	Jojna	44	
Borensztajn	Rywen	16	
Borensztajn	Sura	14	
Borensztajn	Bajla	12	
Borensztajn	Szmul	56	handlarz (tradesman)
Borensztajn	Joel	28	
Brajtsztajn	Hune	60	handlarz (tradesman)
Brajtsztajn	Rywka	60	

Last Name	First Name	Age	Occupation
Braun	Dawid	28	handlarz (tradesman)
Braun	Gitla	27	
Bryn	Berek	36	handlarz (tradesman)
Bryn	Gitla	28	
Bryn	Moszek	4	
Brzezinska	Estera	40	handlowiec (trader)
Caly	Mendel	43	krawiec (tailor)
Caly	Rifka	41	
Caly	Idel	6	
Centner	Hersz	44	robotnik (worker)
Centner	Sura	41	
Centner	Josef	37	
Centner	Dwojra	34	
Chalemska	Ruchla	40	handlowiec (trader)
Chalemska	Perla	60	handlowiec (trader)
Chudy	Fajwel	42	
Chudy	Chana	40	
Chudy	Gitla	12	
Dancygier	Rywen	24	handlarz (tradesman)
Dancygier	Lajb	36	czapnik (hatmaker)
Dancygier	Ryfla	34	
Dancygier	Hawa	28	
Dancygier	Moszek	58	czapnik (hatmaker)
Dancygier	Cywia	56	
Dancygier	Herszyk Majer	28	handlarz (tradesman)
Dancygier	Ruchla	34	
Dancygier	Cypra	28	handlarz (tradesman)
Dawidowicz	Wolek	46	handlarz (tradesman)
Dembinski	Chaim	42	handlarz (tradesman)
Dembinski	Hinda	40	
Dembinski	Sura	38	
Dembinski	Gitla	10	
Dembinski	Szulim	40	handlarz (tradesman)
Gelman	Juda	42	ogrodnik (gardener)
Gelman	Mariem	36	ogrodnik (gardener)
Gelman	Rojza	14	
Gelman	Hinda	16	
Goldman	Gitla	38	
Goldman	Hawa	8	
Goldman	Cypra	12	
Gostynski	Aron	65	szewc (shoemaker)
Gostynski	Sura	62	
Gotelf	Fajga	45	handlarz (tradesman)

Last Name	First Name	Age	Occupation
Gotelf	Ruchla	24	
Hamburg	Sender	46	handlarz (tradesman)
Hamburg	Bajla	44	
Herbolin	Natan	56	handlarz (tradesman)
Jastrzembski	Jakub	41	handlarz (tradesman)
Kelmer	Hersz	40	rzeznik (butcher)
Kelmer	Dwojra	38	
Kelmer	Laja	8	
Kelmer	Cywia	6	
Kirszbaum	Janas	30	rzeznik (butcher)
Kirszbaum	Estera	28	
Kirszbaum	Fana	8	
Kirszbaum	Szmul	6	
Kleczerwski	Dawid	30	handlowiec (trader)
Kleczerwski	Nysym	28	handlowiec (trader)
Kleczerwski	Gitla	28	handlowiec (trader)
Klinger	Hersz	39	szewc (shoemaker)
Klinger	Sara	34	
Kolski	Hejnoch	28	
Kolski	Ryfka	27	
Kolski	Beniamin	2	
Kuwent	Nuchem	38	szewc (shoemaker)
Lajzerowicz	Juda	39	kupiec (merchant)
Lajzerowicz	Hinda	37	
Laskowski	Henoch	40	krawiec (tailor)
Laskowski	Gotla	38	
Lejzerowicz	Froim	56	handlarz (tradesman)
Lejzerowicz	Tauba	54	handlarz (tradesman)
Libfrajnd	Mindla	34	handlarka (tradeswoman)
Libfrajnd	Estera	28	handlarka (tradeswoman)
Libfrajnd	Lajzer	62	kupiec (merchant)
Libfrajnd	Mindel	34	
Libfrajnd	Moszek	8	
Lipszyc	Dwojra	38	handlarz (tradesman)
Lipszyc	Laja	30	
Lipszyc	Jeol	18	
Listek	Sura	32	
Listek	Ruchla	8	
Mastbaum	Dawid	38	krawiec (tailor)
Mastbaum	Dwojra	36	
Mastbaum	Joel	10	
Michalowicz	Godel	44	krawiec (tailor)
Michalowicz	Ryfka	40	

Last Name	First Name	Age	Occupation
Michalska	Fajga	40	szewc (shoemaker)
Michalska	Bajla	14	
Michalska	Jenta	10	
Miedzynski	Fiszel	70	nauczyciel (teacher)
Miedzynski	Gitla	67	
Morgentaler	Lajzer	42	handlarz (tradesman)
Moszkowicz	Juda	40	krawiec (tailor)
Moszkowicz	Gitla	38	
Moszkowicz	Hidna	8	
Nyselmaum	Hersz	70	handlarz (tradesman)
Oberman	Josef	36	handlarz (tradesman)
Oberman	Aron	52	handlarz (tradesman)
Oberman	Genendla	56	
Oberman	Hinda	28	
Pancer	Gitla	28	
Pancer	Moszek	40	rzeznik (butcher)
Pancer	Fajwel	6	
Plocki	Dawid	60	handlarz (tradesman)
Plocki	Cypra	60	
Rajch	Estera	62	handlarz (tradesman)
Rejdenberg	Nita	50	handlarka (tradeswoman)
Rejdenberg	Sura	40	
Rosenkranc	Abram	24	handlarz (tradesman)
Rosenkranc	Sura	22	
Rosenkranc	Gitla	30	
Rozenberg	Altek	45	piekarz (baker)
Rozenberg	Laja	44	
Rozenberg	Hersz	26	
Rozenberg	Nusyn	22	
Rozendorf	Majer	56	handlarz (tradesman)
Rozendorf	Blima	54	
Rozendorf	Chana	30	
Rozendorf	Herszon	24	
Rozengarten	Szyja	68	nauczyciel (teacher)
Rozengarten	Zlata	26	
Rubin	Icek	48	kupiek (merchant)
Rubin	Estera	44	
Rubin	Godel	20	
Sieradzki	Fajwel	46	rzeznik (butcher)
Sieradzki	Sara	44	
Sieradzki	Laja	18	
Sloma	Abram	50	handlarz (tradesman)
Szanowski	Izrael	40	szewc (shoemaker)

Last Name	First Name	Age	Occupation
Szanowski	Hana	30	
Szanowski	Mindla	15	
Szczygiel	Szmul	44	rzeznik (butcher)
Szczygiel	Gitla	40	
Szczygiel	Ruda	12	
Szczygiel	Hersz	8	
Szwarc	Fiszel	28	rzeznik (butcher)
Szwarc	Hejwet	27	
Szwarc	Gitla	20	
Szwarc	Cywja	18	
Toronczyk	Hejnoch	39	handlarz (tradesman)
Toronczyk	Mariem	37	
Toronczyk	Hinda	8	
Urbach	Mendel	41	handlarz (tradesman)
Zajfert	Josek	40	kamasznik (bootmaker)
Zajfert	Ruchla	41	
Zajfert	Szmul	6	
Zlotnik	Chaim	38	zegarmistrz (watchmaker)
Zolna	Frajda	39	
Zolna	Szyja	18	handlarz (tradesman)
Zygielman	Hersz	48	krawiec (tailor)
Zygielman	Jenta	44	
Zygier	Hejnoch	28	electromonter (electrician)
Zygier	Hude	22	ogrodnik (gardener)
Zyk	Aron	40	handlarz (tradesman)
Zyk	Mariem	36	
Zyk	Cypra	2	

Zychliners in Yad Vashem's database of victims

[Not included in the original book]

Editors' note: The names of individuals in Yad Vashem's central database of Shoah victims are compiled from various sources, including the lists published in the memorial books of the towns. After cross-referencing the names of Zychliners in Yad Vashem's database with the list of martyrs that appeared in the original Zychlin book (see pages 210-228 of this English edition), we removed from the list below the names of the individuals who were already included in the book's list. Please be aware that the list may contain errors or oversights. We apologize for any such inaccuracies.

The keys for the acronyms in the "Source" and "Fate" columns are located at the end of the list.

Last Name	First Name	Birth Year	Place of Residence	Source	Fate
Abramson	Adela	1893	Grodzisk, Poland	PT	M
Alter	Avraham Morchaj	1885	Zychlin, Poland	PT	M
Alter	Avraham Mordcha	1874	Zychlin, Poland	PT	M
Alter	Avraham Mordekhai	1872	Warszawa, Poland	PP	M
Alter	Ewa Khava Eva	1914	Zychlin, Poland	PT	M
Alter	Icchak Yitzkhak	1915	Zychlin, Poland	PT	M
Alter	Ichak Mair Yitzkhak	1880	Zychlin, Poland	PT	M
Altman	Gustaw Gustav	1886	Wloclawek, Poland	PT	M
Altman	Gustaw Gustav	1886	Wloclawek, Poland	PT	M
Altman	Hana Khana	1886	Wloclawek, Poland	PT	M
Apel	Ester		Zychlin, Poland	PT	M
Apel	Hershel		Zychlin, Poland	PT	M
Apel	Perla	1902	Poland	PT	M
Aronowicz	Chana	1888	Zychlin, Poland	LDF	M
Aronowicz Aronovitz	Rivka	1890	Lodz, Poland	PT	M
Aronowicz Aronovitz	Ryfka Rivka	1902	Lodz, Poland	PT	M
Asante Asanta	Chaja Khaia	1904	Drobin, Poland	PT	M
Aulshtain Olshtein	Yoel		Zychlin, Poland	PT	M
Babe Fuks	Lazer Leizer Eliezer	1880	Zychlin, Poland	PT	M
Babe Fuks	Rita	1909	Zychlin, Poland	PT	M
Babe Fuks	Rywka Rivka	1880	Zychlin, Poland	PT	M
Bajbok Beibuk	Bela Sara Bilha	1913	Zichlin, Poland	PT	M
Bajbok Beibuk	First name unknown	1939	Zichlin, Poland	PT	M
Bajser	Fiszel	1923	Zychlin, Poland	PP	M
Bajzer Biser	Juda Yehuda	1893	Lodz, Poland	PT	M
Bander	Bajla	1914	Wloclawek, Poland	PT	M

Last Name	First Name	Birth Year	Place of Residence	Source	Fate
Bander Bender	Bela	1916	Wloclawek, Poland	PT	M
Bander Bender	Henius		Wloclawek, Poland	PT	M
Baran	Machla Makhla		Zychlin, Poland	PT	M
Baran	Makhla		Zychlin, Poland	PT	M
Baran	Zanvel		Zychlin, Poland	PT	M
Baran	Zeinwel Zainvel	1853	Zychlin, Poland	PT	M
Baum	Jente Iente	1900	Lowicz, Poland	PT	M
Baumelgrin	Rakhel Lea	1900	Zakhlin, Poland	PT	M
Bazora Bzora	Avraham		Zychlin, Poland	PT	M
Bazora Bzora	Chaim Khaim David		Zychlin, Poland	PT	M
Bazora Bzora	Shalom		Zychlin, Poland	PT	M
Bazora Bzora	Yashke Yiska		Zychlin, Poland	PT	M
Beigelmakher	Sheindil	1897	Sosnowiec, Poland	PT	M
Bekerman	Dwora Dvora	1881	Warszawa, Poland	PT	M
Bender	Moishe Moshe	1916	Wloclawek, Poland	PT	M
Bender	Moshe	1896	Zychlin, Poland	PT	M
Bender	Sara	1898	Zychlin, Poland	PT	M
Benzel	Michael Mikhael	1907	Zychlin, Poland	PT	M
Benzel	Yosef Tzvi		Zychlin, Poland	PT	M
Bercholc	Chana Rywka	1930		LLG	PM
Bercholc	Fajga	1903		LLG	PM
Bercholc	Rachela	1931		LLG	PM
Berecz	Rejla	1909	Zychlin, Poland	LDF	M
Berkowicz Berkovitz	Zisel Zysl	1888	Zgierz, Poland	PT	M
Berman	Yehuda Arie	1880	Zychlin, Poland	PT	M
Berman	Fraida Rivka	1882	Zychlin, Poland	PT	M
Berman	Juda Laib	1880	Zychlin, Poland	PT	M
Bialik	Arje Arie	1908	Zychlin, Poland	PT	M
Bialik	Natan	1880	Zychlin, Poland	PT	M
Bicz	Aharon		Zychlin, Poland	PT	M
Bicz	Dora	1900	Zachlin, Poland	PT	M
Bicz	Ichyel Yekhiel	1899	Zychlin, Poland	PT	M
Bicz	Malka		Zychlin, Poland	PT	M
Bicz	Rakhel		Zychlin, Poland	PT	M
Bicz Bich	Eliezer	1908	Zychlin, Poland	PT	M
Bicz Bich	Haja Khaia Sara	1876	Zychlin, Poland	PT	M
Bicz Bich	Menachem	1924	Zychlin, Poland	PT	M
Bicz Bich	Shmuel Samuel	1900	Zychlin, Poland	PT	M
Biderman	Dora	1928	Zychlin, Poland	PT	M
Biderman	Dvora		Zychlin, Poland	PT	M
Biderman	Frania	1888	Zychlin, Poland	PT	M
Biderman	Franka	1900	Zychlin, Poland	PT	M
Biderman	Halinka	1928	Zichlin, Poland	PT	M

Last Name	First Name	Birth Year	Place of Residence	Source	Fate
Biderman	Jakob Yaakov	1891	Sochaczew, Poland	PT	M
Biderman	Moshe	1895	Zychlin, Poland	PT	M
Biderman	Moshe	1886	Zychlin, Poland	PT	M
Biderman	Moyzesz		Zychlin, Poland	PT	M
Biderman	Sewek	1931	Zychlin, Poland	PT	M
Biderman	Shmuel		Zychlin, Poland	PT	M
Biderman	Shmuel Sevek	1926	Zhikhlin, Poland	PT	M
Biderman	Szyja Yehoshua	1894	Berlin, Germany	PT	M
Biderman	Yehoshua Shiye	1901	Berlin, Germany	PT	M
Bielawska	Nacha Roza	1897	Lowicz, Poland	PT (d)	M
Bindet	Frajdl Freidel	1883	Kiernozia, Poland	PT	M
Blushtein	Yehosha Yehoshua		Zychlin, Poland	PT	M
Blushtin Blaushtein			Zychlin, Poland	PT	M
Blushtin Blushtein	Alta Alte		Zychlin, Poland	PT	M
Bock Buk	Miriam	1923	Warszawa, Poland	PT	M
Bock Buk	Motel	1920	Warsaw, Poland	PT	M
Bock Buk	Yaakov	1914	Warszawa, Poland	PT	M
Boim	Hava Khava		Zychlin, Poland	PT	M
Boim Opatovski Baum	Chaja Khaia	1895	Radom, Poland	PT	M
Bol Bul	Fela	1922	Zychlin, Poland	PT	M
Bol Bul	Jacob Yaakov	1890	Zychlin, Poland	PT	M
Bol Bul	Riva	1895	Zychlin, Poland	PT	M
Bomba	David		Zychlin, Poland	PT	M
Bomba	Gershon Gerson		Zychlin, Poland	PT	M
Bomba	Hamol Khamul		Zychlin, Poland	PT	M
Bomba	Moshe		Zychlin, Poland	PT	M
Bomba	Shalom		Zychlin, Poland	PT	M
Borenstein Bornshtein	Jakob Yaakov	1860	Lipno, Poland	PT	M
Borensztajn	Jacob Lajb	1898	Kutno, Poland	PT (d)	M
Borensztein	Fajwel		Zychlin, Poland	T	M
Bornshtein	Avraham	1860	Zychlin, Poland	PT	M
Bornshtein	Dina	1860	Warsaw, Poland	PT	M
Bornstein	Chaim	1888	Zychlin, Poland	PP	M
Bornstein Bornshtein	Yaakov	1856	Lipno, Poland	PT	M
Bornstein Bornshtein	Yaakow Yaakov	1870	Lipno, Poland	PT	M
Bornsztain Bornshtein	Chaia Tzipora	1907	Zychlin, Poland	PT	M
Bornsztain Bornshtein	Ester	1935	Zychlin, Poland	PT	M
Bornsztain Bornshtein	Raizl Lea Reizl	1903	Zychlin, Poland	PT	M
Bornsztajn	Chaim Szoel	1900	Kutno, Poland	PT (d)	M
Borovik Boroviak	Ester	1890	Zychlin, Poland	PT	M
Borowiak Borovik	Avraham		Zychlin, Poland	PT	M
Borowiak Borovik	Khalusha		Zychlin, Poland	PT	M
Borowiak Borovik	Nisym Nisim	1894	Zychlin, Poland	PT	M

Last Name	First Name	Birth Year	Place of Residence	Source	Fate
Borowiak Borovik Boroviak	Brana	1910	Zychlin, Poland	PT	M
Borowski	Mendel	1921	Wittenberg, Germany	LMG	M
Brajtsztajn Britshtein	Chaja Sara Khaia	1889	Glowno, Poland	PT	M
Braun	Ela		Lodz, Poland	PT	M
Braun	Glika		Rypin, Poland	PT	M
Breitstein Breitshtein	Sara Khaia	1889	Glowno, Poland	PT	M
Bretstein Bretshtein	Jisrael Yisrael	1889	Lodz, Poland	PT	M
Bronet	Ruchel Leah	1894	Warsaw, Poland	PT	M
Bronowicz	Tauba Laja	1912		LLG	M
Brzezowska Bzhezhovski	Cyrl	1894	Sochaczew, Poland	PT	M
Brzezowski Bzhozhovski	Tzira		Sochaczew, Poland	PT	M
Bull	Avraham	1887	Zychlin, Poland	PT (d)	M
Bull	Beila	1925	Zychlin, Poland	PT (d)	M
Bull	Dvora		Zychlin, Poland	PT (d)	M
Bull	Mania	1916	Zychlin, Poland	PT (d)	M
Bull	Nekhama	1934	Zychlin, Poland	PT (d)	M
Bull	Rakhel	1930	Zychlin, Poland	PT (d)	M
Bull	Yaakov	1920	Zychlin, Poland	PT (d)	M
Bull	Yeshiyah	1936	Zychlin, Poland	PT (d)	M
Bull	Yitzkhak	1910	Zychlin, Poland	PT (d)	M
Bull Bolel	Beila	1924	Zychlin, Poland	PT	M
Bull Bolel	Icchak Yitzkhak	1913	Zychlin, Poland	PT	M
Bull Bolel	Mirjam Miriam	1918	Zychlin, Poland	PT	M
Bull Bolel	Mosze Moshe	1889	Zychlin, Poland	PT	M
Bull Bolel	Roda	1901	Zychlin, Poland	PT	M
Burenstein Bornshtein	Dina	1877	Warsaw, Poland	PT	M
Burinsztajn Burinshtein	Rejzel Lea Reizl	1918	Zawiercie, Poland	PT	M
Burnstein Bornshtein	Abraham Avraham	1875	Warsaw, Poland	PT	M
Burshtin	Reizel	1899	Woclawek, Poland	PT	M
Bursztein Burshtin	Reizla Reizel	1900	Wloclawek, Poland	PT	M
Buttler Butler	Szajne Sheinia	1882	Zychlin, Poland	PT	M
Bzura Bzora	Avraham		Zychlin, Poland	PT	M
Bzura Bzora	Batia Roiza		Zychlin, Poland	PT	M
Bzura Bzora	Frania Freida	1916	Zychlin, Poland	PT	M
Bzura Bzora	Khaim David		Zychlin, Poland	PT	M
Bzura Bzora	Matatiahu		Zychlin, Poland	PT	M
Bzura Bzora	Perel		Zychlin, Poland	PT	M
Bzura Bzora	Szalom Shalom	1885	Zychlin, Poland	PT	M
Cala	Pinkus	1885	Zychlin, Poland	LMA	M
Center Tzentner	Bila	1924	Zychlin, Poland	PT	M
Center Tzentner	Mojsze Moshe Tzvi	1900	Zychlin, Poland	PT	M
Centner Tzentner	Avraham		Zychlin, Poland	PT	M
Centner Tzentner	Iechok Yitzkhak	1920	Zychlin, Poland	PT	M

Last Name	First Name	Birth Year	Place of Residence	Source	Fate
Centner Tzentner	Jakob Yaakov	1901	Zachlin, Poland	PT	M
Centner Tzentner	Khudes		Zychlin, Poland	PT	M
Centner Tzentner	Mendel		Zychlin, Poland	PT	M
Centner Tzentner	Mendl Mendel	1903	Zychlin, Poland	PT	M
Centner Tzentner	Moshe		Zychlin, Poland	PT	M
Centner Tzentner	Pesa	1921	Zychlin, Poland	PT	M
Centner Tzentner	Rywka Rivka	1901	Zychlin, Poland	PT	M
Centner Tzentner	Shela		Zychlin, Poland	PT	M
Centner Tzentner	Shiye		Zychlin, Poland	PT	M
Centner Tzentner	Toba Tova	1907	Zychlin, Poland	PT	M
Centner Tzentner	Wolf Volf	1922	Zychlin, Poland	PT	M
Charfic Kharpak			Zychlin, Poland	PT	M
Chazen Khazan	Alte Nekha	1883	Wloclawek, Poland	PT	M
Chelminski Jakubowicz	Ester Bluma	1908	Kutno, Poland	PT	M
Chelminski Khelminski	Frajdl Freidel	1912	Zychlin, Poland	PT	M
Chelminski Khelminski	Jenta Yenta	1910	Zychlin, Poland	PT	M
Chelminski Khelminski	Lejbl Leibel	1880	Zychlin, Poland	PT	M
Chelmski Khelemski	Josef Yosef	1895	Zychlin, Poland	PT	M
Chelmski Khelemski	Mosze Moshe	1882	Zychlin, Poland	PT	M
Chelmski Khelemski	Perl Perel	1880	Zychlin, Poland	PT	M
Chelmski Khelemski	Riwka Rivka	1907	Zychlin, Poland	PT	M
Chelmski Khelemski	Yosef	1905	Zychlin, Poland	PT	M
Chlminski Khelminski	Faiga Golda Feiga	1885	Zychlin, Poland	PT	M
Chohen Kohen	Arie Yosef		Zychlin, Poland	PT	M
Chohen Kohen	Ester Dina		Zychlin, Poland	PT	M
Chohen Kohen	Khava Khana		Zychlin, Poland	PT	M
Chohen Kohen	Sara Miriam		Zychlin, Poland	PT	M
Chohen Kohen	Shmuel		Zychlin, Poland	PT	M
Chohen Kohen	Yehoshua		Zychlin, Poland	PT	M
Chohen Kohen	Yekhiel		Zychlin, Poland	PT	M
Chrzastowski	Ester		Zychlin, Poland	PT	M
Chrzastowski	Ester	1910	Wloclawek, Poland	PT	M
Chszastowski	Benus	1937	Wloclawek, Poland	PT	M
Chszastowski Chrzastowski	Benush Benus	1937	Wloclawek, Poland	PT	M
Chszastowski Chrzastowski	Esther Ester		Wloclawek, Poland	PT	M
Chudy Khudi	Hana Khana	1880	Zychlin, Poland	PT	M
Ciepelinski Tzipelinski	Natan	1919	Radzyn, Poland	PT	M
Ciepelinski Tzipelinski	Seindl Sheindl	1917	Miedzyrzec, Poland	PT	M
Cukier Tzuker	Lejb Leib	1905	Ciechocinek, Poland	PT	M
Cwajghaft Tzveighaft	Gutman	1889	Lodz, Poland	PT	M
Cwajghaft Tzvighaft	Gutman	1887	Lodz, Poland	PT	M
Cwajghaft Tzvighaft	Israel Yehiel Yitzhak	1894	Lodz, Poland	PT	M
Cwajghaft Tzvighaft	Yaakov David	1892	Lodz, Poland	PT	M

Last Name	First Name	Birth Year	Place of Residence	Source	Fate
Cwajghaft Tzvighaft	Yonas Ionas	1866	Lodz, Poland	PT	M
Czastkowski Chonstkovski	Khaia Rivka		Lipno, Poland	PT	M
Czastkowski Chonstkovski	Raca Ratza	1890	Lipno, Poland	PT	M
Dambinsky Dembinski	Chaim Khaim	1899	Zychlin, Poland	PT	M
Dambinsky Dembinski	Chana Khana	1909	Zyrardow, Poland	PT	M
Dambinsky Dembinski	Nekhama		Zychlin, Poland	PT	M
Dambinsky Dembinski	Yokheved	1912	Zychlin, Poland	PT	M
Dambinsky Dembinski	Zacharia	1906	Zychlin, Poland	PT	M
Davidovits Davidovitz	Mordekhai		Zychlin, Poland	PT	M
Davidovits Davidovitz	Zelda		Zychlin, Poland	PT	M
Dawidowitsch Davidovitz	Rachel Rakhel		Dabie, Poland	PT	M
Dawidowitz Davidovitz	Rachel Matl		Dabie, Poland	PT	M
Degenszajn	Zeev Wolf	1893	Skierniewice, Poland	PT	M
Dimand Diamant	Moshe Yekhiel	1900	Lodz, Poland	PT	M
Ditman	Malka	1904	Zychlin, Poland	PT	M
Ditman	Yekhiel Khil Hil	1900	Zychlin, Poland	PT	M
Dorn	Mair Meir	1888	Bruxelles, Belgium	PT	M
Dorn	Majer	1894	Zychlin, Poland	DL	M
Dziedzic	Majer	1878	Zychlin, Poland	PP	M
Elberg	Cypora Tzipora	1910	Kutno, Poland	PT	M
Elberg	Elja Alia Meir	1905	Kutno, Poland	PT	M
Elberg	Jochewet Yokheved	1905	Gostynin, Poland	PT	M
Elberg	Krusa	1912	Kutno, Poland	PT	M
Elechenowicz Elekhnovitz	Jozef Yosef	1887	Lodz, Poland	PT	M
Elensztejn	Nysan	1897	Zychlin, Poland	LDF	M
Eliash	Lea		Zychlin, Poland	PT	M
Eliash	Sara		Zychlin, Poland	PT	M
Eliash	Yitzkhak		Zychlin, Poland	PT	M
Elshtein	Nekha		Zychlin, Poland	PT	M
Elzner	Jankel	1902	Zychlin, Poland	LMA	M
Erdberg	Chaim	1880		LLG	M
Erdberg	Chawa	1912		LLG	PM
Erdberg	Dwojra	1880		LLG	PM
Erdberg	Pesa	1916		LLG	PM
Ettinger	Mariem	1893	Warsza, Poland	PT	M
Fabrikant	Chaja Khaia	1892	Antwerpen, Belgium	PT	M
Fabrykant Fabrikant	Khaia Rivka	1892	Lyon, France	PT	M
Fajbuszak Feibushak	Ciwia Tzipa	1883	Brzezin,	PT	M
Flakser	Jenta Yenta	1891	Wloclawek, Poland	PT	M
Flaster	Estera	1886	Krosniewice, Poland	PT	M
Flint	Bela		Zychlin, Poland	PT	M
Flint	Ester		Zichlin, Poland	PT	M
Flint	Ester		Zechlin, Poland	PT	M

Last Name	First Name	Birth Year	Place of Residence	Source	Fate
Flint	Mordekhai		Zechlin, Poland	PT	M
Flint	Mosze Moshe	1902	Zechlin, Poland	PT	M
Frenkel	Mair Meir	1905	Sanniki, Poland	PT	M
Fridman	Yehuda		Zychlin, Poland	PT	M
Friedman	Leah	1913	Lodz, Poland	PT	M
Friedmann Fridman	Michael Mikhael	1897	Bolimow, Poland	PT	M
Frydman	Lajb	1905	Lodz, Poland	PP	M
Gajer Geier	Dawid David	1890	Kutno, Poland	PT	M
Gala	Pinkhas Pinkus	1855	Zychlin, Poland	LDF	M
Gasierowski Gonsherovski	Rachel Malka		Wloclawek, Poland	PT	M
Gecel Getzel	Dina	1862	Zychlin, Poland	PT	M
Gecel Getzel	Pinchas Pinkhas	1892	Zychlin, Poland	PT	M
Geizler	Yehudit		Wloclawek, Poland	PT	M
Gelbard	Jeusze Yehoshua	1920	Lodz, Poland	PT	M
Gelbart	Hersz Lajb	1892	Lodz, Poland	PT	M
Gelbart	Jda Ita	1907	Zychlin, Poland	PT	M
Gelbart	Malka	1887	Gombin, Poland	PT	M
Gelbart	Szamaj Shamai	1900	Zychlin, Poland	PT	M
Gelbert	Fraida		Zychlin, Poland	PP	M
Gelbert Gelbart	Boroch Barukh	1882	Dobrin, Poland	PT	M
Gelbert Gelbart	Zisha	1884	Plock, Poland	PT	M
Gelman	First name unknown		Zichlin, Poland	PP	M
Gelman	Freda Freida	1880	Zychlin, Poland	PT	M
Gelman	Israel Yisrael	1880	Zychlin, Poland	PT	M
Gelman	Rachel Rakhel	1920	Zychlin, Poland	PT	M
Gelman	Radja		Zichlin, Poland	PP	M
Gelman	Rivka		Zichlin, Poland	PP	M
Gelman	Yisroel		Zichlin, Poland	PP	M
Gersht	Ioselei		Zychlin, Poland	LMYB	M
Gerszt Gersht	Hersz Moshe	1910	Zychlin, Poland	PT	M
Gerszt Gersht	Sheina Yiska	1909	Zychlin, Poland	PT	M
Gerszt Gersht	Sheva		Zychlin, Poland	PT	M
Gerszt Gersht	Yitzkhak		Zychlin, Poland	PT	M
Getzel	Chawa Khava	1895	Zychlin, Poland	PT	M
Glater	Rifka	1903	Zychlin, Poland	DL	M
Glewinski Glevinski	Jakob Yaakov Leib	1883	Zichlin, Poland	PT	M
Glycensztein Glitzenshtein	Mose Moshe	1898	Lodz, Poland	PT	M
Glycensztein Glitzenshtein	Shoshana Rozia	1903	Zychlin, Poland	PT	M
Goldberg	Avigdor		Lodz, Poland	PT	M
Goldberg	Chana Ruchel		Kutno, Poland	PT	M
Goldberg	David		Zechlin, Poland	PT	M
Goldberg	Dvora		Lodz, Poland	PT	M
Goldberg	Ezryl Azril	1878	Zechlin, Poland	PT	M

Last Name	First Name	Birth Year	Place of Residence	Source	Fate
Goldberg	Hinda		Lodz, Poland	PT	M
Goldberg	Izrael Yisrael	1915	Zachlin, Poland	PT	M
Goldberg	Jakob Yaakov	1910	Zechlin, Poland	PT	M
Goldberg	Lea	1880	Zachlin, Poland	PT	M
Goldberg	Leibush		Lodz, Poland	PT	M
Goldberg	Moses Moshe	1890	Zychlin, Poland	PT	M
Goldberg	Noakh		Lodz, Poland	PT	M
Goldberg	Rivka Roiza	1899	Konstantinov, Poland	PT	M
Goldberg	Ryvka Rivka	1913	Zachlin, Poland	PT	M
Goldberg	Sara	1912	Zachlin, Poland	PT	M
Goldberg	Sara	1912	Zychlin, Poland	PT	M
Goldberg	Tuvia		Lodz, Poland	PT	M
Goldberg	Uziel		Zychlin, Poland	PT	M
Goldberg	Volf	1912	Zechlin, Poland	PT	M
Goldberg	Wolf Volf	1912	Zechlin, Poland	PT	M
Goldberg	Yehiel Yekhiel	1929	Zychlin, Poland	PT	M
Goldberg	Yehudit Dvora	1894	Leczyca, Poland	PT	M
Goldberg	Yosef	1893	Lodz, Poland	PT	M
Goldfarb	Avraham		Zichlin, Poland	PT	M
Goldfarb	Avraham	1932	Zychlin, Poland	PT (d)	M
Goldfarb	David Volf	1923	Zychlin, Poland	PT (d)	M
Goldfarb	Moshe	1922	Zychlin, Poland	PT (d)	M
Goldfarb	Rivka	1892	Zychlin, Poland	PT (d)	M
Goldfarb	Riwka Rivka	1890	Zychlin, Poland	PT	M
Goldfarb	Yaakov	1935	Zichlin, Poland	PT (d)	M
Goldman	Gedalja Gdaliyahu		Zachlin, Poland	PT	M
Goldman	Roza		Gombin, Poland	PT	M
Goldnberg Goldenberg	Jojniy Yona Yonatan	1926	Kostantin, Poland	PT	M
Goldsztajn	Izrael	1907	Zychlin, Poland	PP	M
Goldsztajn Goldshtein	Ester	1910	Zachlin, Poland	PT	M
Gomska	Chajem Khaim	1904	Dobrzyn, Poland	PT	M
Gomska	Gitel	1902	Dobzin, Poland	PT	M
Gomska	Mordechai	1893	Dobzhin, Poland	PT	M
Gomska	Noach Noakh	1882	Dubzyn, Poland	PT	M
Gonsierowska Gonsherovsk	Rahel Malka Rakhel		Wloclawek, Poland	PT	M
Gostynski Gostinski	Mania	1882	Tomaszow, Poland	PT	M
Goteiner	Fishl Shlomo	1885	Lodz, Poland	PT	M
Gothelf	Golda	1897	Anvers, Belgium	PP	M
Gothelf	Laja	1897	Zychlin, Poland	LDF	M
Granek	Faja	1912	Zychlin, Poland	LDF	M
Granitz	Chana Khana	1897	Zychlin, Poland	PT	M
Grinholtz Levkovitz	Ite Sara Yuta	1906	Lodz, Poland	PT	M
Grynberg Grinberg	Chana Khana	1880	Sochaczew, Poland	PT	M

Last Name	First Name	Birth Year	Place of Residence	Source	Fate
Gurka	Izrael	1903	Zychlin, Poland	LMN	M
Gurka	Moshe Mozes	1896	Zychlin, Poland	LMN	M
Hacohen	Khava		Zichlin, Poland	PT	M
Hacohen	Mordekhai Kiva	1870	Zichlin, Poland	PT	M
Hajak Kheiek	Ester		Zychlin, Poland	PT	M
Halter	Jehuda Yehuda Iudl	1910	Kolo, Poland	PT	M
Hamburg	Aleksander	1894	Zychlin, Poland	PT	M
Hamburg	Beile		Zychlin, Poland	PT	M
Hamburg	Bela	1895	Zychlin, Poland	PT	M
Hamburg	Bela	1891	Zychlin, Poland	PT	M
Hamburg	Gutl		Zychlin, Poland	PT	M
Hamburg	Henrik	1901	Sosnowiec, Poland	PT	M
Hamburg	Jakev Yaakov		Zychlin, Poland	PT	M
Hamburg	Jakob Yaakov	1890	Zychlin, Poland	PT	M
Hamburg	Khana Bluma	1910	Zychlin, Poland	PT	M
Hamburg	Rakhel		Zychlin, Poland	PT	M
Hamburg	Sender	1889	Zychlin, Poland	PT	M
Hamburg	Yaakov	1886	Zychlin, Poland	PT	M
Hamburg	Yisrael	1900	Dąbrowa, Poland	PT	M
Hamer	Dvora	1912	Warszawa, Poland	PT	M
Helcner Heltzner	Idl Jidel Pavel	1898	Zachlin, Poland	PT	M
Helmer	Arie	1903	Zychlin, Poland	PT	M
Helmer	Avraham Moshe	1888	Lodz, Poland	PT	M
Helmer	Avraham Moshe	1893	Lodz, Poland	PT	M
Helmer	Batia	1860	Wloclawek, Poland	PT	M
Helmer	Chaja Khaia		Zychlin, Poland	PT	M
Helmer	Ester	1876	Zichlin, Poland	PT	M
Helmer	Feiga Feige	1918	Zichlin, Poland	PT	M
Helmer	Helen	1930	Zichlin, Poland	PT	M
Helmer	Jakob	1885	Wloclawek, Poland	PT	M
Helmer	Jenta Yenta	1904	Zechlin, Poland	PT	M
Helmer	Jsua Yehoshua	1904	Zichlin, Poland	PT	M
Helmer	Michael Mekhael	1902	Zichlin, Poland	PT	M
Helmer	Noakh	1886	Zichlin, Poland	PT	M
Helmer	Slomo Shlomo Leib	1897	Zichlin, Poland	PT	M
Helmer	Sol	1906	Lowicz, Poland	PT	M
Helmer	Tova	1887	Zichlin, Poland	PT	M
Hendeles	Bunim	1915	Zychlin, Poland	PT	M
Hendeles	Masha Moshe	1887	Zychlin, Poland	PT	M
Hendeles	Nachum Nakhum	1885	Zychlin, Poland	PT	M
Hermelin	Elimelic Elimelekh	1912	Zachlin, Poland	PT	M
Herszkowier Korn		1916	Zychlin, Poland	LDF	M
Hodes			Zichlin, Poland	PT	M

Last Name	First Name	Birth Year	Place of Residence	Source	Fate
Hoffman Hofman	Ester	1934	Dabrowice, Poland	PT	M
Hoffman Hofman	Ita	1922	Dabrowice, Poland	PT	M
Hoffman Hofman	Jenta Bina	1896	Dabrowice, Poland	PT	M
Hoffman Hofman	Mendel		Dabrowice, Poland	PT	M
Hoffman Hofman	Zacharie Zakharia	1890	Dabrowice, Poland	PT	M
Holcman Holtzman	Bela	1894	Zychlin, Poland	PT	M
Holcman Holtzman	Bina	1931	Zychlin, Poland	PT	M
Holcman Holtzman	Bina	1931	Zychlin, Poland	PT	M
Holcman Holtzman	Heniek	1925	Zychlin, Poland	PT	M
Holcman Holtzman	Henio	1925	Zychlin, Poland	PT	M
Holcman Holtzman	Leib Leon	1898	Zychlin, Poland	PT	M
Holzman Holtzman	Haja Khaia Sara	1905	Gabin, Poland	PT	M
Holzman Holtzman	Lea		Gombin, Poland	PT	M
Honig	Riwka Rivka	1900	Lodz, Poland	PT	M
Hordes	Moshe	1892	Zychlin, Poland	PT	M
Hudes	First name unknown		Lodz, Poland	PT	M
Hudes	First name unknown		Zychlin, Poland	PT	M
Hudes	Natan		Lodz, Poland	PT	M
Iashchemski	Khaim		Zychlin, Poland	PT	M
Ickoviz Itzkovitz	Rosa Roza	1895	Zychlin, Poland	PT	M
Ignazian	Dawid Moisze			PP	M
Ignazian	Dawid Mojsze			PP	KMS
Infeld	Rywka Rivka	1880	Lodz, Poland	PT	M
Itzkovich Itzkovitz	Pinkhas		Zychlin, Poland	PT	M
Itzkovich Itzkovitz	Roza Shoshana		Zychlin, Poland	PT	M
Jackubowicz Yakubovitz	Shoya Yeshayahu	1891	Zachlin, Poland	PT	M
Jakobowicz Yakubovitz	Frida	1926	Zychlin, Poland	PT	M
Jakobowicz Yakubovitz	Frida		Zychlin, Poland	PT	M
Jakobowicz Yakubovitz	Yehuda	1928	Zychlin, Poland	PT	M
Jakobowicz Yakubovitz	Yehuda		Zychlin, Poland	PT	M
Jakobowicz Yakubovitz	Yekhiel Meir	1895	Warszawa, Poland	PT	M
Jakobowicz Yakubovitz	Yitzkhak	1890	Zychlin, Poland	PT	M
Jakobowicz Yakubovitz	Yitzkhak	1890	Zychlin, Poland	PT	M
Jakoubowski	Maurice	1901	Zychlin, Poland	LMA	M
Jakubovicz Yakubovitz	Moszek Moshe	1880	Sochaczew, Poland	PT	M
Jakubowicz	Fajga	1917	Radom, Poland	LRG	PM
Jakubowicz Yakubovitz	David Yoel		Zychlin, Poland	PT	M
Jakubowicz Yakubovitz	Eliezer	1916	Zychlin, Poland	PT	M
Jakubowicz Yakubovitz	Miriam	1914	Zychlin, Poland	PT	M
Jakubowicz Yakubovitz	Nacha Nekha	1910	Zychlin, Poland	PT	M
Jakubowicz Yakubovitz	Sara		Zychlin, Poland	PT	M
Jakubowicz Yakubovitz	Szlamo Shlomo	1900	Zychlin, Poland	PT	M
Jakubowski	Chemia	1904	Zychlin, Poland	LMA	M

Last Name	First Name	Birth Year	Place of Residence	Source	Fate
Jakubowski	Chemja	1904	Zychlin, Poland	LDF	M
Jankowska Iankovski	Estera Ester	1880	Grabow, Poland	PT	M
Jastrzebski	Barukh	1890	Kalisz, Poland	PT	M
Jastrzebski	Lezer Eliezer	1890	Lodz, Poland	PT	M
Jastrzebski Iashchemski	Baruch Barukh	1888	Kalisz, Poland	PT	M
Jastrzebski Iashchemski	Chuma Khuma	1880	Zichlin, Poland	PT	M
Jastrzebski Iashchemski	Miriam	1900	Kalisz, Poland	PT	M
Jastrzebski Iashchemski	Mosza Moshe	1895	Kalisz, Poland	PT	M
Jastrzebski Iashchemski	Rochel Rakhel	1870	Lodz, Poland	PT	M
Jastrzebski Iashchemski	Szajna Sheina	1893	Kalisz, Poland	PT	M
Jastrzebski Iashchemski	Yetul Etol	1905	Kalisz, Poland	PT	M
Jastrzębski Iashchemski	Riwka Rivka Lea	1878	Zychlin, Poland	PT	M
Kac Katz	Abrahim Avraham	1872	Zychlin, Poland	PT	M
Kalski	Ita	1895	Piatek, Poland	PT	M
Kalski	Rachel Laia	1895	Ozorkow, Poland	PT	M
Kanarek	Mendel	1914	Zychlin, Poland	LMA	M
Kanarek	Samuel	1900	Zychlin, Poland	LMA	M
Kanarek Kanarik	Mordekhai	1898	Zichlin, Poland	PT	M
Kano	Rywka Maryem	1880	Anderlecht, Belgium	PT	M
Kaplan	Abraham	1895	Zychlin, Poland	DL	M
Kaplan	Abraham Avraham	1885	Wuppertal, Germany	PT	M
Kaplan	Telca	1900	Wuppertal, Germany	PT	M
Karmel	Jochewed Yokheved	1900	Zychlin, Poland	PT	M
Karmel	Nachum Nakhum	1897	Zychlin, Poland	PT	M
Karmel	Rivka		Zychlin, Poland	PT	M
Karo	Abram Avraham	1900	Zychlin, Poland	PT	M
Karten	Mascha	1913	Viersen, Germany	LMG	M
Katz	Jozef	1923	Zychlin, Poland	M	M
Katzenelenbogen	Chaja Khaia Sara	1892	Opoczno, Poland	PT	M
Kelmer	Abe	1923	Zychlin, Poland	PT	M
Kelmer	Abraham	1906	Zychlin, Poland	LDF	M
Kelmer	Abram	1906	Zychlin, Poland	LMA	M
Kelmer	Bayla	1920	Zychlin, Poland	PT	M
Kelmer	Berayna	1922	Zychlin, Poland	PT	M
Kelmer	Fayvel	1925	Zychlin, Poland	PT	M
Kelmer	First name unknown	1930	Zychlin, Poland	PT	M
Kelmer	Hana Leah	1905	Zychlin, Poland	PT	M
Kelmer	Hersch	1905	Zychlin, Poland	PT	M
Kelmer	Hirsh	1903	Zychlin, Poland	PT	M
Kelmer	Jacob	1928	Zychlin, Poland	PT	M
Kelmer	Jacob	1897	Zychlin, Poland	PT	M
Kelmer	Joshua	1865	Zychlin, Poland	PT	M
Kelmer	Moshe	1926	Zychlin, Poland	PT	M

Last Name	First Name	Birth Year	Place of Residence	Source	Fate
Kelmer	Rosa	1895	Zychlin, Poland	PT	M
Kelmer	Yocheved	1870	Zychlin, Poland	PT	M
Kelmer Kalmar	Aizyk Aizik	1892	Zichlin, Poland	PT	M
Kelmer Kalmar	Shmuel Samuel	1887	Lodz, Poland	PT	M
Kerstein	Avrum Yizchock	1909	Zychlin, Poland	PT	M
Kerstein	Chava		Zychlin, Poland	PT	M
Kerstein	Henoch		Zychlin, Poland	PT	M
Kesman	Mose Moshe	1887	Lodz, Poland	PT	M
Kesman		1915	Zychlin, Poland	PT	M
Kesman Kisman	Eidusza Idusha	1917	Zhichlin, Poland	PT	M
Kesman Kisman	Simcha Simkha	1890	Zychlin, Poland	PT	M
Kesman Kosman	Abraham Avraham	1915	Zichlin, Poland	PT	M
Kibel	Yochewet Iokhevet	1888	Warsza, Poland	PT	M
Kidibert Kilbert	Aron	1893	Zychlin, Poland	LDF	M
Kigiel	Lejb	1896	Zytomierz, Ukraine	PP	M
Kilbert	Aron	1893	Zychlin, Poland	LMA	M
Kilbert	Dawid David	1911	Zychlin, Poland	PT	M
Kilbert	Eliezer	1886	Lodz, Poland	PT	M
Kilbert	Josek	1885	Zychlin, Poland	PP	M
Kilbert	Leib		Lodz, Poland	PT	M
Kilbert	Majlich Melekh	1896	Lodz, Poland	PT	M
Kilbert	Mendel	1898	Krosniewice, Poland	PT	M
Kilbert	Tuvia		Lubicz, Poland	PT	M
Kirshtein	Chawe Khava	1919	Lodz, Poland	PT	M
Kirshtein	Elka	1879	Zichlin, Poland	PT	M
Kirshtein	Ewa Eva	1922	Lodz, Poland	PT	M
Kirshtein	Yaakov		Lodz, Poland	PT	M
Kirstein Kirshtein	Dwora Dvora	1923	Zychlin, Poland	PT	M
Kirstein Kirshtein	Yaakov		Lodz, Poland	PT	M
Kirszberg Kirshberg	Pnina Perale Perel		Zychlin, Poland	PT	M
Kirsztajn Kirshtein	Tzvia Tova	1905	Zychlin, Poland	PT	M
Kirsztein Kirshtein	Avram Yitzkhak	1885	Zechlin, Poland	PT	M
Kirsztein Kirshtein	Chaja Khaia	1915	Zichlin, Poland	PT	M
Kirsztein Kirshtein	Chawa Khava	1920	Lodz, Poland	PT	M
Kirsztein Kirshtein	Elka	1889	Lodz, Poland	PT	M
Kirsztein Kirshtein	Fischl Fishel	1910	Zychlin, Poland	PT	M
Kirsztein Kirshtein	Gitel	1887	Zechlin, Poland	PT	M
Kirsztein Kirshtein	Jakov Yaakov	1887	Lodz, Poland	PT	M
Kirsztein Kirshtein	Jona Yona	1907	Zychlin, Poland	PT	M
Kirsztein Kirshtein	Liba	1924	Zichlin, Poland	PT	M
Kirsztein Kirshtein	Racl Ratzel	1912	Zechlin, Poland	PT	M
Kirsztein Kirshtein	Tauba	1922	Zechlin, Poland	PT	M
Kiwent	Jankiel	1917	Zychlin, Poland	LMA	M

Last Name	First Name	Birth Year	Place of Residence	Source	Fate
Klar	Icek	1899	Zychlin, Poland	PP	M
Klejnot Klind	Szmerl Shmariahu	1906	Zechlin, Poland	PT	M
Klingbajl	Hudes	1875	Kutno, Poland	PP	M
Klingbeil	Hadasa	1879	Kutno, Poland	PT	M
Klinger	Avraham	1903	Zychlin, Poland	PT	M
Klinger	Rafael	1878	Zychlin, Poland	PT	M
Klinger	Rakhel	1880	Zichlin, Poland	PT	M
Klinger	Sheina Roda	1906	Zichlin, Poland	PT	M
Klinger	Yonatan	1911	Zhichlin, Poland	PT	M
Klinger Klanger	Jakob Yaakov	1884	Kombin, Poland	PT	M
Klinshot Kleinshot	Geizel Gotshalk		Zichlin, Poland	PT	M
Klinshot Kleinshot	Tova		Zychlin, Poland	PT	M
Klinshot Kleinshot	Yossef Yosef		Zychlin, Poland	PT	M
Klum	Moshe	1878	Ozarow, Poland	PT	M
Kohen	Chawa Khava		Zichlin, Poland	PT	M
Kohen	Mendel		Warsha, Poland	PT	M
Kohen	Nakhman		Zichlin, Poland	PT	M
Kohen	Yaakov Yehuda	1890	Zichlin, Poland	PT	M
Kohn Kohen	Menachem Mendel	1904	Zichlin, Poland	PT	M
Kohn Kohen	Nchemia Nekhemia		Zychlin, Poland	PT	M
Kohn Kohen	Nechama Nekhama		Zychlin, Poland	PT	M
Kohn Kohen	Rachel Rakhel		Zhichlin, Poland	PT	M
Kohn Kohen	Ryfka Rivka	1892	Sanniki, Poland	PT	M
Kon	Abram Moszek	1931		LLG	PM
Kon	Binem	1904		LLG	PM
Kon	Icek Lajb	1898		LLG	PM
Kon	Marja Mina	1930		LLG	PM
Kopel	Pinkus	1907	Zychlin, Poland	PP	M
Koper Kuper	Moshe Khaim	1887	Warszawa, Poland	PT	M
Kopolovitz	Odis Udes		Zychlin, Poland	PT	M
Kopolowitz Kopolovitz			Zychlin, Poland	PT	M
Koppel	Chaja Ruchla	1901	Berlin, Germany	LDB	M
Koppel	Chaja Ruchla	1901	Berlin, Germany	LMG	M
Koren	Chaya Sara	1917	Zychlin, Poland	PT	M
Koren	Debora Lyba	1922	Zychlin, Poland	PT	M
Koren	Fraida Freida	1895	Zychlin, Poland	PT	M
Koren	Hershl Hershel	1893	Zychlin, Poland	PT	M
Koren	Jacob	1925	Zychlin, Poland	PT	M
Koren	Jacob	1934	Zychlin, Poland	PT	M
Koren	Mendel Menachem	1923	Zychlin, Poland	PT	M
Koren	Rocha Leah	1920	Zychlin, Poland	PT	M
Koren	Toba Ester	1918	Zychlin, Poland	PT	M
Korn	Dwora	1914	Zychlin, Poland	PT	M

Last Name	First Name	Birth Year	Place of Residence	Source	Fate
Korn	Ester Tova		Zychlin, Poland	PT	M
Korn	Frajda Freida	1878	Zychlin, Poland	PT	M
Korn	Hirsz Tzvi	1872	Zychlin, Poland	PT	M
Korn	Jakob Yaakov	1911	Zychlin, Poland	PT	M
Korn	Khava Sara		Zychlin, Poland	PT	M
Korn	Mendel		Zychlin, Poland	PT	M
Korn	Mendel	1913	Zychlin, Poland	PT	M
Korn	Rakhel Lea		Zychlin, Poland	PT	M
Korn	Rakhel Lea		Zychlin, Poland	PT	M
Korn	Rivka Zahava		Zychlin, Poland	PT	M
Korn	Rivka Zahava		Zychlin, Poland	PT	M
Korn	Tzipora		Zychlin, Poland	PT	M
Korn	Yaakov		Zychlin, Poland	PT	M
Kosman	Sara	1890	Zichlin, Poland	PT	M
Kosses	Hans	1922	Zechlin, Poland	LDB	M
Kotonowski Kotonovski	Aharon		Zychlin, Poland	PT	M
Kotonowski Kotonovski	Hena	1900	Zychlin, Poland	PT	M
Kotonowski Kotonovski	Khana		Zychlin, Poland	PT	M
Kotonowski Kotonovski	Yona		Zychlin, Poland	PT	M
Kotonowski Kutnovski	Yitzkhak		Zychlin, Poland	PT	M
Kovnat	Avraham Shmuel		Zychlin, Poland	PT	M
Kovnat	Bunim		Zychlin, Poland	PT	M
Kovnat	Dvora		Zichlin, Poland	PT	M
Kovnat	Ester		Zychlin, Poland	PT	M
Kovnat	Joseph		Zychlin, Poland	PT	M
Kovnat	Joseph Yosef		Zychlin, Poland	PT	M
Kovnat	Khana		Zychlin, Poland	PT	M
Kovnat	Malka		Zychlin, Poland	PT	M
Kovnat	Shlomo		Zychlin, Poland	PT	M
Kovnat	Yehoshua Feibush		Zychlin, Poland	PT	M
Kowent Kisilewicz	Ester	1935	Zychlin, Poland	PT	M
Kowent Kisilewicz	Malka	1893	Zychlin, Poland	PT	M
Kowent Kisilewicz	Yosef	1928	Zychlin, Poland	PT	M
Kowent Kovnat	Avraham Shmuel	1918	Zychlin, Poland	PT	M
Kowent Kovnat	Beila		Zychlin, Poland	PT	M
Kowent Kovnat	Bunim	1924	Zychlin, Poland	PT	M
Kowent Kovnat	Dvora	1880	Zychlin, Poland	PT	M
Kowent Kovnat	Ester		Lodz, Poland	PT	M
Kowent Kovnat	Gitil		Sochaczew, Poland	PT	M
Kowent Kovnat	Khana	1925	Zychlin, Poland	PT	M
Kowent Kovnat	Shlomo	1922	Zychlin, Poland	PT	M
Kowent Kovnat	Shlomo		Zychlin, Poland	PT	M
Kowent Kovnat	Yisrael	1876	Zychlin, Poland	PT	M

Last Name	First Name	Birth Year	Place of Residence	Source	Fate
Kowent Kovnat	Yosef	1910	Zychlin, Poland	PT	M
Kowent Kovnat	Yosef		Lodz, Poland	PT	M
Kowent Kuvent	Beila		Zychlin, Poland	PT	M
Krajcer Kreitzer	Golda Riwka Zahava	1901	Gostynin, Poland	PT	M
Kraut	Binem	1899	Zichlin, Poland	DL	M
Kraut	Szaja Shaia		Lodz, Poland	PT	M
Kraut Kroit	Bunem	1899	France	PT	M
Kraut Kroit	Lajbl Leibel	1897	Lodz, Poland	PT	M
Kraut Kroit	Pola	1902	Lodz, Poland	PT	M
Kriza Krize	Golda Ruchel Gold		Nowy Sacz, Poland	PT	M
Krize	Avraham Noakh	1899	Zychlin, Poland	PT	M
Kubec Kovach	Chana Khana	1904	Warszawa, Poland	PT	M
Kujawski	Henry	1916	Krosniewice, Poland	PT	M
Kurstein Kirshtein	Lea	1924	Zychlin, Poland	PT	M
Kurstein Kurshtein	Avraham Yitzkhak	1889	Zychlin, Poland	PT	M
Kurstein Kurshtein	Chaja Khaia Genendl	1894	Zychlin, Poland	PT	M
Kurstein Kurshtein	Elka	1897	Lodz, Poland	PT	M
Kurstein Kurshtein	Fischel Fishel	1917	Zychlin, Poland	PT	M
Kurstein Kurshtein	Khava		Lodz, Poland	PT	M
Kurstein Kurshtein	Liba		Zychlin, Poland	PT	M
Kurstein Kurshtein	Ryfka Rivka	1918	Zychlin, Poland	PT	M
Kurstein Kurshtein	Tova		Zychlin, Poland	PT	M
Kutner	David	1899	Zychlin, Poland	LDF	M
Kutner Skrobek	David Aron	1899	Warszawa, Poland	PT	M
Kutnovski	Icchak Yitzkhak	1906	Zychlin, Poland	PT	M
Kutnovski	Mosze Moshe	1888	Wloclawek, Poland	PT	M
Kutnowski	Abraham		Wloclawek, Poland	PT	M
Kutnowski	Liba		Wloclawek, Poland	PT	M
Kutnowski	Moszek Zelig		Wloclawek, Poland	PT	M
Kutnowski Kutnovski	Aharon		Zychlin, Poland	PT	M
Kutnowski Kutnovski	Chana Khana	1884	Zychlin, Poland	PT	M
Kutnowski Kutnovski	Jona Yona	1880	Zychlin, Poland	PT	M
Kutnowski Kutnovski	Khanan		Zychlin, Poland	PT	M
Kutnowski Kutnovski	Khanan		Wloclawek, Poland	PT	M
Kutnowski Kutnovski	Laja Lea	1902	Wloclawek, Poland	PT	M
Kutnowski Kutnovski	Leja Lea	1906	Zychlin, Poland	PT	M
Kutnowski Kutnovski	Liba	1890	Wloclawek, Poland	PT	M
Kutnowski Kutnovski	Menasze Menashe	1897	Zychlin, Poland	PT	M
Kutnowski Kutnovski	Sheva		Zychlin, Poland	PT	M
Kutnowski Kutnovski	Zakharia		Zychlin, Poland	PT	M
Kutnowski Kutnovski	Zakhariahu		Wloclawek, Poland	PT	M
Kuvent	Bajla Bila	1878	Zychlin, Poland	PT	M
Kuvent	Bela	1902	Zichlin, Poland	PT	M

Last Name	First Name	Birth Year	Place of Residence	Source	Fate
Kuvent	Gitlya	1914	Zhikhlin, Poland	PP	M
Kuvent	Iosif	1906	Zhikhlin, Poland	PP	M
Kuvent	Josef Yosef		Zichlin, Poland	PT	M
Kuvent	Liba Rojza Shoshana		Zichlin, Poland	PT	M
Kuvent	Yisrael		Zychlin, Poland	PT	M
Kuwent	Faiwel	1937	Zychlin, Poland	PT	M
Kuwent	Hersz	1910	Zychlin, Poland	M	M
Kuwent	Mordechai	1900	Zychlin, Poland	PT	M
Kuwent	Mordechai	1900	Gostynin, Poland	PT	M
Kuwent Kovnat	Cwija Tzvia	1908	Zychlin, Poland	PT	M
Kuwent Kovnat	Mordekhai	1905	Zychlin, Poland	PT	M
Kuwent Kovnat	Yehoshua Perel		Zychlin, Poland	PT	M
Kuwent Kuvent	Berl	1930	Zychlin, Poland	PT	M
Kuwent Kuvent	Bluma	1902	Zychlin, Poland	PT	M
Kuwent Kuvent	Chana Roda Khana	1918	Zychlin, Poland	PT	M
Kuwent Kuvent	Eljasz Eliahu	1898	Zychlin, Poland	PT	M
Kuwent Kuvent	Gitla Leya Gitel Lea	1905	Zychlin, Poland	PT	M
Kuwent Kuvent	Gucia Gucha	1920	Zychlin, Poland	PT	M
Kuwent Kuvent	Mordka Mordekhai	1902	Zychlin, Poland	PT	M
Kuwent Kuvent	Sala	1938	Zychlin, Poland	PT	M
Kuwent Kuvent	Sara	1936	Zychlin, Poland	PT	M
Kuwent Kuvent	Szmaja Shemaia	1908	Zychlin, Poland	PT	M
Kuwent Kuvent	Yehoshua Shraga	1936	Zychlin, Poland	PT	M
Kuwent Kuvent	Yisrael Moshe	1873	Zychlin, Poland	PT	M
Kuwent Kuvent	Yosef	1905	Zychlin, Poland	PT	M
Kuwent Kuvent		1940	Zychlin, Poland	PT	M
Kuwent Kuvent Rozenkrantz	Blima Rojza Roza	1900	Zychlin, Poland	PT	M
Kuwent Kuvent Rozenkrantz	Brana	1930	Zychlin, Poland	PT	M
Kuwent Kuvent Rozenkrantz	Sala	1935	Zychlin, Poland	PT	M
Kuwent Kuvent Rozenkrantz	Szlama Shlomo	1933	Zychlin, Poland	PT	M
Kuyavsky Kuiavski	Abraham Avraham	1883	Lodz, Poland	PT	M
Kuzbek	Rika		Zychlin, Poland	PT	M
Kviwski	Ester		Lutz, Poland	PT	M
Lajzerowicz	Simon Israel	1903	Zychlin, Poland	LMA	M
Lajzerowicz Leizerovitz	Efraim	1885	Zychlin, Poland	PT	M
Landau	Edmund	1880	Warszawa, Poland	PP	M
Landsman Landesman	Jechiel Yekhiel	1896	Zychlin, Poland	PT	M
Landsman Landesman	Tzvia		Zychlin, Poland	PT	M
Lansman	Chil	1896	Kutno, Poland	PT	M
Laski	Freida		Gombin, Poland	PT	M
Lasman Lesman	Benjamin Beniamin	1868	Zgierz, Poland	PT	M
Lasman Lesman	Genya		Zychlin, Poland	PT	M
Lasman Lesman	Ida	1893	Lodz, Poland	PT	M

Last Name	First Name	Birth Year	Place of Residence	Source	Fate
Lasman Lesman	Lajb Efraim Leib	1908	Zychlin, Poland	PT	M
Lasman Lesman	Mosze Moshe	1864	Lodz, Poland	PT	M
Lasman Lesman	Perel	1907	Zychlin, Poland	PT	M
Lasman Lesman	Perel	1910	Zychlin, Poland	PT	M
Lasman Lesman	Wolf Dov	1878	Kutno, Poland	PT	M
Lasman Lesman	Zelma		Zychlin, Poland	PT	M
Lassman	Fajwel	1880	Lodz, Poland	PT	M
Lassman	Fiszel	1906	Lodz, Poland	PT	M
Leczycka	Marysia	1925	Zychlin, Poland	PP	M
Leczycki	Jakab	1922	Zychlin, Poland	PP	M
Leczycki	Jakob	1922	Zychlin, Poland	PP	M
Leczycki	Marysia	1925	Zychlin, Poland	PP	M
Leczycki	Romek	1924	Zychlin, Poland	PP	M
Leczycki	Romek	1924	Zychlin, Poland	PP	M
Lederman	Dvora		Zychlin, Poland	PT	M
Lederman	Faivel Shraga		Zychlin, Poland	PT	M
Lederman	Sara		Zychlin, Poland	PT	M
Lederman	Yehuda Leib		Zychlin, Poland	PT	M
Lemberg	Abram Avraham	1868	Zychlin, Poland	PT	M
Lemberg	Aharon	1911	Zychlin, Poland	PT	M
Lemberg	Aron Aharon	1912	Lowicz, Poland	PT	M
Lemberg	Avraham Meir	1896	Zychlin, Poland	PT	M
Lemberg	Benjamin Beniamin	1906	Zychlin, Poland	PT	M
Lemberg	Chana Sara Khana		Zychlin, Poland	PT	M
Lemberg	David		Zychlin, Poland	PT	M
Lemberg	Dawid David		Zychlin, Poland	PT	M
Lemberg	Hendel	1918	Zychlin, Poland	PT	M
Lemberg	Hendel	1920	Zychlin, Poland	PT	M
Lemberg	Hersz Henech	1882	Zychlin, Poland	PT	M
Lemberg	Khana		Zychlin, Poland	PT	M
Lemberg	Lypcsz Lipesh	1922	Zychlin, Poland	PT	M
Lemberg	Lypesz Lipesh	1917	Zychlin, Poland	PT	M
Lemberg	Miriam	1916	Gdansk, Danzig	PT	M
Lemberg	Mirjam Miriam	1916	Gdansk, Danzig	PT	M
Lemberg	Rivka		Gdansk, Danzig	PT	M
Lemberg	Rywka Rivka	1899	Zychlin, Poland	PT	M
Lemberg	Yehuda		Zychlin, Poland	PT	M
Lemberg	Zew Zeev	1891	Zychlin, Poland	PT	M
Lenchinski	Hela Ila		Zychlin, Poland	PT	M
Lenchinski	Marisha Miriam		Zichlin, Poland	PT	M
Lenchinski	Reuven		Zychlin, Poland	PT	M
Lenchinski	Yaakov		Zichlin, Poland	PT	M
Lenczycki Lanchichki	Haim Ruwen	1916	Zychlin, Poland	PT	M

Last Name	First Name	Birth Year	Place of Residence	Source	Fate
Lenczycki Lanchichki	Yenta		Zychlin, Poland	PT	M
Lenczycki Łęczycki	Yejrel Yaroslav	1911	Zychlin, Poland	PT	M
Lesman	Aba		Zychlin, Poland	PT	M
Lesman	Asher	1896	Lodz, Poland	PT	M
Lesman	Aszer Asher	1895	Lodz, Poland	PT	M
Lesman	Jankiel Dawid	1877		LLG	PM
Lesman	Rivka		Woclawek, Poland	PT	M
Lesman	Riwka Rivka	1872	Wloclawek, Poland	PT	M
Lesman	Tova		Zychlin, Poland	PT	M
Lesman	Yackov Yaakov		Zychlin, Poland	PT	M
Levi	Asher		Zychlin, Poland	PT	M
Levi	Asher	1892	Zhikhlin, Poland	PT	M
Levi	Ester	1912	Lodz, Poland	PT	M
Levi	Moshe	1920	Kroshnivitz, Poland	PT	M
Levi Neifeld	Henia		Broszniow, Poland	PT	M
Levi Neifeld	Tova	1918	Broszniow, Poland	PT	M
Levin	Yerucham Yerukham	1899	Sobota, Poland	PT	M
Levin Lewin	Ester Estera	1912	Lodz, Poland	PT	M
Levkovitz Lewkuvic	Moshe Aharon	1928	Zichlin, Poland	PT	M
Levy Levi	Usher Asher	1887	Zichlin, Poland	PT	M
Lewin Levin	Feiga	1872	Zychlin, Poland	PT	M
Lewin Levin	Gerszon Gershon	1904	Zychlin, Poland	PT	M
Lewin Levin	Lea	1895	Zechlin, Poland	PT	M
Lewin Levin	Levi		Zychlin, Poland	PT	M
Lewin Levin	Natan	1903	Sobota, Poland	PT	M
Lewin Levin	Nechemia Nekhemia	1894	Zechlin, Poland	PT	M
Lewin Levin	Tzipa		Zychlin, Poland	PT	M
Lewin Levin	Ysrael Yisrael	1870	Zychlin, Poland	PT	M
Lewkuvic	Avraham Yaakov		Zichlin, Poland	PT	M
Lewkuvic Levkovitz	Heniek Eliakim	1923	Zachlin, Poland	PT	M
Lewkuvic Levkovitz	Liba Rojza Shoshana	1926	Zichlin, Poland	PT	M
Lewy Levi	Chanoch Khanokh	1902	Zychlin, Poland	PT	M
Lewy Levi	Gitel	1906	Zychlin, Poland	PT	M
Lewy Levy Levi	Moshele Moshe	1926	Zychlin, Poland	PT	M
Liberman	Beresh	1880	Zychlin, Poland	PT	M
Liberman	Sara Dvora	1880	Sandomierz, Poland	PT	M
Lichtenstein Bornshtein	Ester		Zychlin, Poland	PT	M
Lichtenstein Bornshtein	Lea		Zychlin, Poland	PT	M
Lichtenstein Bornshtein	Rachela Rakhel	1913	Zychlin, Poland	PT	M
Lichtensztein Likhtenshtein	Leibl Leibel	1910	Zychlin, Poland	PT	M
Liebfreund	Bernard	1925	Zychlin, Poland	LFC	M
Lipski	Chejwet	1922	Kutno, Poland	PP	M
Lipski	Gerszon	1916	Kutno, Poland	PP	M

Last Name	First Name	Birth Year	Place of Residence	Source	Fate
Lipski	Szajna Rywka	1893	Zychlin, Poland	PP	M
Lipszic Lifshitz	Gela	1885	Wiskit, Poland	PT	M
Lisak	Gita	1897	Krosniewice, Poland	PT	M
Listek	First name unknown		Zychlin, Poland	PT	M
Listek	Nochcza Nakhche	1922	Zychlin, Poland	PT	M
Listek	Pinchos Pinkhas	1921	Zychlin, Poland	PT	M
Listek	Selde Zelda	1923	Zychlin, Poland	PT	M
Litman	Gecil Gotshalk	1881	Dobrzyn, Poland	PT	M
Logovinskiy Logovinski	Fishel	1906	Zychlin, Poland	PT (d)	KMS
Luksenburg	Ieta		Rypin, Poland	PT	M
Luksenburg	Pesa		Rypin, Poland	PT	M
Luksenburg	Yisrael Mikhael		Rypin, Poland	PT	M
Luxenberg	Yeta		Zychlin, Poland	PT (d)	M
Luxenberg	Yisroel Michael		Zychlin, Poland	PT (d)	M
Maidat Meidat	Bejla Beila	1911	Zychlin, Poland	PT	M
Maidat Meidat	Chana Khana	1915	Zychlin, Poland	PT	M
Maidat Meidat	Feiga		Zychlin, Poland	PT	M
Maidat Meidat	Gitel		Zychlin, Poland	PT	M
Maidat Meidat	Khaia		Zychlin, Poland	PT	M
Maidat Meidat	Mendel		Zychlin, Poland	PT	M
Maidat Meidat	Miriam Mariam	1885	Zychlin, Poland	PT	M
Maidat Meidat	Moisze Moshe	1896	Zychlin, Poland	PT	M
Maidat Meidat	Mordechai	1910	Zychlin, Poland	PT	M
Maidat Meidat	Pesia		Zychlin, Poland	PT	M
Maidat Meidat	Rivka		Zychlin, Poland	PT	M
Maidat Meidat	Szlome Shlomo	1918	Zychlin, Poland	PT	M
Maidat Meidat	Tauba	1914	Zychlin, Poland	PT	M
Maidat Meidat	Yakob Yaakov	1880	Zychlin, Poland	PT	M
Maidat Meidat	Zipe Tzipa	1906	Zychlin, Poland	PT	M
Majdak	Mendel	1920	Zychlin, Poland	LFC	M
Majdet	Icek	1897	Plock, Poland	PT	M
Majranc Mirantz	Hawa Khaia	1890	Zichlin, Poland	PT	M
Manisowitz Manisovitz	Falah Felitzia	1921	Dobrzyn, Poland	PT	M
Manisowitz Manisovitz	Manis	1887	Dobzin, Poland	PT	M
Manisowitz Manisovitz	Toba Tova	1907	Dobrzyn, Poland	PT	M
Manisowitz Manisovitz	Toba Tova	1924	Dobrzyn, Poland	PT	M
Marcusfeld Markusfeld	Dvora	1902	Zichlin, Poland	PT	M
Marcusfeld Markusfeld	Nekhama			PT	M
Markovics Markovitz	Malka	1898	Lovich, Poland	PT	M
Markus	Chaya Rachel	1902	Zychlin, Poland	PT	M
Markus	David Yitzkhak		Zychlin, Poland	PT	M
Markus	Hersh Moshe		Zychlin, Poland	PT	M
Markus	Khaim		Zychlin, Poland	PT	M

Last Name	First Name	Birth Year	Place of Residence	Source	Fate
Markus	Khana Hudes		Zychlin, Poland	PT	M
Markus	Pesakh		Zychlin, Poland	PT	M
Markus	Szlomo Shlomo	1900	Zychlin, Poland	PT	M
Markus	Zelda		Zychlin, Poland	PT	M
Menche	Brucha	1883	Zychlin, Poland	PP	M
Menche Mankhe	Riwka Rivka	1892	Kutno, Poland	PT	M
Mendiuk	Rakhel	1916	Krzemieniec, Poland	PT	M
Mest Mast	Avraham Yaakov	1885	Zychlin, Poland	PT	M
Michalovitz Mikhalovich	Ester		Zychlin, Poland	PT	M
Michalovitz Mikhalovich	Godel	1885	Zychlin, Poland	PT	M
Michalovitz Mikhalovich	Keila	1900	Zychlin, Poland	PT	M
Michalovitz Mikhalovich	Moshe	1890	Zychlin, Poland	PT	M
Miedzinski Midzinski	Perla	1895	Wloclawek, Poland	PT	M
Morgenstein	Jenta Yenta	1918	Zaklin, Poland	PT	M
Morgenstein	Tauba Tova	1912	Zaklin, Poland	PT	M
Morgentaler	Aron Aharon	1888	Wloclawek, Poland	PT	M
Morgentaler	Aron Aharon	1890	Wloclawek, Poland	PT	M
Morgentaler	Cesia Tzesia	1918	Wloclawek, Poland	PT	M
Morgentaler	Eliezer Leon	1889	Zychlin, Poland	PT	M
Morgentaler	Mindl Mindel	1900	Zychlin, Poland	PT	M
Morgentaler	Rivka		Wloclawek, Poland	PT	M
Moskat Czolek	Roza	1877	Lodz, Poland	PT	M
Moskovic Moshkovitz	Chana Khana	1887	Lodz, Poland	PT	M
Moskowic Moskovich	Jeudit Yehudit	1906	Lenczyca, Poland	PT	M
Motyl Motil	Reisla Reizl	1903	Gostynin, Poland	PT	M
Mrocki	Ichak		Zechlin, Poland	PT	M
Muszkat	Irka	1932	Zichlin, Poland	PT	M
Nachmanowicz	Tauba	1888	Lodz, Poland	PT	M
Naifeld	Tova	1924	Zychlin, Poland	PT	M
Najdorf Noidorf	Szajndel Sheindl	1892	Zychlin, Poland	PT	M
Najdorf Noidorf	Yaakov Eliahu	1891	Zychlin, Poland	PT	M
Najman Neiman	Icchak Yitzkhak Tzvi	1901	Zychlin, Poland	PT	M
Naszelewicz Nashelevitz	Chana Khana	1910	Zychlin, Poland	PT	M
Naszelewicz Nashelevitz	Ciwia Tzivia	1883	Zychlin, Poland	PT	M
Naszelewicz Nashelevitz	Lejbisz Leibish	1908	Zychlin, Poland	PT	M
Naszelewicz Nashelevitz	Mordechai	1880	Zychlin, Poland	PT	M
Naszelewicz Nashelevitz	Mosze Moshe	1906	Zychlin, Poland	PT	M
Naszelewicz Nashelevitz	Rachel Rakhel	1906	Zychlin, Poland	PT	M
Naszelewicz Nashelevitz	Tzivia		Zychlin, Poland	PT	M
Neifeld	Henia		Zychlin, Poland	PT	M
Neikof	Toibe		Kutno, Poland	PT	M
Neiman	Leizer Eliezer	1898	Wloclawek, Poland	PT	M
Neufeld Noifeld	Aharon Leib	1905	Zychlin, Poland	PT	M

Last Name	First Name	Birth Year	Place of Residence	Source	Fate
Neufeld Noifeld	Chana Khana	1900	Zychlin, Poland	PT	M
Neufeld Noifeld	Chawa Khava	1881	Zychlin, Poland	PT	M
Neufeld Noifeld	Nachum Nakhum	1881	Zychlin, Poland	PT	M
Neuman Neiman	Leizer	1898	Wlodslovek, Poland	PT	M
Neumark Noimark	Hersh Yaakov		Zychlin, Poland	PT	M
Niedobior	Leosia Lea		Kutno, Poland	PT	M
Nifeld Noifeld	Aaron Aharon	1910	Zechlin, Poland	PT	M
Noifeld	Nachum Nakhum	1886	Zechlin, Poland	PT	M
Oberman	Mirla Mirl	1905	Lodz, Poland	PT	M
Oblengorsky Oblengorski	Dina	1887	Lodz, Poland	PT	M
Olewski Olevski	Naftali	1918	Osieciny, Poland	PT	M
Oliwenstein Olivenshtein	Perec Peretz	1909	Warszawa, Poland	PT	M
Oliwenstein Olivenshtein	Zeev		Warszawa, Poland	PT	M
Opalen	Aron Moshe	1909	Zychlin, Poland	PT	M
Opalen	Greina Gruna	1939	Zychlin, Poland	PT	M
Opalen	Leah Sara	1909	Wloclawek, Poland	PT	M
Opaljon Opalion	Aron Moshe Aharon	1912	Wloclawek, Poland	PT	M
Opaljon Opalion	Fajwel Simcha	1888	Zychlin, Poland	PT	M
Opaljon Opalion	Hendel Gitel		Zychlin, Poland	PT	M
Opaljon Opalion	Ruchel Rivka Rakhel	1924	Zychlin, Poland	PT	M
Opaljon Opalion	Shajna Sheina		Zychlin, Poland	PT	M
Opatovski	Gronim Gronam	1914	Zychlin, Poland	PT	M
Opatowski Opatovski	Meir	1886	Zychlin, Poland	PT	M
Opatowski Opatovski	Meir	1892	Zychlin, Poland	PT	M
Opatowski Opatovski	Pola	1896	Zychlin, Poland	PT	M
Opatowski Opatovski	Pola Perel	1900	Zychlin, Poland	PT	M
Opolion	Israel Chaim		Zychlin, Poland	PT	M
Opotovski Opatovski	Zalman David	1912	Zychlin, Poland	PT	M
Opotovski Opatovski	Abraham Avraham	1916	Zychlin, Poland	PT	M
Opotovski Opatovski	Icze Icie	1880	Zychlin, Poland	PT	M
Opotovski Opatovski	Makhle Malka	1880	Zychlin, Poland	PT	M
Opotovski Opatovski	Wolf Volf	1910	Zychlin, Poland	PT	M
Orenbakh	Pesa		Klodawa, Poland	PT	M
Orner	Abraham Avraham	1889	Kutno, Poland	PT	M
Orner	Abram	1890	Zychlin, Poland	PP	M
Osowska Osovski	Minia	1917	Kutno, Poland	PT	M
Osowski Osovski	Frida Freida	1892	Kutno, Poland	PT	M
Pels Peltz	Szprinca Shprintza	1906	Warszawa, Poland	PT	M
Perec	Cyrla	1897	Zychlin, Poland	PP	M
Perl	Yerachmiel		Zychlin, Poland	PT	M
Pietrowski	Ita	1913	Zychlin, Poland	LDF	M
Piotrkowski	Chevet		Lodz, Poland	PT	M
Plocki Plotzki	Cyrla Tzirel	1868	Zychlin, Poland	PT	M

Last Name	First Name	Birth Year	Place of Residence	Source	Fate
Plocki Plotzki	Dawid David	1870	Zychlin, Poland	PT	M
Plonska Palunski	Chawa Khava Lea	1885	Zychlin, Poland	PT	M
Plonska Palunski	Ester	1912	Zychlin, Poland	PT	M
Plonska Palunski	Regina Rivka	1913	Zychlin, Poland	PT	M
Plonski	Aron Aharon	1890	Lodz, Poland	PT	M
Plonski	Benjamin Beniamin	1882	Zychlin, Poland	PT	M
Plonski	Marisia Miriam	1915	Zychlin, Poland	PT	M
Plonski	Noech Noakh	1899	Zychlin, Poland	PT	M
Plonsky Plonski	Hadasa	1913	Zychlin, Poland	PT	M
Pomeranc Pomerantz	Abraham Avraham	1910	Wloclawek, Poland	PT	M
Poznanski	Hersz Tzvi	1897	Zychlin, Poland	PT	M
Poznanski	Neha Nekha		Zychlin, Poland	PT	M
Poznanski	Nekha		Zychlin, Poland	PT	M
Poznanski	Nekha		Zychlin, Poland	PT	M
Poznanski	Sara	1898	Zychlin, Poland	PT	M
Poznanski	Yaakov		Zychlin, Poland	PT	M
Poznanski	Yaakov		Zychlin, Poland	PT	M
Poznanski	Yakov Yaakov		Chelmno, Poland	PT	M
Princ Printz	Arie	1905	Zichlin, Poland	PT	M
Princ Printz	Chaia Khaia	1908	Zichlin, Poland	PT	M
Princ Printz	First name unknown		Zichlin, Poland	PT	M
Princ Printz	First name unknown		Zichlin, Poland	PT	M
Prinz Printz	Bendit Bendet	1887	Zaklin, Poland	PT	M
Probs Props	Ita	1894	Zychlin, Poland	PP	M
Prync	Aron Dawid	1899	Radom, Poland	LRG	PM
Przedecki Pashdetzki	Aron Aharon		Wloclawek, Poland	PT	M
Pytel	J	1899	Zychlin, Poland	LDF	M
Pytel	Joseph	1899	Zychlin, Poland	LMA	M
Pytel Pitel	Masza Masha	1914	Zychlin, Poland	PT	M
Pytel Pitel	Noach Noakh	1914	Zychlin, Poland	PT	M
Radziwiller	Tauba Fraida	1902	Anderlecht, Belgium	PT	M
Radzynski	Ruchla	1908	Zychlin, Poland	DL	M
Radzynski Ratzinski	Rozia Shoshana	1908	Bruxelles, Belgium	PT	M
Redlich	Hana Dobrysz Dobrisz	1888	Zychlin, Poland	PP	M
Reicher Reiber	Rywka Rivka	1890	Kolo, Poland	PT	M
Reselbach	Sarah	1890	Lodz, Poland	PT	M
Reszelbach	Abram	1893		LLG	PM
Reszelbach	Chana Bajla	1925		LLG	PM
Reszelbach	Jocheta	1929		LLG	PM
Reszelbach	Pesach	1923		LLG	PM
Reszelbach	Pesach Adolf	1923	Zychlin, Poland	PP	M
Reszelbach	Sura	1892		LLG	PM
Rister	Eljahu Eliahu	1898	Zychlin, Poland	PT	M

Last Name	First Name	Birth Year	Place of Residence	Source	Fate
Rister	Mnucha Menukha	1900	Zychlin, Poland	PT	M
Rister	Yaakov		Zychlin, Poland	PT	M
Robin	Moshe	1917	Zichlin, Poland	PT	M
Rochman Rokhman	Slomo Shlomo	1916	Zychlin, Poland	PT	M
Rojtberg	Szloma	1910	Luck, Poland	PP	M
Rosemberg	Cypra	1907	Zychlin, Poland	LDF	M
Rosenbaum Rozenbaum	Roza Shoshana	1905	Zychlin, Poland	PT	M
Rosenberg	Heroch	1892	Zychlin, Poland	LMA	M
Rosenberg	Pinkhas Wolf	1884		LLG	PM
Rosenberg Rozenberg	Alte Alter	1900	Zychlin, Poland	PT	M
Rosenberg Rozenberg	Etka Ester	1897	Wloclawek, Poland	PT	M
Rosenberg Rozenberg	Lea	1905	Zychlin, Poland	PT	M
Rosenberg Rozenberg	Meir	1900	Zychlin, Poland	PT	M
Rosenberg Rozenberg	Mosze Moshe	1902	Zychlin, Poland	PT	M
Rosenberg Rozenberg	Rivka		Zychlin, Poland	PT	M
Rosenberg Rozenberg	Rivka		Zychlin, Poland	PT	M
Rosenberg Rozenberg	Rivka		Zychlin, Poland	PT	M
Rosenberg Rozenberg	Runia Ronia	1928	Wloclawek, Poland	PT	M
Rosenberg Rozenberg	Yosef	1909	Zychlin, Poland	PT	M
Rosenfeld	Jzreel	1920	Lodz, Poland	PP	M
Rosenfeld	Rachela	1895	Lodz, Poland	PP	M
Rosenfeld	Rozia	1910	Sochaczew, Poland	PP	M
Rosenkranc	Abel	1900	Zychlin, Poland	LMA	M
Rosenkranc Rozenkrantz	Mojsze Moshe		Zychlin, Poland	PT	M
Rosenkranz	Fischel	1867	Regensburg, Germany	LMG	M
Rosenkranz Rozenkrantz	Feivish Feibish	1895	Leczyca, Poland	PT	M
Rosenthal Muskat Rozental	Emalia Amalia	1880	Leipzig, Germany	PT	M
Rosenthal Rozental	Yosef Iosef	1878	Leipzig, Germany	PT	M
Rotkop	Dvora	1890	Lodz, Poland	PT	M
Rozenbaum	Chana	1895		LLG	PM
Rozenberg	Abram		Zychlin, Poland	PT	M
Rozenberg	Aharon	1910	Zichlin, Poland	PT	M
Rozenberg	Aharon	1910	Zychlin, Poland	PT	M
Rozenberg	Alte	1892	Zychlin, Poland	PT	M
Rozenberg	Bejla Bela	1902	Zachlin, Poland	PT	M
Rozenberg	Bela	1900	Zychlin, Poland	PT	M
Rozenberg	Chaia Idel	1880	Zichlin, Poland	PT	M
Rozenberg	David	1877	Zichlin, Poland	PT	M
Rozenberg	Efraim		Zichlin, Poland	PT	M
Rozenberg	Ester Malka	1911	Zichlin, Poland	PT	M
Rozenberg	Fajwysz Feibush	1907	Zychlin, Poland	PT	M
Rozenberg	Feibush Feivish	1901	Zychlin, Poland	PT	M
Rozenberg	First name unknown		Zychlin, Poland	PT	M

Last Name	First Name	Birth Year	Place of Residence	Source	Fate
Rozenberg	First name unknown		Zychlin, Poland	PT	M
Rozenberg	Gilda	1914	Belostok, Poland	PP	M
Rozenberg	Gilda	1914	Belostok, Poland	PP	M
Rozenberg	Godel		Zychlin, Poland	PT	M
Rozenberg	Hershel		Zychlin, Poland	PT	M
Rozenberg	Jakob Yaakov	1912	Zychlin, Poland	PT	M
Rozenberg	Jakob Yaakov	1911	Zychlin, Poland	PT	M
Rozenberg	Jojne Yona	1900	Zachlin, Poland	PT	M
Rozenberg	Josef Yosef	1908	Warszawa, Poland	PT	M
Rozenberg	Khaia	1880	Zychlin, Poland	PT	M
Rozenberg	Mair Meir	1900	Zychlin, Poland	PT	M
Rozenberg	Malka	1902	Zgerzh, Poland	PT	M
Rozenberg	Mania	1922	Gabin, Poland	PT	M
Rozenberg	Matl		Zychlin, Poland	PT	M
Rozenberg	Menashe	1882	Gombin, Poland	PT	M
Rozenberg	Menashe	1909	Zychlin, Poland	PT	M
Rozenberg	Mojsze Moshe	1903	Zychlin, Poland	PT	M
Rozenberg	Pinkhas Wolf	1887		LLG	PM
Rozenberg	Rene		Zychlin, Poland	PT	M
Rozenberg	Reza Reze	1904	Zychlin, Poland	PT	M
Rozenberg	Rivka		Zychlin, Poland	PT	M
Rozenberg	Rivka		Zichlin, Poland	PT	M
Rozenberg	Rivka		Zychlin, Poland	PT	M
Rozenberg	Riwa Riva	1892	Zychlin, Poland	PT	M
Rozenberg	Sara		Zychlin, Poland	PT	M
Rozenberg	Schlomo Shlomo	1897	Zychlin, Poland	PT	M
Rozenberg	Shmil Shmuel	1872	Zychlin, Poland	PT	M
Rozenberg	Toba Tova	1924	Zakhlin, Poland	PT	M
Rozenberg	Tova Ester	1909	Zychlin, Poland	PT	M
Rozenberg	Yaakov	1917	Gombin, Poland	PT	M
Rozenberg	Yaakov Chaim	1869	Wloclawek, Poland	PT	M
Rozenberg	Yonas Ionas		Zychlin, Poland	PT	M
Rozenberg	Yurek Iurek	1923	Wloclawek, Poland	PT	M
Rozenblum	Riwka Luba Rivka	1885	Zychlin, Poland	PT	M
Rozencwajg Rozentzveig	Golda	1890	Lodz, Poland	PT	M
Rozenfeld	Rakhel	1883	Lodz, Poland	PT	M
Rozenkopf	Avraham		Zychlin, Poland	PT	M
Rozenkopf	Golda Zahava	1914	Zychlin, Poland	PT	M
Rozenkopf	Moshe		Zychlin, Poland	PT	M
Rozenkranc Rozenkrantz	Mosze Moshe	1897	Zychlin, Poland	PT	M
Rozenkrantz	Chawa Khava	1897	Lodz, Poland	PT	M
Rozenkrantz	Keila		Zychlin, Poland	PT	M
Rozenkrantz	Rivka Lea	1912	Zychlin, Poland	PT	M

Last Name	First Name	Birth Year	Place of Residence	Source	Fate
Rozenkrantz	Yeta	1912	Zychlin, Poland	PT	M
Rozenkranz Rozenkrantz	Aba	1909	Zychlin, Poland	PT	M
Rozental	Jakov Yaakov		Zychlin, Poland	PT	M
Rozental	Yaccov Yhoda		Zechlin, Poland	PT	M
Roznblum Rozenblum	Bejrisz Ber	1880	Zychlin, Poland	PT	M
Rubin	Avraham Shmuel		Plock, Poland	PT	M
Rubin	Baruch	1911	Zychlin, Poland	PP	M
Rubin	Baruch	1911	Zychlin, Poland	PP	M
Rubin	Benjamin Beniamin	1910	Zychlin, Poland	PT	M
Rubin	Chana Khana	1894	Zychlin, Poland	PT	M
Rubin	David	1920	Zichlin, Poland	PT	M
Rubin	Emalja Amalia Mala	1916	Zychlin, Poland	PT	M
Rubin	Frymet Frumet	1914	Zychlin, Poland	PT	M
Rubin	Gedalja Gedalia	1920	Zychlin, Poland	PT	M
Rubin	Gitel Gitla		Zychlin, Poland	PT	M
Rubin	Hershel		Zychlin, Poland	PT	M
Rubin	Hersz Hersh	1907	Plock, Poland	PT	M
Rubin	Israel Yisrael	1894	Zychlin, Poland	PT	M
Rubin	Mosje Hersz	1901	Zychlin, Poland	DL	M
Rubin	Mosze Moshe	1908	Zychlin, Poland	PT	M
Rubin	Rivka		Zychlin, Poland	PT	M
Rubin	Sara		Zichlin, Poland	PT	M
Rubin	Toibe Tauba	1914	Zychlin, Poland	PT	M
Rubin	Yitzkhak Yehuda		Zichlin, Poland	PT	M
Rubin			Zychlin, Poland	PT	M
Ryster	Eli		Zichlin, Poland	PT	M
Ryster	Feia		Zichlin, Poland	PT	M
Rzerznik Rezer	Ruchla Rakhel	1900	Lodz, Poland	PT	M
Sachoczewski	Zach	1908	Zychlin, Poland	PP	M
Sadovski	Avraham		Zychlin, Poland	PT	M
Sadovski	Moshe Hersh		Zychlin, Poland	PT	M
Sadovski	Rivka		Zychlin, Poland	PT	M
Sadovski	Toibe Ester		Zychlin, Poland	PT	M
Sanicki	Malka		Zychlin, Poland	PT	M
Sanicki	Pessa	1899	Zichlin, Poland	PT	M
Sanicki		1898	Zychlin, Poland	PT	M
Sanicki Sanitzki	Manya Mania	1928	Zychlin, Poland	PT	M
Sanicki Sanitzki	Pesel	1896	Zychlin, Poland	PT	M
Sanicki Sanitzki	Yesef Yosef	1896	Zychlin, Poland	PT	M
Sapirsztajn Shafirshtein	Bajla Bila		Pabianice, Poland	PT	M
Sarna	Berek	1925	Zychlin, Poland	PP	M
Sarna	Berek	1925	Zychlin, Poland	PP	M
Schapira Shapira	Sara Ite		Lodz, Poland	PT	M

Last Name	First Name	Birth Year	Place of Residence	Source	Fate
Schapszewicz Shapshevich	Chana Yehudit Idis		Zychlin, Poland	PT	M
Scheibe Shaibe	Roda	1882	Konstantynów, Poland	PT	M
Schwarc Shvartz	First name unknown		Zichlin, Poland	PT	M
Schwarc Shvartz	Selda Zelda	1903	Zichlin, Poland	PT	M
Schwarz Shvartz	Fischel Fishel	1903	Jochlin, Poland	PT	M
Schwarz Shvartz	Sheya Moshe		Jochlin, Poland	PT	M
Seczewinski Sechevinski	Icko Yitzkhak Meir	1906	Zachlin, Poland	PT	M
Senderovicz Senderovitz	Icze Icie	1900	Zychlin, Poland	PT	M
Senderowicz Senderovitz	Chana Khana	1906	Zychlin, Poland	PT	M
Senderowicz Senderovitz	Dvora		Zychlin, Poland	PT	M
Senderowicz Senderovitz	Moshe		Zychlin, Poland	PT	M
Senderowicz Senderovitz	Tauba		Zychlin, Poland	PT	M
Shaten	Ita		Zychlin, Poland	PT	M
Shigel	Shmuel		Zychlin, Poland	PT	M
Shlechtus Hirsch	Avraham		Zychlin, Poland	PT	M
Shlechtus Shlakhtus	Moshe		Zychlin, Poland	PT	M
Shlechtus Shlakhtus	Tirza Tirtza		Zychlin, Poland	PT	M
Shlekhter	Rela		Plock, Poland	PT	M
Shmukler	Icha Icie		Zychlin, Poland	PT	M
Shvarts Shvartz	Haya Khaia		Zychlin, Poland	PT	M
Shvartz	Feiga		Zychlin, Poland	PT	M
Shvartz	Leibish		Zychlin, Poland	PT	M
Shvartz	Makhli		Zychlin, Poland	PT	M
Shvartz	Mendel		Zychlin, Poland	PT	M
Shvartz	Tankhum	1936	Zychlin, Poland	PT	M
Shvartz	Yaakov	1916	Zychlin, Poland	PT	M
Shvartz	Zalman		Zychlin, Poland	murdered	M
Shvartz	Zalman Binem	1902	Kolo, Poland	PT	M
Shwartz Shvartz	Hinka Khinka		Zychlin, Poland	PT	M
Shwartz Shvartz	Shaya Shaia		Zychlin, Poland	PT	M
Sieger	Abram	1898	Zychlin, Poland	PP	M
Sieger	Abram	1898	Zychlin, Poland	PP	M
Sieger	Abram	1898	Zychlin, Poland	PP	M
Sieradzky Sheratzki	Fayvel Faivel	1900	Zychlin, Poland	PT	M
Sigel	Roda		Zychlin, Poland	PT	M
Sloma	Abraham Avraham	1920	Zychlin, Poland	PT	M
Sloma	Avraham Yitzkhak	1885	Zhichlin, Poland	PT	M
Sloma	Bella Sara Bila	1920	Zychlin, Poland	PT	M
Sloma	Chaim Meir Khaim	1897	Zychlin, Poland	PT	M
Sloma	Ester	1918	Brussels, Belgium	PT	M
Sloma	Ester		Zhichlin, Poland	PT	M
Sloma	Estera Malka	1918	Zychlin, Poland	DL	M
Sloma	Israel Yisrael	1923	Zichlin, Poland	PT	M

Last Name	First Name	Birth Year	Place of Residence	Source	Fate
Sloma	Moshe		Zhichlin, Poland	PT	M
Sloma	Mosze Moshe	1913	Zychlin, Poland	PT	M
Sloma	Ryvka Rivka	1900	Zychlin, Poland	PT	M
Sloma	Sara	1925	Zychlin, Poland	PT	M
Sloma	Sara	1889	Zechlin, Poland	PT	M
Sloma	Sara		Zychlin, Poland	PT	M
Sloma	Sara		Zhichlin, Poland	PT	M
Sloma	Schalom Shalom	1924	Zychlin, Poland	PT	M
Sloma	Schalom Shalom	1919	Zechlin, Poland	PT	M
Sloma	Shoshana		Zhichlin, Poland	PT	M
Sloma	Yisrael		Zhichlin, Poland	PT	M
Sloma	Yitzkhak Mordekhai	1917	Zychlin, Poland	PT	M
Sloma Hamburg	Bajla Bilha	1888	Zychlin, Poland	PT	M
Slomon Salomon	Avraham		Zichlin, Poland	PT	M
Slomon Salomon	Chaim Khaim Meir		Zichlin, Poland	PT	M
Slomon Salomon	Rivka		Zichlin, Poland	PT	M
Slomon Salomon	Sulem Shalom		Zychlin, Poland	PT	M
Slomon Salomon	Yitzkhak Mordche		Zychlin, Poland	PT	M
Sochaczewski	Zack	1908	Zychlin, Poland	PP	M
Sochaczewski Sokhachevsk	Laja Lea		Kutno, Poland	PT	M
Stempa	Andzia		Kolo, Poland	PT	M
Sternfeld Shternfeld	Rivka Rifka	1890	Lowicz, Poland	PT	M
Stul	Mordehay	1922	Paris, France	PP	M
Surname unknown	Adela Eidel	1889	Grodzisk Mazow, Poland	PT	M
Surname unknown	Frajda Freida		Zychlin, Poland	PT	M
Surname unknown	Khaim		Zychlin, Poland	PT	M
Surname unknown	Misha	1938	Zichlin, Poland	PT (d)	M
Surname unknown	Rakhel		Zychlin, Poland	PT	M
Surname unknown	Rakhel	1923	Zichlin, Poland	PT (d)	M
Surname unknown	Sara	1894	Zychlin, Poland	PT	M
Szabo Goldstein	Bela	1893	Tokaj, Hungary	LMH	M
Szabo Goldstein	Gyula	1897	Tokaj, Hungary	LMH	M
Szanovska Shenovski	Feiga	1914	Zechlin, Poland	PT	M
Szczawinska Shchavinski	Hinda		Zychlin, Poland	PT	M
Szczawinski	Lutek	1915	Zychlin, Poland	M	M
Szczawinski	Mendel	1920	Zychlin, Poland	PP	M
Szczawinski Shchavinski	Mendel		Zychlin, Poland	PT	M
Szczawinski Shchavinski	Motel		Zychlin, Poland	PT	M
Szenowski Shenovski	Chaim Khaim	1937	Zychlin, Poland	PT	M
Szerakowiak Sherakoviak	Malka	1903	Lodz, Poland	PT	M
Szerakowiak Sherakoviak	Riwka Rachel	1889	Zgierz, Poland	PT	M
Szlam Shtanke	Zalman	1903	Rypin, Poland	PT	M
Sztulzaft Shtulzaft	First name unknown		Zychlin, Poland	PT	M

Last Name	First Name	Birth Year	Place of Residence	Source	Fate
Sztulzaft Shtulzaft	First name unknown		Zychlin, Poland	PT	M
Sztulzaft Shtulzaft	Szifri Shprintza	1907	Zychlin, Poland	PT	M
Sztulzaft Shtulzaft	Szlojme Shlomo	1900	Zychlin, Poland	PT	M
Szwarc	Abram Moszek	1905	Krosniewice, Poland	LMA	M
Szwarc Shvartz	David	1890	Zychlin, Poland	PT	M
Szwarc Shvartz	Dawid David	1890	Zychlin, Poland	PT	M
Szwarc Shvartz	Feiga	1897	Wloclawek, Poland	PT	M
Szwarc Shvartz	Raca Ratza	1869	Zychlin, Poland	PT	M
Szwarcberg Shvartzberg	Khaim		Lowicz, Poland	PT	M
Szwarcberg Shvartzberg	Malka	1889	Zychlin, Poland	PT	M
Tadelas	Rochel		Zichlin, Poland	PP	M
Tajczer	Benjamin	1907	Krzemieniec, Poland	PP	M
Tatarka	Ester		Zychlin, Poland	PT	M
Tatarka	Josef Ber		Poland	PT	M
Tatarka	Laja		Zychlin, Poland	PT	M
Tatarka	Szymszon		Zychlin, Poland	PT	M
Tatarko	Abraham	1883	Zychlin, Poland	PT	M
Tatarko	Hana	1909	Zychlin, Poland	PT	M
Tatarko	Hershl Hershel	1907	Zychlin, Poland	PT	M
Tatarko	Josef	1912	Zychlin, Poland	PT	M
Tatarko	Judith Yehudit	1914	Zychlin, Poland	PT	M
Tatarko	Mindl Mindel	1910	Zychlin, Poland	PT	M
Tatarko	Tauba Towa	1886	Zychlin, Poland	PT	M
Tatarko	Toba Tova	1887	Zychlin, Poland	PT	M
Teitelbaum	Ryfka	1888	Lodz, Poland	PT	M
Toroncyk Torunchik	Hersz Tzvi		Zychlin, Poland	PT	M
Toronczyk Torunchik	Chaim Khaim		Zychlin, Poland	PT	M
Toronczyk Torunchik	Rozia Shoshana	1872	Zychlin, Poland	PT	M
Trojanovski Troinovski	Golda	1883	Zgierz, Poland	PT	M
Tuszinski Tushinski	Szifcia Shifra	1902	Zychlin, Poland	PT	M
Tuszynska Tushinski	Ryfcia Rivka Lea	1905	Zychlin, Poland	PT	M
Tuszynski Tushinski	Becalel Betzalel	1905	Warszawa, Poland	PT	M
Tuszynski Tushinski	Betzalel	1899	Warszawa, Poland	PT	M
Tuszynski Tushinski	Rywka Rivka	1907	Zychlin, Poland	PT	M
Tuszynski Tushinski	Salomon Shlomo	1890	Zychlin, Poland	PT	M
Tuszynski Tushinski	Szlomo Shlomo	1880	Zychlin, Poland	PT	M
Tuszynski Tushinski	Szyfra Shifra	1900	Zychlin, Poland	PT	M
Tzinamon	Anszel		Zychlin, Poland	LMYB	M
Undeciphered Family Name	Aron Szyja		Zychlin, Poland	PP	M
Urbakh Orbakh	Balcia Beila	1915	Zychlin, Poland	PT	M
Urbakh Orbakh	Balcia Beila	1915	Wloclawek, Poland	PT	M
Urbakh Orbakh	Beila	1915	Wloclawek, Poland	PT	M
Urbakh Orbakh	Bunim		Zychlin, Poland	PT	M

Last Name	First Name	Birth Year	Place of Residence	Source	Fate
Urbakh Orbakh	Chaja Ester Khaia	1888	Zychlin, Poland	PT	M
Urbakh Orbakh	Frania	1889	Zychlin, Poland	PT	M
Urbakh Orbakh	Israel Yisrael Yosef	1887	Wloclawek, Poland	PT	M
Urbakh Orbakh	Israel Yozef Yisrael	1887	Zychlin, Poland	PT	M
Urbakh Orbakh	Khaia Ester	1886	Wloclawek, Poland	PT	M
Urbakh Orbakh	Mendel	1891	Zychlin, Poland	PT	M
Urbakh Orbakh	Mendel Menakhem		Zychlin, Poland	PT	M
Urbakh Orbakh	Mikhael		Zychlin, Poland	PT	M
Urbakh Orbakh	Raizil Roza Reizl	1914	Zychlin, Poland	PT	M
Urbakh Orbakh	Rakhel	1870	Zychlin, Poland	PT	M
Urbakh Orbakh	Reizl Reizel	1914	Wloclawek, Poland	PT	M
Urbakh Orbakh	Reizl Roza Reizel	1914	Wloclawek, Poland	PT	M
Vays	Khil Iosif	1921	Gantsevichi, Poland	PP	M
Vays	Khil Iosif	1921	Zhikhlin, Poland	PP	M
Veikselfish	Chana Tova	1914		PT	M
Veikselfish	Yekhiel			PT	M
Viezhbinski	Khana Ieta		Wloclawek, Poland	PT	M
Viner	Yosef		Zychlin, Poland	PT	M
Vitman	Ester	1909	Zychlin, Poland	PT	M
Vitman	Meir	1904	Zychlin, Poland	PT	M
Vodzislavski	Yisrael Zeev	1880	Warszawa, Poland	PT	M
Vogel	Milka Sara	1918	Hermannsbad, Poland	LMA	M
Volman	Aharon		Zychlin, Poland	PT	M
Volman	Khaia		Zychlin, Poland	PT	M
Vrubel	Efraim		Zachlin, Poland	PT	M
Vrubel	Miriam		Zachlin, Poland	PT	M
Vrubel	Rakhel		Zychlin, Poland	PT	M
Vrubel	Reuven		Zichlin, Poland	PT	M
Vrubel	Sara		Warsza, Poland	PT	M
Vrubel	Shmuel Nisan		Zichlin, Poland	PT	M
Vrubel	Simkha		Zychlin, Poland	PT	M
Vrubel	Tova		Zychlin, Poland	PT	M
Wajdeslawska Vodzislavski	Karola Kreina	1906	Zychlin, Poland	PT	M
Wajdeslawski Vodzislavski	Abram Avraham	1897	Zychlin, Poland	PT	M
Wajdeslawski Vodzislavski	Symcha Simkha	1912	Zychlin, Poland	PT	M
Wajdet Veidet	Jechak Yitzkhak Iche	1880	Zychlin, Poland	PT	M
Wajdet Veidet	Mordcha Ber	1875	Przedecz, Poland	PT	M
Wajkselfisz Veikselfish	Eljau Eliahu	1911	Lipno, Poland	PT	M
Wajnsztajn Veinshtein	Bela	1912	Kutno, Poland	PT	M
Walach	Abramek		Zychlin, Poland	PT	M
Walach	Laja		Zychlin, Poland	PT	M
Walach	Szaja		Zychlin, Poland	PT	M
Walach	Szajndel	1896	Zychlin, Poland	PP	M

Last Name	First Name	Birth Year	Place of Residence	Source	Fate
Walach	Szajndl		Zychlin, Poland	PT	M
Waldman Valdman	Aron		Zichlin, Poland	PT	M
Waldman Valdman	Moshe		Zichlin, Poland	PT	M
Waldman Valdman	Regine Regina	1912	Zichlin, Poland	PT	M
Walis Velis	Hadas	1888	Pabianice, Poland	PT	M
Warcka Vartzki	Bentzion		Kutno, Poland	PT	M
Warcka Vartzki	Rozia	1887	Kutno, Poland	PT	M
Warmwasser Varmvaser	Malka	1898	Lodz, Poland	PT	M
Warszawiak Varshavyak	Abraham Avraham	1891	Krosniewice, Poland	PT	M
Wartcki Vartzki	Ben Cyjon Bentzion	1906	Kutno, Poland	PT	M
Wasilewski Vasilevski	Brajne Breina	1882	Zychlin, Poland	PT	M
Wasilewski Vasilevski	Icchak Yitzkhak	1880	Zechlin, Poland	PT	M
Welis Velis	Aszer Asher	1909	Zychlin, Poland	PT	M
Widawski Vidavski	Rachel Rakhel Lea	1903	Ozorkow, Poland	PT	M
Wionzowska Vionzovski	Dwojra Dvora Zelda	1870	Lodz, Poland	PT	M
Wodislawski Vodislavski	Frumet	1904	Sosnowiec, Poland	PT	M
Wodka	Dwojra Rajzla	1909	Zychlin, Poland	DL	M
Wojdeslawski	Abram	1897	Lask,	LMA	M
Wojdeslawski	Israel Zeev	1880	Warszawa, Poland	PT	M
Wojdeslawski Vodzislavski	Jacob Yaakov David	1876	Zychlin, Poland	PT	M
Wojdeslawski Vodzislavski	Szmul Shmuel		Zychlin, Poland	PT	M
Wojdyslawska Vodzislavski	Sara	1875	Lodz, Poland	PT	M
Wolkowicz Volkovitz	Josef Yosef	1902	Zychlin, Poland	PT	M
Wolkowicz Volkovitz	Josef Yosef	1906	Poland	PT	M
Wolkowicz Volkovitz	Szamay Shamai	1895	Zychlin, Poland	PT	M
Wolman Volman	Aharon	1918	Poland	PT	M
Wolman Volman	Chaja Tzipora	1882	Blonie, Poland	PT	M
Wolman Volman	Khaia	1920	Lodz, Poland	PT	M
Wrobel Vrubel	Chana Khana	1882	Zgierz, Poland	PT	M
Wrobel Vrubel	Golda	1900	Zgierz, Poland	PT	M
Wroclawski Vrotzlavski	Ita	1870	Lodz, Poland	PT	M
Wygdorczyk Vigdorchik	Mendel	1880	Zychlin, Poland	PT	M
Wygdorczyk Vigdorchik	Mirjam Miriam	1882	Zychlin, Poland	PT	M
Wygdorczyk Vigdorchik	Rachel Rakhel	1915	Zychlin, Poland	PT	M
Wyszegrodzki	Barukh	1917	Dombrowice, Poland	PT	M
Wyszegrodzki	Ester Blima	1921	Dombrowice, Poland	PT	M
Wyszegrodzki	Sheina Gitel	1912	Dombrowice, Poland	PT	M
Yakubovich Yakubovitz	Feigele Feigel Feiga		Zychlin, Poland	PT	M
Yakubovitz	Blime		Kutno, Poland	PT	M
Yakubovitz	Moshe		Zychlin, Poland	PT	M
Yakubovitz	Yehoshua		Zychlin, Poland	PT	M
Zafern Gliksman	Ela		Lodz, Poland	PT (d)	M
Zafran	Chaia Khela	1920	Zichlin, Poland	PT (d)	M

Last Name	First Name	Birth Year	Place of Residence	Source	Fate
Zafran	Chawa Khava	1901	Zychlin, Poland	PT	M
Zafran	Eva	1904	Zichlin, Poland	PT (d)	M
Zafran	Hilel		Zachlin, Poland	PT	M
Zafran	Hilel	1911	Zychlin, Poland	PT (d)	M
Zafran	Israel Yisrael	1898	Zychlin, Poland	PT	M
Zafran	Khaia		Zachlin, Poland	PT	M
Zafran	Khaia	1923	Hrubieszow, Poland	PT	M
Zafran	Menakhem		Zychlin, Poland	PT	M
Zafran	Moshe	1879	Zychlin, Poland	PT (d)	M
Zafran	Mundek	1924	Zychlin, Poland	PT (d)	M
Zafran	Rakhel		Zychlin, Poland	PT	M
Zafran	Rakhel	1932	Zichlin, Poland	PT (d)	M
Zafran	Tzesha	1892	Zychlin, Poland	PT	M
Zafran	Yekhiel		Zechlin, Poland	PT	M
Zafran	Yisrael		Zychlin, Poland	PT	M
Zafran	Yisrael		Zychlin, Poland	PT (d)	M
Zaiontz	Sara		Gombin, Poland	PT	M
Zajbert Zibert	Cypojra Tzipora		Zychlin, Poland	PT	M
Zajbert Zibert	Rojza Roize		Zychlin, Poland	PT	M
Zajdel	Moshe		Zychlin, Poland	PT	M
Zajdman Zeidman Gelbart	Jechiel Yekhiel Meir	1892	Gombin, Poland	PT	M
Zajfert	Telca	1900	Zychlin, Poland	DL	M
Zalkowicz Zelkovitz	Abram Avraham	1920	Zachlin, Poland	PT	M
Zalkowicz Zelkovitz	Faiga Feiga	1917	Zychlin, Poland	PT	M
Zalkowicz Zelkovitz	Maisze Mashia	1915	Zichlin, Poland	PT	M
Zalkowicz Zelkovitz	Sara	1870	Zychlin, Poland	PT	M
Zalmanovitz	Hinda	1895	Sosnowiec, Poland	PT	M
Zandberg	Alte Sara		Zychlin, Poland	PT	M
Zandberg	Avigdor	1922	Zichlin, Poland	PT	M
Zandberg	Ester		Zychlin, Poland	PT	M
Zandberg	Esther Frida	1930	Zychlin, Poland	PT	M
Zandberg	Haim Khaim Volf	1902	Zychlin, Poland	PT	M
Zandberg	Hersh		Zychlin, Poland	PT	M
Zandberg	Hirshel		Zychlin, Poland	PT	M
Zandberg	Inda Hinda		Zychlin, Poland	PT	M
Zandberg	Joseph Hirsh	1934	Zychlin, Poland	PT	M
Zandberg	Khaim Volf		Zychlin, Poland	PT	M
Zandberg	Liba	1904	Zychlin, Poland	PT	M
Zandberg	Mindl Ita	1928	Zichlin, Poland	PT	M
Zandberg	Moshe		Zichlin, Poland	PT	M
Zandberg	Pesach Pesakh		Zychlin, Poland	PT	M
Zandberg	Rakhel		Zychlin, Poland	PT	M
Zandberg	Roiza Rivka		Zychlin, Poland	PT	M

Last Name	First Name	Birth Year	Place of Residence	Source	Fate
Zandberg	Rose	1922	Zychlin, Poland	PT	M
Zandberg	Roza		Zychlin, Poland	PT	M
Zandberg	Sara Alte		Zychlin, Poland	PT	M
Zandberg	Shlomo		Zychlin, Poland	PT	M
Zandberg	Toibe Hinda	1926	Zychlin, Poland	PT	M
Zandberg	Tova		Zychlin, Poland	PT	M
Zandberg	Victor Viktor		Zychlin, Poland	PT	M
Zandberg	Yeta		Zychlin, Poland	PT	M
Zandberg	Zalman		Zychlin, Poland	PT	M
Zander	Mina	1918	Rupin, Poland	PT (d)	M
Zander	Pinkhas Meir	1887	Rupin, Poland	PT	M
Zander	Pinkhas Meir		Rupin, Poland	PT (d)	M
Zander	Sara		Rupin, Poland	PT (d)	M
Zander	Yekhezkel		Rupin, Poland	PT (d)	M
Zandman Zendman	Avraham	1872	Zychlin, Poland	PT	M
Zawieruchi Kroit	Chana Khana	1916	Lodz, Poland	PT	M
Zawieruchi Kroit	Jakub Yaakov Eliahu	1895	Siedlce, Poland	PT	M
Zegelman Zigelman	Cyla Tzila		Zychlin, Poland	PT	M
Zeibart	Eliezer Leizer		Zichlin, Poland	PT (d)	M
Zhezhinski	Feiga Tzipora	1914	Rupin, Poland	PT (d)	M
Zieg Tzig	Rywka Rivka	1895	Lowicz, Poland	PT	M
Zieg Zig	Aron Aharon David		Zychlin, Poland	PT	M
Zieg Zig	Bela	1873	Zychlin, Poland	PT	M
Zieg Zig	Brajna Breina	1880	Zychlin, Poland	PT	M
Zieg Zig	Israel Yisrael	1875	Zychlin, Poland	PT	M
Zieg Zig	Josef Yosef	1870	Zychlin, Poland	PT	M
Zieg Zig	Rywka Rivka	1900	Zychlin, Poland	PT	M
Ziger	Dow Dov	1885	Zichlin, Poland	PT	M
Ziger	First name unknown		Zichlin, Poland	PT	M
Ziger	Gytl Gitel	1908	Zychlin, Poland	PT	M
Ziger	Hanoch Khanokh	1910	Zichlin, Poland	PT	M
Ziger	Jechiel Yekhiel	1916	Zichlin, Poland	PT	M
Ziger	Lewi Levi	1915	Zychlin, Poland	PT	M
Ziger	Riwka Rivka	1912	Zichlin, Poland	PT	M
Ziger	Rywka Rivka	1907	Zychlin, Poland	PT	M
Ziger	Yaakov		Zichlin, Poland	PT	M
Zik	Brana Breina	1881	Zychlin, Poland	PT	M
Zik	Maite Meite		Zychlin, Poland	PT	M
Zik	Rakhel		Zichlin, Poland	PT	M
Zik	Tzira		Zychlin, Poland	PT	M
Zik	Yisrael		Zichlin, Poland	PT	M
Zik Zak	Rivka Bakha	1904	Zychlin, Poland	PT	M
Zilberberg	Azriel		France	PT	M

Last Name	First Name	Birth Year	Place of Residence	Source	Fate
Zislender	Yosef	1890	Potsk, Poland	PT	M
Zlotak	Jakub	1878	Zychlin, Poland	PP	M
Zlotak	Salek Israel	1919	Zychlin, Poland	LMA	M
Zlotek	Moshe		Zychlin, Poland	PT	M
Zlotnik	Szmuel Shmuel	1902	Zichlin, Poland	PT	M
Zolna	Fiszel	1934		LLG	PM
Zolna	Zelek	1907		LLG	PM
Zolty Zhulti	Esther Ester	1892	Zychlin, Poland	PT	M
Zolty Zhulti	Herch Tzvi	1870	Zychlin, Poland	PT	M
Zolty Zhulti	Izchak Yitzkhak	1890	Zychlin, Poland	PT	M
Zolty Zhulti	Lea	1875	Zychlin, Poland	PT	M
Zolty Zhulti	Lea		Zychlin, Poland	PT	M
Zolty Zhulti	Leah Lea	1852	Zychlin, Poland	PT	M
Zolty Zhulti	Tzvi Hershel		Zychlin, Poland	PT	M
Zolty Zhulti	Yitzkhak		Zychlin, Poland	PT	M
Zolty Zhulti	Zwi Tzvi Hersh	1850	Zychlin, Poland	PT	M
Zubersger	Azriel	1902	Zychlin, Poland	LDF	M
Zukert Tzukert	Beile Beila		Zychlin, Poland	PT	M
Zukert Tzukert	Israel Yisrael Meir		Zachlin, Poland	PT	M
Zurawski Zhuravski	Avraham Yitzkhak	1900	Zychlin, Poland	PT	M
Zurawski Zhuravski	Ester Yenta	1901	Zychlin, Poland	PT	M
Zurawski Zhuravski	Hersh Volf		Zychlin, Poland	PT	M
Zychlinska	Estera	1915	Zychlin, Poland	M	M
Żychliński Rozental	Yaakov Yehuda		Zychlin, Poland	LMYB	M
Zychlinski Zikhlinski	Efraim	1918	Zychlin, Poland	PT	M
Zychlinski Zikhlinski	Roda Ruda	1887	Zychlin, Poland	PT	M
Zychlinsky Zikhlinski	Smuel Shmuel	1885	Zychlin, Poland	PT	M
Zygar Ziger	Laja Lea	1920	Zychlin, Poland	PT	M
Zygelman Zigelman	Chaskel Yekhezkel	1891	Zychlin, Poland	PT	M
Zygelman Zigelman	Hersh Tzvi	1917	Zychlin, Poland	PT	M
Zygelman Zigelman	Moshe	1921	Zychlin, Poland	PT	M
Zyger	David		Izbica Kujawska, Poland	PT	M
Zyger	Sheindl Shindel		Izbica Kujawska, Poland	PT	M
Zyger Ziger	Chaja Khaia	1916	Zychlin, Poland	PT	M
Zyger Ziger	Mirjam Miriam	1872	Zychlin, Poland	PT	M
Zyger Ziger	Mordcha Mordekhai	1897	Zychlin, Poland	PT	M
Zyger Ziger	Mosche Moshe	1898	Gostynin, Poland	PT	M
Zyger Ziger	Slomo Shlomo	1870	Zychlin, Poland	PT	M
Zygier	Gabryel Jehosz	1937		LLG	PM
Zygier	Jankiel Lajb	1914		LLG	PM
Zygier	Liba	1917		LLG	PM
Zygier Ziger	Mordekhai Shmuel	1890	Gostynin, Poland	PT	M
Zygier Ziger	Berisz Dov Berish	1880	Zychlin, Poland	PT	M

Last Name	First Name	Birth Year	Place of Residence	Source	Fate
Zygier Ziger	Heinoch Khanokh	1909	Zychlin, Poland	PT	M
Zygier Ziger	Jakob Yaakov	1920	Zychlin, Poland	PT	M
Zygier Ziger	Jechiel Yekhiel	1918	Zychlin, Poland	PT	M
Zygier Ziger	Jechiel Yekhiel	1922	Zychlin, Poland	PT	M
Zygier Ziger	Jechil Yekhiel	1917	Zychlin, Poland	PT	M
Zygier Ziger	Mordekhai	1897	Zychlin, Poland	PT	M
Zygier Ziger	Mordekhai		Zychlin, Poland	PT	M
Zygier Ziger	Mordekhai		Zychlin, Poland	PT	M
Zygier Ziger	Naftali		Zychlin, Poland	PT	M
Zygier Ziger	Naftali		Zychlin, Poland	PT	M
Zygier Ziger	Noach Noakh	1907	Zychlin, Poland	PT	M
Zygier Ziger	Rachel Rakhel	1885	Zychlin, Poland	PT	M
Zygier Ziger	Regine Rivka	1911	Zychlin, Poland	PT	M
Zygier Ziger	Sara	1896	Zychlin, Poland	PT	M
Zygier Ziger	Szlomo Shlomo	1870	Zychlin, Poland	PT	M
Zygier Ziger	Yaakov Volf	1926	Zychlin, Poland	PT	M
Zygier Ziger	Yakow Yaakov	1886	Zychlin, Poland	PT	M
Zygier Ziger	Yehoszua Yehoshua	1894	Zychlin, Poland	PT	M
Zyk Zik	Aharon David	1905	Zychlin, Poland	PT	M
Zylberberg Zilberberg	Ezriel Azriel		Amsterdam, Netherlands	PT	M
Zylbersztejn	Laja		Zychlin, Poland	LDF	M
Zyslender Zislender	Fraidl Fridl	1885	Zychlin, Poland	PT	M

Keys to acronyms			
Source		**Fate**	
DL	Deportation list	M	Murdered
LDB	List deportation - Berlin	PM	Presumably murdered
LDF	List deportation - France	KMS	Killed in military service
LFC	List Flossenbuerg camp inmates		
LLG	List Lodz ghetto inmates		
LMA	List Jews murdered in Auschwitz		
LMG	List murdered Jews - Germany		
LMH	List murdered Jews - Hungary		
LMN	List murdered Jews - Netherlands		
LMYB	List murdered Jews - Yizkor books		
LRG	List Radom ghetto inmates		
M	Mauthausen personal card file		
PP	List persecuted persons		
PT	Page Testimony		
PT (d)	Page Testimony (digital)		
T	List Theresienstadt inmates		

Zychlin memorial monuments in Israel and Poland

[Not included in the original book]

Cemetery of Holon, Israel, 1984.
Dedicated by the Organization of Zychliners in Israel.
Image source: Wikimedia Commons.

Zychlin Municipal Park, Poland, 2022.
Dedicated by the Municipality of Zychlin and the Zychlin Group of the
Association of Descendants of Jewish Central Poland.
Image source: Towarzystwo Przyjaciół Ziemi Kutnowskiej.

INDEX OF NAMES

Note: The names that appear in the book's following lists are not included in this index:
"List of Martyrs", p. 210+
"List of Jews murdered on the day before deportation", p. 280+
"Zychliners in Yad Vashem's database of victims", p. 285+

www.ingramcontent.com/pod-product-compliance
Lightning Source LLC
Chambersburg PA
CBHW082004150426

42814CB00005BA/221

* 9 7 8 1 9 5 4 1 7 6 5 1 5 *